Dag Hammarskjöld will go down in history as one of the few great international figures of the post-war period. In his eight and a half years as Secretary-General of the United Nations (from 1953, when he succeeded Trygve Lie, to his tragic death in a plane crash in Northern Rhodesia in September 1961), he showed himself to be a man of outstanding ability and devotion to his work. His contribution to the standing of the United Nations, during a peculiarly troubled period of its history, and to the cause of world peace, is incalculable.

Dag Hammarskjöld believed that public speaking was an important part of the Secretary-General's duties, as a means of spreading understanding of the problems of international and human relations, and he wrote and delivered a very great number of speeches during his years of office in spite of infinite other demands upon his time. All of them were prepared with great care and were meant to be pondered and re-read. Although he spoke and wrote much more than could be included in a publication of this length, there has been room to reproduce most of his more important speeches in full. Others appear in extracts. To them have been added a number of statements and addresses which he delivered in capacities other than as Secretary-General and which reflect the breadth of his interests.

Altogether, the volume provides a complete view of his policies and of his philosophy.

Wilder Foote, the editor, was Director of the Press and Publications Division of the UN Secretariat until December 1960. In this capacity he served for more than thirteen years as press spokesman for Trygve Lie and Dag Hammarskjöld, and assisted in the preparation of the annual reports of the Secretary-General throughout this period. He was also one of the very few people who knew Dag Hammarskjöld as a personal friend.

The Servant of Peace

A Selection of the Speeches and Statements of

Dag Hammarskjöld

The
Servant of Peace

A Selection of the
Speeches and Statements of

Dag Hammarskjöld

Secretary-General of the United Nations
1953-1961

Edited and introduced by
WILDER FOOTE

THE BODLEY HEAD
LONDON

© This selection Dag Hammarskjöld's estate 1962
Printed and bound in Great Britain for
The Bodley Head Ltd
10 Earlham Street, London, wc2
by William Clowes and Sons Ltd, Beccles
Set in Monotype Ehrhardt
First published 1962

CONTENTS

*   *   *

INTRODUCTION

Dag Hammarskjöld, the man, is gone and the world will long mourn this grievous and irreparable loss. But his work and words remain with us. They are not lost. They can continue to help our efforts to find our way through times of gravest danger and new opportunity towards a world society with firmer foundations of international order in support of peace, freedom, equality and justice. All those who share in the responsibility for seeking to shape the development in this direction, whether they be national leaders or conscientious citizens, will find in study and understanding of the record of his service as Secretary-General of the United Nations a rich and, indeed, indispensable source of guidance and inspiration.

There is the record of action as administrator, as conciliator and negotiator, as representative to governments of the law of the Charter and of the overriding common interest, and as inspirer and executor of pioneering actions by international organization in support of peace. There is also the record of interpretation and analysis of the Charter and of the developing role of the institutions of the United Nations, always in firm relationship to the realities of present-day international life, to problems of individual attitudes and responsibility and to faith in the possibilities of creative social evolution.

Much of the record of action can be traced in the official records of the United Nations. There can be found thousands of pages of reports, statements and debates in the General Assembly, the Security Council and other organs on every question in which the Secretary-General bore responsibility or exercised influence. A simple list of his more important public acts is sufficient to indicate their scope and significance. From his mission to Peking in January 1955 in behalf of the imprisoned American fliers, to his last mission to the Congo in September 1961, it also includes:

Continuous efforts in every year to keep the Palestine question from exploding into war and to make progress toward lasting solutions;

Organization in 1955 and 1958 of two great international scientific conferences on the peaceful uses of atomic energy which broke down Cold War barriers to the fruitful exchange of knowledge in this field;

The attempt by 'quiet diplomacy' in October 1956 to achieve a peaceful solution of the Suez Canal crisis on the basis of the six principles to which the foreign ministers of the United Kingdom, France and the United Arab Republic agreed in his office; this attempt was interrupted by the armed Suez intervention two weeks later but was resumed after that resort to force was successfully nullified by the United Nations and was finally brought to a conclusion satisfactory in most respects on the very basis of the original six principles;

The creation of the United Nations Emergency Force (UNEF)—the first force formed and directed by international organization—the withdrawal of the British, French and Israeli forces from Egypt, and the clearance of the Suez Canal by a United Nations fleet in the period between November 1956 and April 1957;

Repeated but rejected efforts at this time to be of constructive service in the Hungarian crisis, caused by Soviet armed intervention;

The creation of the United Nations Observation Group in Lebanon and a United Nations Office in Jordan; these, together with a successful appeal in the General Assembly to the spirit of Arab unity, made possible the solution of the Lebanon and Jordan crises in 1958 and the withdrawal of American and British forces from these countries;

The use of the good offices of a personal representative of the Secretary-General in 1959 in restoring diplomatic relations which had been broken between Cambodia and Thailand and the stationing of a special personal representative in Laos early in 1960 in an effort to contribute to a solution of the Laotian problem;

The launching in the Congo in July 1960 of the greatest, most dangerous and difficult of United Nations operations and securing for it in its first weeks unanimous support of both East and West in the Security Council.

Throughout this period he also worked to give more significance to the part played by the United Nations in helping the economically under-developed and newly independent countries in their struggle for a life of freedom and dignity in the community of nations. He saw moral support from the World Organization and encouragement of a sense of solidarity with it as of high importance. He gave this support through personal visits and diplomacy with the leaders of the young and weak countries on the one hand and with leaders of the industrially advanced countries in a position to provide capital and experts on the other hand. The latter were not yet generally willing to allocate to United Nations programs more than a small fraction of the resources provided in their bilateral aid programs, but this deficiency he offset in part by the steps he took to strengthen the quality and effectiveness of the United Nations multilateral technical assistance and administrative missions, its regional Economic Commissions and the coordination with the Specialized Agencies of the United Nations family, as well as to give to the Economic and Social Council more of a policy-making role in international economic cooperation.

Of course, the official records cannot provide a complete record of action by Dag Hammarskjöld as Secretary-General. The personal influence he exercised through his continuous contacts with the Permanent Delegates and his frequent talks and correspondence with virtually all the leaders of government of the Member States in their capitals or at United Nations Headquarters formed a vital part of his total contribution. Some of this part of the record will inevitably be lost as memories fade and the participants pass on. But enough could be salvaged by prompt research to round out the official records sufficiently to give them reality and life. Authoritative accounts of this record in all its aspects will be of great value to those who carry on the work for international order.

This book is intended to serve a different, though related purpose. It is not a selection from the records of action. It is a selection from the other part of the record—from the speeches, statements and comments in which he developed his philosophy and policies for the role of the United Nations and its relationship to the main currents in international life.

The reader will find reflected in the pages that follow qualities which helped to make Dag Hammarskjöld that most rare of persons in human affairs—a man of true inner greatness in a position of high leadership. He was sustained and inspired by pure and firmly founded beliefs and ideals about life and human relationships to which he was true in word and act. To these he joined a very brilliant, orderly, pragmatic and subtle mind, capable of lightning

speed in both comprehension and construction, yet strictly disciplined. He always had a firm grip on realities and he could be as disappointed by wishful thinking or shallow optimism as by cynicism
or self-serving. His interests were as wide-ranging as those of a man
of the Renaissance while his sympathies for the human predicament
drew their inspiration straight from the ethics of the Gospels. He
was infinitely careful in the planning and execution of all he attempted, in calm acceptance and understanding of human limitations—
including his own—and of the often harsh realities with which he
must work. At the same time his courage was that of the medieval
mystics to whom he refers in his confession of faith, who 'had found
strength to say *yes* to every demand which the needs of their neighbors made them face'. This, combined with his natural mental and
physical endurance, carried him through 18 and 20 hour working
days for weeks on end in times of crisis.

He rejected alike beliefs in the inevitability of progress or of
catastrophe. He considered abstract constructions of constitutional
arrangements for a future world order to be of limited value. He
had a strong sense of the continuity of history and of the possibilities of organic growth into better forms of organization for
society which could result from human endeavours in this direction
renewed and carried forward from one generation to another. The
work must be pragmatic and experimental, performed with a deep
sense of duty and with equal humility. For, as he said at the University of Chicago: 'Working at the edge of the development of
human society is to work at the brink of the unknown. Much of
what is done will one day prove to have been of little avail. That is
no excuse for the failure to act in accordance with our best understanding, in recognition of its limits but with faith in the ultimate
result of the creative evolution in which it is our privilege to
cooperate.'

These qualities of mind and character infused and shaped the
approaches to the problems of international relationships and international organization that are developed in the speeches and statements included in this volume. They speak and should speak for
themselves, but something may usefully be said concerning the
main themes.

'Ours is a work of reconciliation and realistic construction,' Dag
Hammarskjöld told the General Assembly when he accepted his
election as Secretary-General on 10 April 1953. This sentence

continued to define the core of his views of the role of the United Nations as he elaborated them throughout his terms of office. The Charter established the principles and purposes which should guide the work by the governments and the Secretariat. He saw and increasingly sought to interpret these objectives as an evolutionary extension to the relations between nations of democratic principles which have won general acceptance within national life—equal political rights, equal economic opportunity, acceptance of rules of justice and equity, the peaceful settlement of all conflicts in conformity with these rules and abstention from the use of force save in the common interest as constitutionally determined.

The institutions of international organization were tools or instruments needed by the governments in working toward these objectives. These institutions were incomplete, imperfect and experimental, but they also represented indispensable steps along the evolutionary road to that stronger international order he believed must one day be achieved. He recognized the reasons for the greater weight given by the governments to armed alliances and regional groupings in the pursuit of international power politics, but he believed the opportunities opened by the United Nations for moving towards firmer ground for the security of all than an ever-mounting arms race were under-estimated. Since a universal system of collective security remained beyond reach for the present, the work must be carried out primarily by the processes 'of reconciliation and realistic construction'.

From the beginning Dag Hammarskjöld gave emphasis to the importance of making the United Nations more effective as an instrument of negotiation. The conference machinery and formal quasi-parliamentary proceedings were valuable in themselves but they were only a framework for the substance of diplomacy. He was constantly exploring and testing ways of making multilateral diplomacy better serve the goals of reconciliation on the basis of the Charter, by reducing the weight of public propaganda and increasing the element of genuine private negotiation. There are frequent discussions in his speeches and reports of the special values added by the United Nations to the practice of such a diplomacy of reconciliation and of the informal and formal methods by which he sought this end. By persuasion and example he did a great deal to influence the development and he has left guide-lines which, if followed, can lead to further progress.

Though the Charter does not use the word 'universality' in its membership provisions, he believed this principle to be implicit in its inner logic. If one of the Organization's primary purposes was to serve as an instrument of negotiation in the work of reconciliation and peaceful settlement, it did not make sense, as a matter of principle, to keep outside nations which must necessarily be parties to the negotiation if it were to get anywhere.

He welcomed unreservedly the great influx of new Member nations from Africa and Asia, partly because their membership as independent States was an expression of the Charter principle of equal political rights for nations and partly because he saw the task of reconciliation between the West and Asia and Africa as one of the greatest of our times, as important as reconciliation between the two power blocs in the Cold War and one in which the United Nations had practical opportunities to make a more significant immediate contribution. Questions of procedure raised by the sudden doubling of membership, the need to enlarge the Security Council and the Economic and Social Council to make them more representative, the inexperience of the leaders of many of the new nations—these were secondary problems for which answers could be found in adaptations of the rules and by practical experience. He recognized the need to maintain an equitable political balance between the rights of the majority and of the principal possessors of power but he saw this as an old problem dating from 1945. Again, the answers should be sought empirically and in the inner play of the realities of political life. He preferred this approach to schemes for weighted voting which, besides, went against a basic democratic principle of the Charter—equal political rights for large and small. Finally, he rejected utterly the idea that nations could be divided into classes of the responsible and the irresponsible. The lesson of history was only too clear that neither wealth nor power nor age was any guarantee of responsibility in the conduct of national policy.

In the negotiation of issues between the two sides in the Cold War Dag Hammarskjöld accepted the pursuit of direct talks outside the formal procedures of the United Nations as in line with the Charter injunction to Members in Article 33 to seek solutions first of all by negotiation or other peaceful means of their own choice. He consistently dismissed charges of by-passing the Organization that were raised against these procedures. However, he did not hesitate to remind the Great Powers of the overriding constitutional responsibility of the United Nations for disarmament and for dealing with any threats to the peace which might arise from the failure of direct negotiation on such questions as Berlin. On the urgency of renewed efforts to break out of the stalemate of distrust in which disarmament negotiations were locked he held strong views and expressed himself in stronger words than was his custom about the 'nightmare' of the arms race and the increasing risks which its continuance entailed. He spoke also for the rights and interests of the very many other nations whose own security and future life were involved in the outcome of these negotiations. Finally, he saw possibilities for improving the prospects of progress by bringing such negotiations within those United Nations procedures for private and conference diplomacy which he did so much to explore and develop, either within the framework of the Security Council or in some other manner. Though he never pressed the point, the successive breakdowns in bilateral Cold War negotiations at all levels from the Summit down should lead to renewed consideration of the values he believed could be added by using such procedures and by bringing to bear the mediating influences which the United Nations is capable of generating.

Dag Hammarskjöld's conception of the scope for effective use of the United Nations as an instrument in the work of 'realistic construction' widened as he and the governments increasingly tested its powers for executive action over the years. The Suez crisis was the first great test, the Lebanon and Jordan affair another and the Congo the most severe of all. Beyond these he saw in the sudden emergence of African independence as a whole a challenge not only to reconciliation but to realistic construction for which the Organization was a uniquely adapted instrument. The help so much needed by the weak and inexperienced new nations in finding their way to a peaceful political, economic and social evolution could best be provided in ways that were truly disinterested and divorced from power politics by the United Nations, for the United Nations was their organization by equal right with all the others. It was not an outsider in Africa. Even with the far too limited financial resources yet available for multilateral economic, technical and operational assistance he saw opportunity for the Organization to exert a decisive influence upon the development. The United Nations constituted for the young nations of Africa their best hope of

2

keeping the Cold War out of their continent and of gaining a chance to grow to political maturity and strength in genuine freedom and peace. As splits and rivalries appeared among the African states during the Congo crisis he appealed again and again for 'African solidarity within the United Nations' as the only reply to the threat of foreign interventions and widespread war.

From 1956 onward the Secretary-General became increasingly the executive for field operations by the United Nations in support of peace, acting under general mandates from the Security Council or General Assembly. UNEF, the Observation Group in Lebanon, the UN 'presence' in Jordan, the civilian and military operations in the Congo, were all trail-blazing innovations in the forms of action available to the Organization. In each of these crises there was grave danger of the Cold War spreading into new areas of conflict in the Middle East and Africa. That danger so far has been averted, entirely aside from the other contributions made to the pacification of conflicts arising within the region.

Although he warned against expecting the Secretary-General to shoulder responsibilities that rightly belonged to Member governments, Dag Hammarskjöld believed the United Nations could serve increasingly for such executive action in preventing the Cold War from spreading and in gradually narrowing the margins of this conflict. He believed this was equally in the interest of both sides, if not for better reasons because the dangers of another course were too high for either side. He saw a truly international Secretariat, bound to neutrality among all national interests and to service only of the Organization as a whole, as a vital instrument for this purpose. The same principle and the same need would apply to the execution of any agreements that might later be reached for controlled disarmament. He was fully aware of the political risks involved in pioneering an evolution that some would say was ahead of the times and others would find an obstacle to national ambitions or a threat to long-held positions, but he believed the risks for world peace would be far greater if the evolution were not pursued. Therefore it must be pursued.

The Soviet Union's reversal of policy, from support of the UN Congo operations to attacks upon them, and upon the very concept of the international civil servant, was a heavy blow. The danger was compounded by certain voices raised in the West too, and in other parts of the world. These did not generally join in open attack but they indicated a shared desire, for various reasons, to attempt to stop the evolution and turn the clock back. Together they have placed in jeopardy prospects for further growth in the effectiveness of the United Nations, and even of its very existence as anything more than a standing conference machinery of a type that the nations had found inadequate as far back as 1919. But the battle is far from lost. Stands have changed in the past and can be changed again, or somehow by-passed. Before he died Dag Hammarskjöld, at Oxford and in his last annual report, discussed calmly and fully the fundamental issues involved and the grave consequences of a step backward. He has left behind other weapons of example and reason as well. With their help the work of construction can be carried on if there are enough men and leaders of sense and good will who will unite to use them. His own firmly held belief had been expressed to press correspondents at the beginning of his second term—'faith that the future will be all right because there will always be enough people to fight for a decent future'.

In the course of his speeches about the United Nations and world problems he returned again and again to questions of individual attitudes and responsibility. These were what counted, far more than institutions. He spoke to the universities, to the churches, to scientists, to business, to political leaders, to many others on this theme. An address at Johns Hopkins University was entitled, 'International Service' but its main subject was not the Secretariat or diplomacy. It was about individual responsibility for international service in the world of today. The 'walls of distrust' preventing true communication between man and man and people and people troubled him greatly and he fought to break them down in all directions. At the University of Lund and elsewhere he dealt with the new relationships between the West and Asia and Africa in terms of the problems of understanding for the individual Westerner and for the individual Asian and African. International-mindedness had nothing to do with a 'rootless cosmopolitanism'. It should instead grow from roots firmly anchored in your own culture and traditions but reaching outward to meet with understanding and respect all the others with different cultures and traditions.

*　　*　　*

The preceding paragraphs are intended as a general indication in summary form of the main themes to be found elaborated in this

volume with all the interplay of comprehension, analysis and insights to which Dag Hammarskjöld's qualities of mind and character
gave him access. He considered speech-making to be an important
part of the Secretary-General's duties, not as a propaganda operation but as a contribution to understanding of the problems of
international and human relations and of the United Nations as an
instrument in helping to meet these problems. He could accept only
a few of the thousands of invitations he received because of the
many other demands upon his time and he spoke only when he
could think out and prepare his speeches personally. He disliked
oratory and his speeches were never platform performances. They
were meant to be pondered and re-read.

He spoke and wrote much more as Secretary-General than could
be included in a publication of this length, but most of his speeches
are here in full, together with shorter statements of significance or
special interest and those Introductions to his Annual Reports of
greatest value for the future. In other cases extracts have been used
when they could stand by themselves. Some titles have been added
to assist identification, and purely formal introductory or concluding
sentences have usually been omitted. In all other cases where dele-
tions have been made they are indicated. These have been done
with care to avoid any alteration of meaning or balance.

A few of his statements to the Security Council or General
Assembly have been included, especially those giving his understanding of the duties of his office at the times of his elections and
of the Suez and Congo crises. In the fall and winter of 1960–61 it
was his task to reply again and again to incessant Soviet attacks upon
the Congo operation and the Secretariat. The responses chosen for
inclusion here reflect the unshaken courage and integrity with which
Dag Hammarskjöld faced all the fire that a Great Power could
direct against the Secretary-General.

For reasons given in a later explanatory note (see page 63) two
addresses he gave to the Swedish Academy and one to the Swedish
Tourist Association in capacities other than as Secretary-General
and on subjects other than those directly related to the United
Nations have also been included, as well as a few shorter statements
reflecting other interests. Some excerpts from the voluminous transcripts of his press conferences have been chosen to round out the
picture. His extemporaneous comments have a flavor of their own
and he also tended to use his press conferences to express opinions

or advance ideas which it would have been difficult or impossible for him to do in more formal circumstances. The delegations soon discovered this and regularly read and dispatched the transcripts to their foreign offices.

The arrangement is mainly chronological, though shorter extracts and comments made in the same general period have in some cases been grouped together. An arrangement by subject matter would have been impossible without doing violence to many texts that were presented as coherent entities and to a sequence inspired in part by successive experiences and the historical course of developments. Notes have been kept to a minimum, but there are a full table of contents and an index to assist reference to Dag Hammarskjöld's views on specific topics and events. English is the original language of the contents except in the few cases noted where his speeches were written in Swedish. The English spelling style used in the speeches and statements as originally issued at the United Nations has been retained.

Finally, I am most grateful for advice and assistance in the preparation of this volume to old friends and colleagues with whom I worked as Director of Press and Publications at the United Nations.

WILDER FOOTE

Camden, Maine
1 May, 1962

OLD CREEDS IN A NEW WORLD

Written for Edward R. Murrow's radio program 'This I Believe,' a series of statements of personal philosophy and spiritual belief by prominent men and women later published in book form under the same title. This statement is included in Volume 2, published in 1954.*

The world in which I grew up was dominated by principles and ideals of a time far from ours and, as it may seem, far removed from the problems facing a man of the middle of the twentieth century. However, my way has not meant a departure from those ideals. On the contrary, I have been led to an understanding of their validity also for our world of today. Thus, a never abandoned effort frankly and squarely to build up a personal belief in the light of experience and honest thinking has led me in a circle; I now recognize and endorse, unreservedly, those very beliefs which were once handed down to me.

From generations of soldiers and government officials on my father's side I inherited a belief that no life was more satisfactory than one of selfless service to your country—or humanity. This service required a sacrifice of all personal interests, but likewise the courage to stand up unflinchingly for your convictions.

From scholars and clergymen on my mother's side I inherited a belief that, in the very radical sense of the Gospels, all men were equals as children of God, and should be met and treated by us as our masters in God.

Faith is a state of the mind and the soul. In this sense we can understand the words of the Spanish mystic, St. John of the Cross: 'Faith is the union of God with the soul.' The language of religion is a set of formulas which register a basic spiritual experience. It must not be regarded as describing, in terms to be defined by philosophy, the reality which is accessible to our senses and which we can analyse with the tools of logic. I was late in understanding what this meant. When I finally reached that point, the beliefs in which I was once brought up and which, in fact, had given my life direction even while my intellect still challenged their validity, were recognized by me as mine in their own right and by my free choice.

I feel that I can endorse those convictions without any compromise with the demands of that intellectual honesty which is the very key to maturity of mind.

The two ideals which dominated my childhood world met me fully harmonized and adjusted to the demands of our world of today in the ethics of Albert Schweitzer, where the ideal of service is supported by and supports the basic attitude to man set forth in the Gospels. In his work I also found a key for modern man to the world of the Gospels.

But the explanation of how man should live a life of active social service in full harmony with himself as a member of the community of the spirit, I found in the writings of those great medieval mystics for whom 'self-surrender' had been the way to self-realization, and who in 'singleness of mind' and 'inwardness' had found strength to say *yes* to every demand which the needs of their neighbors made them face, and to say *yes* also to every fate life had in store for them when they followed the call of duty, as they understood it. Love— that much misused and misinterpreted word—for them meant simply an overflowing of the strength with which they felt them-selves filled when living in true self-oblivion. And this love found natural expressions in an unhesitant fulfillment of duty and in an unreserved acceptance of life, whatever it brought them personally of toil, suffering—or happiness.

I know that their discoveries about the laws of inner life and of action have not lost their significance.

PART I

1953–1957

STATEMENTS
AFTER ELECTION TO OFFICE

9 April 1953–4 December 1953

THE INTERNATIONAL PUBLIC SERVANT

*Statement to the press on arrival at International
Airport, New York, 9 April 1953.*

On this occasion, when I am landing in New York to take up my
new responsibilities, you may well expect me to have something to
say to you. I should, myself, like to do more at this first meeting on
American soil than just to introduce myself. But yet, there are only
a few very general remarks which I feel that I could—and should—
make here and now.

I will tell you why.

First a personal reason. I want to do a job, not to talk about it—
not even afterwards, so much the less in advance.

But further. Of course, I—like all of you, like all engaged in
diplomatic or political activity—have my views and ideas on the
great international issues facing us. But those personal views of
mine are not—or should not be—of any greater interest to you
today than they were just a couple of weeks ago. Those views are
mine as a private man. In my new official capacity the private man
should disappear and the international public servant take his place.
The public servant is there in order to assist, so to say from the
inside, those who take the decisions which frame history. He should
—as I see it—listen, analyze and learn to understand fully the forces
at work and the interests at stake, so that he will be able to give the
right advice when the situation calls for it. Don't think that he—in
following this line of personal policy—takes but a passive part in
the development. It is a most active one. But he is active as an
instrument, a catalyst, perhaps an inspirer—he serves.

Irrespective of the political responsibilities of the Secretary-
General to which I have just referred, he has an important, indeed
an overwhelming job as chief administrator of the UN Secretariat.

27

To me it seems a challenging task to try and develop the UN administrative organization into the most efficient instrument possible. My experience from other administrations tells me that even in the best one there is always much to improve. On the other hand, I feel that an administration inspired by sound self-criticism, never blunted by conceit or false loyalties, and self-improving in that spirit, has a just claim to the respect and confidence of the governments and the public.

In articles recently published it has been said that I am interested in mountaineering. That's true. But I have never climbed any famous peaks. My experience is limited to Scandinavia where mountaineering calls more for endurance than for equilibristics, and where mountains are harmonious rather than dramatic, matter of fact (if you permit me such a term in this context) rather than eloquent. However, that much I know of this sport that the qualities it requires are just those which I feel we all need today: perseverance and patience, a firm grip on realities, careful but imaginative planning, a clear awareness of the dangers but also of the fact that fate is what we make it and that the safest climber is he who never questions his ability to overcome all difficulties.

A WORK OF RECONCILIATION
AND REALISTIC CONSTRUCTION

Statement before the Plenary Session of the General Assembly, 10 April 1953 after his election as Secretary-General.

In the message by which the President of the Security Council informed me of the decision to recommend me as Secretary-General of the United Nations he drew attention to 'the immense importance of this post, especially at the present time.' With humility I accept an election, expressing a confidence in me which I have still to justify—with a humility inspired as much by my knowledge of personal limitations as by my awareness of the extraordinary responsibility which you impose on me by your election.

My background is, as you know, the civil service of my country—
a civil service strengthened by a long tradition and firmly founded
on law. It is in the bodies by which the nations of Europe are trying
to shape the future of that part of the world that I have gathered
the experience I have of international cooperation. There I have
learned the vital importance of loyalty, devotion and integrity of
those engaged in the work.

I bring to this task a firm will to devote myself without any reserve
to the work carried out by the United Nations organization in
pursuit of its high aims. I am here to serve you all. In so doing I
shall count on your understanding, on your advice and on your will
to give to what I have to say the attention that it may deserve. I am
animated by a desire to meet all problems with an open mind. It is
for you to judge how I succeed. It is for you to correct me if I fail.

Ours is a work of reconciliation and realistic construction. This
work must be based on respect for the laws by which human civilization has been built. It likewise requires a strict observance of the
rules and principles laid down in the Charter of this Organization.
My work shall be guided by this knowledge.

This great Organization grew out of the pain and turmoil of the
last war. It welded together in what should be a continued cooperation for world peace all those who had fought against oppression.
By all who have sacrificed themselves, by all sacrificing themselves
in the fight for freedom and peace this Organization has—in the
words of one of the greatest leaders of democracy—been 'consec-
rated far above our poor power to add or detract'. May I quote also
these other words from the Gettysburg address. 'The world will
little note, nor long remember, what we say here, but it can never
forget what they did. . . . It is for us, the living, rather to be dedicated here to the unfinished task which they have, thus far, so
nobly advanced. It is rather for us to be here dedicated to the great
task remaining before us.'

In concluding may I remind you of the great memory just cele-
brated by the Christian world, may I do so because of what that
memory tells us of the redeeming power of true dedication to peace
and good will toward men. We are of different creeds and convictions. Events and ideas which to some of us remain the very basis
of our faith are elements of the spiritual heritage of man which are
foreign to others. But common to us all, and above all other convictions stands the truth, once expressed by a Swedish poet when he

said that the greatest prayer of man does not ask for victory but for peace.*

I have not gone into any of the specific problems facing this Organization, some of them now harassing all minds. But I have tried to indicate the spirit in which I shall go to the work when called upon to take part in the efforts of the United Nations Organization to justify the hopes of all its members.

FROM LEAGUE OF NATIONS TO
UNITED NATIONS

Extract from Address to the Staff of the UN Office at the Palais des Nations, Geneva, 26 May 1953.

Most of you certainly have been to the museum arranged in this house, with collections commemorating the days of the League of Nations. There we see portraits of Nansens and Cecils, Stresemanns and Briands, of decades between the two wars. The memory of these men is justly honoured by us. They were pioneers for an internationalism, universal in scope and with world peace as its aim, which, whatever its shortcomings, represents one of the elements in our world of today on which we have to base what hope we may have in future.

The organization whose life and contribution is reflected in our museum belongs already to the past, but many of those who worked in it are with us. From personal experience they can tell of the change taken place between the days of the League of Nations and the days of the United Nations. Although perhaps profiting from wider support of the common man than our predecessors, we have to work in a much harsher climate. Where our predecessors dreamt of a new heaven, our greatest hope is that we may be permitted to save the old earth. Behind that hope, however, are now rallied all peoples of the world.

You may not agree with me, but it is my personal conviction that in order to keep alive that internationalism of which I spoke, in order to translate it into action, we must work harder and hope for

* Erik Axel Karlfeldt 1864-1931, member of the Swedish Academy, awarded the Nobel Prize in Literature, 1931.

less than those who built the League. The museum is not a tomb. The memory it celebrates is a challenge and a source of strength for those who have the privilege of serving the organizations which now embody the hope of peace. We are expected to succeed where our predecessors failed. We remember their selflessness and courage, but we know that even more may be required of us, if only in order to save what they achieved. . . .

ON DEFEATISM

Extract from Remarks to the United Nations Correspondents Association, 10 July 1953.

. . . I have repeatedly quoted a phrase coined by Paul Valéry ('Ceux qui préfèrent se noyer à nager dans les conditions de l'eau'). It expresses the simple truth that, when trying to change our world, we have to face it as it is. Those are lost who dare not face the basic facts of international interdependence. Those are lost who permit defeats to scare them back to a starting point of narrow nationalism. Those are lost who are so scared by a defeat as to despair about the future. For all those, the dark prophecies may be justified. But not for those who do not permit themselves to be scared, nor for the Organization which is the instrument at their disposal in the fight— an instrument which may be wrecked, but, if that happens, would have to be, and certainly would be, recreated again and again. . . .

TRIBUTE TO A MEDIATOR

From Statement on the Occasion of the Rededication of the Memorial Plaque for Count Folke Bernadotte at UN Headquarters, 24 July 1953.

On 17 September* it will be five years since the day when Count Folke Bernadotte gave his life in Jerusalem while carrying out the assignment, entrusted to him by the United Nations, of establishing and maintaining a truce in Palestine and of bringing about an

* It was to be on 17 September 1961 that Dag Hammarskjöld took off on the flight from Leopoldville to Ndola that ended in the fatal crash early the following morning.

armistice. He died as he had lived—gallantly, unselfishly—in the service of the highest ideals of humanity. He served with a true humility of spirit which ennobled his work. No human life was too mean for his compassion, no obstacle was too great for his effort, no risk was too high—if the end was to give another measure of relief to a suffering and war-torn humanity. . . .

But it is not a precious memory only which we honor today. We bow before an ideal of life, and an example of profound faith, faith in the dignity but also in the good sense and fundamental decency of men. Without this ideal and this faith, who would seek to follow the course of patient negotiation, of ceaseless effort to conciliate, to mediate, to compose differences, to appeal to men's reason in order to build agreement ? This ideal of public service and this faith in the ultimate triumph of good will are a living reality. They are the foundation upon which the United Nations itself is built.

Sometimes the reality becomes obscured and the patient effort of mediation may seem to lead only to frustration and futility. Then the name upon this plaque will stand as an affirmation of living truth. Bernadotte's life is a pledge which the first Mediator of the United Nations has given, that the effort to realize by honest agreement on earth peace and good will toward men is worthy of the greatest sacrifice a true man can bring. . . .

THE WEAPONS OF THE SECRETARIAT

Extract from Message for UN Staff Day at Geneva,
4 December 1953.

. . . Why are the standards and the independence of the Secretariat so important ? The more I see of the work in the United Nations, the more convinced I feel of this importance. Countries are arming in order to be able to negotiate from a position of strength. The Secretariat too has to negotiate, not only in its own interest, but for the cause of peace and a peaceful development of our world. The weight we carry is not determined by physical force or the number of people who form the constituency. It is based solely on trust in our impartiality, our experience and knowledge, our maturity of judgment. Those qualities are our weapons, in no way secret weapons, but as difficult to forge as guns and bombs. The

Secretariat has an essential part to play in the world affairs of today. We *will* play it if we accept the price for building up our position of strength. We must reject a role of insignificance subject to constant criticism and shirking the risks of a full part in our world. We must choose a role of responsibility and independence, sacrificing part of the illusory safety you may derive from a locked door. . . .

THE UNITED NATIONS
AND THE POLITICAL SCIENTIST

*Address at Luncheon given by the American Political
Science Association, Washington, D.C.,
11 September 1953.*

The political scientists had a great share in the creation of the United Nations Organization. And they are doing much in the class-room, in publications and by their daily influence on public affairs to explain, to strengthen and to help the Organization. Meeting you here today it is natural for me to try and explain how the United Nations' world looks from the inside—to a social scientist who long ago had to abandon scientific work but who, in the back of his mind, in whatever job he has had to try, has given much thought to the challenge that the special activities in which he was engaged presented to his scientific imagination and conscience.

The area covered by your Association is very wide—certainly as wide as, but probably not any wider than, that covered by the United Nations. On one of the frontiers of UN activities we find the highly specialized economist working with his statistical tools, at another frontier the expert on public relations and their psychology. At still another frontier the diplomatic expert with his background in international political history. And at a fourth frontier you have the man specializing in problems of internal administration and institutional developments.

The United Nations and its activities reflect acute needs of our time. The diversification and the scope of its various problems and efforts mirror the diversification and problems of the present social and political situation. In this way the United Nations' experiences are indicative of the challenge of our time to the social sciences and the social scientists.

In many respects what is done in the United Nations is to apply to practical problems of today conclusions drawn in studies already made in various spheres of the social sciences. In other cases the United Nations embarks upon pioneer work, elaborating its own approaches and presenting practical conclusions to be studied by—and perhaps also challenged by—the independent social scientists. I am tempted to describe the situation in the famous phrase of Max Weber: To a large extent the United Nations is living off truth, as established by the social scientists, but it has also to live for truth, in its creative intellectual and practical activities.

I think that the spheres in which the United Nations, and those working inside its Secretariat, have the greatest wealth of new material to offer to the social scientists for their studies are first, the sphere of institutional problems, proper to a world-wide international administration, and second, that of diplomatic techniques and of international relations as elaborated in an international body, serving all countries irrespective of the split of our world and the differences of national interests represented among the governments by which it has been established.

It would take me too far to go into any detail. It would, indeed, be presumptuous on my part to try to do so. My imagination as an ex-teacher of the University of Stockholm may lead me into temptation, but twenty years of political life have not dulled my scientific conscience nor muffled its warning against large conclusions from inconclusive evidence.

However, let me indicate briefly the nature of the problems I have in mind in the two specific spheres to which I have referred —problems which seem to me to present a challenge to the social scientists.

I imagine that a few of you have already given some thought to the very peculiar organizational and institutional problems developing in an international administration. One of those problems has recently had the honour of figuring even in the newspaper headlines. I refer to the implications of a truly international status for such an administration, a status of full independence.* Other problems which affect the day-to-day work and are just as important, are scarcely noted by the public and certainly only partly known to those scientists who are interested in the field of public administration. Let me mention a few of them briefly.

In the United Nations Secretariat we have nearly sixty different nationalities represented. None of us can make ourselves entirely free from our own background, and why should we ? Is not the national accent and the national experience very often a great asset in international cooperation ? It certainly is, but at the same time it may introduce an element of division. It may tend to split what

---

* Refers to U.S. governmental investigations in 1952 and 1953 of the loyalty of its nationals in the Secretariat. See Address at Oxford University, page 340, for discussion of the issues involved.

should be a unity into separate compartments. For the Secretary-General of the United Nations and his collaborators it is necessary to find ways to make the national elements an asset, to overcome the divisive influences and try to create a unity in which the diversity of the national backgrounds of the members of the administration is fully respected and preserved, but in such a way as to be an asset, rather than a liability in the work. I am sure it must be evident to you how difficult and challenging a problem this is.

Another problem in international administration is closely connected with the ways in which such an administration is influenced by different administrative traditions and national legal ideologies. I would like to give you a practical example of significance. In the United Nations Administration as it is now set up, you find a blend between administrative traditions typical of various parts of the world. For example from the American administrative practice the United Nations has derived a tradition calling for a high degree of specialization, from the European side a tradition calling for a high degree of permanency of employment and professional flexibility. The American system of specialization, as is well known, creates a need for a comparatively larger number of officials. But this number varies from time to time both upward and downward as changes are made in policies and programs and this in turn leads to less emphasis upon, and fewer safeguards for, permanency of tenure. The European system, on the other hand, works with a smaller number of officials and the employees are supposed to be able to adjust to a variety of different responsibilities. This European system makes it possible to give to the employment a high degree of permanency, where the tendency to rigidity is counterbalanced by the flexibility of service. When you combine such traditions, as is being done in the United Nations, you are really trying out a new technique, natural in the light of prevailing circumstances, but fraught with difficulties, and so far insufficiently explored. By methods of trial and error we have to work towards an equilibrium between the various elements, adjusted to the special needs of a universal international administration.

The general problem just mentioned leads up to a whole series of questions which will have to be settled in the light of further experience. Let me mention only two. How is the specialized scientific expert to be fitted into the framework of the international administration? What is his proper function and what kind of

status should he be given ? And further, how is the problem created
by the aging of specialized employees—a problem facing all
administrations—to be solved in an international administrative
system ?

But let me leave this field and say just a few words also about the
sphere where the United Nations Administration is pioneering into
fields where it may be said to break new ground for the political
scientists. Traditional diplomatic techniques are, of course, in
principle, bilateral. That is true even if many nations happen to be
represented at the conference table. A truly multilateral approach
to diplomacy does not come into being until an instrument is
created which represents a denationalized platform for negotiations
or a denationalized instrument for a number of governments. In
the Annual Report to the Eighth Assembly I have said that I believe
we have only begun to explore the full potentialities of the United
Nations as an instrument for multilateral diplomacy, especially the
most fruitful combinations of public discussion on the one hand and
private negotiations and mediation on the other. I added that the
opportunities are there to be tested and used.

This is a fascinating field where the experience of classical diplomacy, the successes and the errors of the League of Nations and of
the United Nations, and the knowledge of the technique and
psychology of a public debate utilizing to the full the modern media,
all have to be taken into account by the political scientist as well as
by those who are put in positions where they have to explore
possibilities by action. Looking at my present job from the point of
view of the social scientist, but looking at it also just as much from
the point of view of somebody deeply engaged in the common effort
to save peace and to build a world of peace, I cannot find any part
of my present task more challenging than the one which consists in
trying to develop all the potentialities of that unique diplomatic
instrument which the Charter has created in the institution called
the Secretary-General of the United Nations.

At this point I would like to depart from the beaten track of my
prepared text and venture into wider fields even at the risk of losing
my way.

I called the Secretariat and the institution named the Secretary-
General instruments the full potentialities of which should be
further explored. Instruments for whom ? Well, of course, for the
governments, but to be handled by the men and women assigned to

the various posts in the Administration. I would not say anything here about *how* they are using the instruments. That would take me into the field of policy-making which I think is more properly discussed from other platforms. But I would like to indicate *what* they need as a background for the proper handling of the instruments, because these needs throw light on the challenge of our time to the political sciences in the spheres where the United Nations is in no way a pioneer but gratefully may reap where others have sown.

The Secretary-General—and I use him as a symbol for all of the Secretariat—is facing a public relations problem of a delicate and difficult nature. He is not out to 'sell' anything. His is not a propaganda operation. But he has to try and reach the minds and hearts of people so as to get the United Nations' efforts firmly based in public reaction. As I said, we are not selling anything, but we feel that what we are doing is something that should have the support of the simple reactions of plain men, if we manage to tell them our story in the right way. So, the question of public relations to the Secretary-General develops into a question of human relations.

Human relations. The United Nations has to activate in its support people's urge to live together and work together in peace and decency. For that reason the United Nations has to try to create a new awareness of human and national interdependence. In order to be able to do so it will have to understand what makes so difficult the development of such an awareness. It will have to understand—and challenge—the fear that motivates so much of human action, the fear that is our worst enemy but which, somehow, seems to taint at least some corner of the heart of every man.

So the Secretary-General of the United Nations is led into very wide fields which are under the reign of political science. In his efforts he may have to enter the world of 'An American Dilemma' and the land of 'The Lonely Crowd', and he must give such knowledge its proper background in the broodings of the de Tocquevilles and Schumpeters.

When tackling the question of interdependence the United Nations must try and analyze for itself what determines group relations of the kind which international political history so often mirrors. I have already mentioned the element of fear but there are other factors. We would be misled if we thought about international relations only in terms of diplomatic history. Economic policies and power politics are other forces doing their work in the background. We move here in the shadow of Burckhardt. We have to listen to those who analyze the dynamics of the great population movements and the national revivals. Finally we may arrive at a point where we have to analyze the situation with the finest tools of political economy in order to see how material factors determine or clash with human reactions.

You may feel that my departure from the beaten path has led me very far indeed, when I try to cover in one sweeping movement spheres studied by the theoretical economist, the historian and the student of the human mind. However, all the parts of political and social science are linked together. The man mastering all the various aspects does not exist. But each of us may be able to make a contribution and so to build up a picture which, although far from complete, gives us a rough map of the waters that we have to sail.

The ultimate challenge to the political sciences—and to us all— is whether man shall master his world and his history or let himself be mastered by a world and a history which after all is made by man. There cannot be more than one reply to this question. Man must master his world, but in order to do so, he must know it.

THE NEW 'SANTA MARIA'

Address at Dinner in his honor given by the American Association for the United Nations in cooperation with the New York University Institute for Review of United Nations Affairs, New York, 14 September 1953.

All of us in this room tonight are here because of our concern for the things that the United Nations stands for and for the proper place of the United Nations in our world. I am sure this concern is shared by the many families who are not physically present but have just now joined in our program from their homes by means of radio and television. You, who *are* present as members and friends of the American Association for the United Nations, and of the New York University Institute for Review of United Nations Affairs, are here because you believe in the United Nations, you want it to succeed, and each of you, within the circle of your influence, is working for it to succeed. In this, the hopes and prayers of millions more are with you.

Thus, you and I are in the same boat together. It is true that while you are volunteers, I may be considered a draftee who had not much of a choice when the draft call came for the job I hold. But my commitment to what the United Nations stands for is and always has been freely given. My recent experiences have strengthened my conviction that the job I hold in the United Nations is one that rightly commands the utmost that can be given to it.

So we are truly together, in the same boat. We are together in our concern and in our hopes, together also in our determination to use to the best of our ability the means at our disposal, with perseverance and firm trust in the future.

The *Baghavad-Gita* echoes somewhere an experience of all ages and all philosophies in these words: 'Work with anxiety about results is far inferior to work without such anxiety, in calm self-surrender.' These are words of worldly wisdom which we can all share. But they also express a deep faith. We will be happy if we can make that faith ours in all our efforts.

On the seas we sail we have to face all the storms and stresses created by the ideological, economic and social conditions of our world. Aboard this new *Santa Maria* we have to meet the impatience of those sailors who expect land on the horizon tomorrow, also the cynicism or sense of futility of those who would give up and leave us drifting impotently. On the shores we have all those who are against the whole expedition, who seem to take a special delight in blaming the storms on the ship instead of the weather. Well, let us admit that this comparison with the crew of Columbus soon after he set sail on the *Santa Maria* has some truth also in its negative implications. We have still to prove our case.

I think you will agree that it will help us to have frequent recourse to our compass and the Guide to Navigation for our civilization that historical experience and the new knowledge and techniques of science and technology have placed in our hands.

In the classical Chinese collection of poetic philosophy, ascribed to Tao-Tse-Tung, it is said somewhere that whoever wants to grip the world and shape it will fail, because the world is a spiritual thing that cannot be shaped. On first reaction, this might seem to be the antithesis of the spirit that animated Columbus. But this is not so. The history of mankind is made by man, but men partly make it blindly. No one can foresee with certainty what will emerge from the give and take of the forces at work in any age. For that reason history often seems to run its course beyond the reach of any man or nation. We cannot mould the world as masters of a material thing. Columbus did not reach the East Indies. But we can influence the development of the world from within as a spiritual thing. In this sense Columbus would have been a pioneer for a new age even if he himself had never reached America.

As individuals and as groups we can put our influence to the best of our understanding and ability on the side of what we believe is right and true. We can help in the movement toward those ends that inspire our lives and are shared by all men of good will—in terms very close to those of the Charter of the United Nations—peace and freedom for all, in a world of equal rights for all.

In the annual report to the General Assembly I expressed my conviction that our time is basically characterized by two movements in civilization—one toward greater social justice within nations, and the other toward greater political and economic equality and justice between nations. I am sure that there are many who would dissent from this proposition. They would say that the basic movements of our time are towards a free society on the one hand and towards totalitarianism on the other.

To them I can only say that I think this is confusing what are the forces at work in the world with specific manifestations of those forces, when utilized by or clashing with ideologies and unguided group reactions. I believe the dictatorships of the few—and the dictatorships of the masses—the devastating wars and the great revolutions that have characterized our generation are to be understood in the light of the basic movements toward social justice and equality within and between nations. When those forces are controlled and guided by constructive and far-seeing policies they yield other effects.

I am thinking of those nations that have managed without violent revolution and without passing dictatorship to create in this century a life for their own peoples not too far from the ideals of freedom and equality for all. I am thinking of the great new independent nations that have been born in the past few years, again without bloodshed, who are now cooperating in fruitful friendship with the nations which formerly had conquered and controlled them.

Thus, it seems to me, the basic movements of our time should not be confused with their various manifestations—war, revolution, dictatorship, peaceful democratic evolution and the peaceful achievement of independence.

The United Nations owes its origin to those who, fifty years ago, surmised at least the basic trends of the twentieth century at its inception and sought in the international field to channel them within a peaceful framework of law and orderly development. The first World War interrupted those first efforts. But after that war the struggle to create patterns for peaceful international progress was renewed and the League of Nations was created. Once more we suffered a catastrophic setback, but the experiment has been repeated for a third time in the United Nations, an international instrument with more potential influence and a wider field of activity than any before envisaged.

I think that all those who will take the trouble to re-read the Charter and examine the work of the United Nations and the Specialized Agencies would agree that the United Nations is 'in tune' with the basic movements of our time in their positive and constructive manifestations. All its pledges and all its work are in the direction of peaceful progress toward greater social justice within nations and greater political and economic equality and justice between nations.

But I must hasten to add, for the benefit of a certain school of thought probably not represented here tonight, that the United Nations has no power to encroach upon the national sovereignty of any state against the will of its government and people. It would indeed not only be against the letter and the spirit of the Charter for the United Nations to attempt to impose its will in domestic matters. It would also be against the elementary wisdom expressed in Tao-Tse-Tung's law of life. You cannot grip the world and shape it as a material thing. You can only influence its development if you recognize and respect it as a thing of the spirit.

Just as the United Nations cannot impose its will in domestic matters, so its existence does not add to the economic burden of its Members, beyond its modest administrative budget. . . . Nor does it create restrictions on the freedom of action of its Member nations beyond the commitments of the Charter—commitments that I believe every civilized community in the world would wish to uphold in any case.

Beyond this, economic burdens and restrictions on freedom of action of any nation are imposed not by the United Nations, but by the facts of international life and the national interests of the countries concerned. Programs of economic and military aid, and the conferences and negotiations through which agreements are sought, are undertaken by governments because they are deemed to be necessary to the national interest and position of the countries concerned and not because of restrictions imposed from outside by charters and treaties.

This again is a case of blaming the ship instead of the weather for the difficulties of steering a safe course in rough seas.

In fact, organized international cooperation as represented by the United Nations and other agencies tends to reduce, rather than increase, the burden upon any single nation in its efforts to prevent war and encourage an orderly evolution toward a more peaceful, just and prosperous world. What would otherwise be a burden on the shoulders of one, is shared by many and the equitability of the sharing is something that can be worked out. But if there is no international organization, no United Nations, then equitability and sharing itself become academic questions. There is a price to be paid for organized international cooperation. But it is a far lesser price than the one that would be exacted from any nation that attempted in this day and generation to 'go it alone'.

Now I come to an even more central question in this examination of our compass and our Guide to Navigation. As you all know, the United Nations Charter is based on what I may call a working hypothesis. This is that all the great nations and groups of nations must belong to it if it is to succeed. The Charter does not quite say that membership should be universal, but that is its spirit.

We know that this hypothesis is being challenged, and challenged not only by those who do not yet fully understand and accept the essential interdependency of our world today, but also by truly internationally minded people animated by the most serious desire to build a better world. Yet it seems to me that the idea of the United Nations as a club to which only the like-minded will be admitted, in which membership is a privilege and expulsion is the retribution for wrong-doing, is totally unrealistic and self-defeating.

Look anywhere in the world today. Is there any solution in sight except peacefully negotiated agreements ? Granted that at a given moment the prospects for such agreements seem dim indeed. What is the alternative ? Only the attempt to establish 'one world' by force of arms. And that is no alternative. Such an attempt would lead to a catastrophe just as fatal to the presumed victor, as to the vanquished. Beyond that, history and social conditions have given us a world so heterogeneous that the conditions simply do not exist for a one world established by force. I believe this should be recognized as true no matter on what ideology you base your j udgment and for whatever way of life you plead.

So we return to our working hypothesis of somehow living together. And we find that the governments of the Great Power members of the United Nations seem to believe in it enough to continue actively working inside the United Nations. We find that in the present division of the world the power of veto often prevents decisions by the Security Council. But we also know that the United Nations as a whole need not be paralyzed. First of all, the application of the veto does not exist in the Assembly and the other organs.

But there is a more important and basic consideration that should be more widely understood. Peaceful settlements of the great issues between nations are not prevented by a veto written into the Charter, but by the hard fact that such settlements require agreement and

acceptance by the parties to it. This would be true even if there
were no provision for a veto in the Security Council. Thus, it is not
primarily a question of this or that voting procedure, but of working
to create conditions of international life more favourable than those
that exist today for the acceptance by the parties concerned of just
and wise solutions to these great issues.

Is there anyone who would tell us that any course of action
tending to make the United Nations less universal than it is would
improve the prospects for finding such solutions by peaceful means ?
In fact, so far, we find no nation willing to risk what is likely to be
the end of a course, once entered, that would make the United
Nations no longer a meeting place for all the world. I believe that
the currents of history and the judgment of the governments alike
are on our side.

When I think of the work before us—you as friends and believers
in the United Nations, and I as Secretary-General—I am reminded
of a famous idea of Dostoevsky in *The Brothers Karamazov*, where
he has one of his heroes say that the future may be one of a struggle
between the State trying to make itself Church and the Church
trying to make itself State.

Applied in international life today, we might say that the United
Nations represents ideals at least professed by all nations, but that
it is not a super-state trying to impose on people any 'right' way of
life or any way of life different from one freely chosen by the people.
On the contrary, it seeks as the repository and voice of a common
heritage of ideals to penetrate the life of states in their international
relations and to influence their conduct toward a wider realization
of those ideals.

I think that such a view of the United Nations as I have outlined
will help all of us who are working for its success, whether as
citizens or officials, in judging wisely each issue as it comes along
and in meeting the various currents of criticism and opposition. No
state, no group of states, no world organization, can grip the world
and shape it, neither by force, nor by any formula of words in a
charter or a treaty. There are no absolute answers to the agonies and
searchings of our time. But all men and women of good will can
influence the course of history in the direction of the ideals expressed
in the Charter.

What does such an approach mean in practical terms for you on
the one hand and for the Secretary-General and the Secretariat on

the other ? You will permit me to take my own role first, not because it is more important but because it may have some bearing upon yours.

I do not conceive the role of the Secretary-General and the Secretariat as representing what has been called a 'third line' in the international debate. Nor is it for him to try and initiate 'compromises' that might encroach upon areas that should be exclusively within the sphere of responsibility of the respective national governments.

On the other side I see the duty of the Secretariat to form, in the first instance, a most complete and objective picture of the aims, motives and difficulties of the Member nations. Acting in that knowledge, it is our duty to seek to anticipate situations that might lead to new conflicts or points of tension and to make appropriate suggestions to the governments before matters reach a stage of public controversy.

Beyond this, the Secretary-General should express with full frankness to the governments concerned and their representatives the conclusions at which he arrives on issues before the Organization. These conclusions must be completely detached from any national interest or policy and based solely on the principles and ideals to which the governments have adhered as Members of the United Nations. In other words, the relationship of the Secretary-General to the governments should be one of a trusted consultant on those considerations following from adherence to the Charter and membership in the United Nations that should be taken into account by the governments in coming to their own policy decisions.

Clearly such a relationship of mutual confidence and trust would be impossible in an atmosphere of publicity. This does not mean that the Secretary-General should not also be a public spokesman for the Organization. Indeed, to explain, interpret and defend the United Nations to the peoples of the world is one of the important duties of his office. But he should never do this in such a way as to contravene his obligations as representative of all Member nations and to the principles of the Organization. He should not permit himself to become a cause of conflict unless the obligations of his office under the Charter and as an international civil servant leave him no alternative.

Thus you see that I conceive the Secretariat and the Secretary-General in their relations with the governments as representatives of a secular 'church' of ideals and principles in international affairs of which the United Nations is the expression.

In a different way those who belong to organized citizens' groups supporting the United Nations in all countries, represent this secular 'church' to their respective national states. It is your role to influence opinion within the circle to which your reach extends toward the course you believe to be right for your country. Whether your circle be small or large, it counts, for it is the sum total of all of them that influences the policies of governments.

Your role is different from mine in this respect. Whereas the international civil servant speaks for the ideals and commitments of the Charter as they may affect the formulation of national policies, you speak for the national interest of your countries in their policies toward and in the United Nations. This is important. You are rightly partisans for the best interests of your country as you see them. When you speak and act for national policies that will strengthen the influence of the United Nations you are doing so because you believe that this is best for your country as well as for humanity.

Your role is of the highest significance. No matter what their private judgment, those in positions of authority cannot go against prevailing public opinion or lead in a direction the public is not prepared to follow. Your influence in what you believe to be the right direction, exercised in the manifold ways that are available to you, is essential to the exercise of statesmanship.

I know there are many occasions when the pressures and the events that lead in the contrary direction seem overwhelming. But just as we cannot shape our world at will like a handful of clay, neither do such pressures and events inexorably lead on to a pre-ordained doom. They are subject to influence and change.

Time is also a great healer and 'playing for time' is an important element in the tactics we must follow in these days of crisis, anxiety and frustration. We all have a tendency to regard the situation as it exists at any single moment as a lasting one, forgetting that we ourselves and the societies which we form are all subject to the law of change. Those people and nations which are to live together in the future, if we succeed in overcoming the immediate risks of war, will not be of the same generation as those who do not see any possibility of living together as they are now and as conditions are today.

Conflicts, not only in human life, but also in the life of nations, are often never resolved, but simply outgrown. Often in history situations have arisen where people were saying, as it is sometimes being said now, that they could neither live together nor fight each other down, and in spite of that, the world has moved on and the situation of despair has become past history.

It is always delicate for a foreigner to speak about a country where he is but a visitor. And it is difficult for him to assess the significance of the spiritual and political history of his host country. I feel, however, you will understand, if, in conclusion, I refer to an American experience to which all the world owes much. The founding fathers of this great nation took upon themselves the responsibility for the creation of a new and independent state on American soil. They did so in a firm trust in the future and with a firm belief in the basic decency of man. In that spirit they managed to weld together in one nation people from many nations of the world. *E pluribus unum* is rightly inscribed on the shield of the United States.

That could also be the motto of the United Nations in its defiance of seemingly insuperable difficulties, in its belief in freedom and in its hope for world unity. Read in the right spirit, the Charter of the United Nations expresses an approach to the political problems of man which would have been well understood by men like Jefferson and Lincoln.

NEW DIPLOMATIC TECHNIQUES
IN A NEW WORLD

*Address to the Foreign Policy Association at a Dinner
given in his honor, New York, 21 October 1953.*

One of the many contradictions of life is the frequency with which
we refer to ourselves as living in a period of change and rapid
development, while, on the other hand, we are so often reluctant
to acknowledge the need for adjustment in our ways to the changes
which actually take place.

I am to talk tonight about 'New Diplomatic Techniques in a
New World.' Is there a new world ? Is there any need for adjustment of diplomatic techniques to that world ?

Diplomacy as a professional activity is certainly one of the most
ancient and conservative. There has always been a need for negotiation between nations and the techniques and psychology of such
negotiations have, at least until recently, undergone no great changes
through all the centuries. I guess that the emissaries of Egypt or
Greece or Rome had to approach their problem in very much the
same way as the emissaries of Napoleon's France, Bismarck's
Germany and Queen Victoria's Great Britain.

However, I do not think that it is an exaggeration to say that the
world with which modern diplomacy has to deal differs from the
world of the nineteenth century in those respects which interest us
here, more than the world of the nineteenth century differed from
its predecessors.

May I give you a little example which seems to me to throw
considerable light on what has happened to us in this field. In
1783, Benjamin Franklin signed on behalf of the United States of
America a treaty of friendship and commerce with the King of
Sweden. The first part of the 22nd Article of that treaty reads in
translation as follows:

> 'In order to favor even further trade between the two sides, it
> is agreed that in case of war between the two nations, which
> we pray to God to avert, a period of nine months after the
> declaration of war shall be given to all tradesmen and all
> citizens on both sides so as to give them time to withdraw with
> everything they own, or to sell the same property wherever

4   49

they like to do so, it being forbidden in any way to hamper such activities and, even more so, to detain the said persons during this period of nine months. On the contrary, they shall be given passports for the time which they consider necessary for their return home. But in case within the said period anything is taken from them or they are subjected to any harm by one of the two sides, their people or citizens, full and satisfactory compensation shall be paid to them.'

War in the period of the Enlightenment was, indeed, very different from what it has since become. At the time to which my quotation belongs one could still speak of war as merely the ultimate resource and extension of diplomacy. Although there were wars even then that occasionally got out of hand and became great wars, war generally was a limited military action, fought for limited objectives without weapons of mass destructive power by small professional armies when other means of diplomatic action had failed to arrive at a settlement. Under such conditions, normal civilian life was only moderately disturbed.

For many reasons arising from the development of the modern state, whether it be a democracy of the masses or a dictatorship of the masses, and of our industrial civilization, general war in the twentieth century means total war, fought not only by mass armies but the entire civilian population.

From the first World War, through the second, and into the age of the hydrogen bomb, the technique of war has been revolutionized in a way which now brings with it destruction of vast areas, death to millions upon millions of the civilian population, and economic and financial ruin with effects lasting over long periods after the fighting stops. All this does not mean that our ancestors in Benjamin Franklin's time were necessarily more civilized than we, but that the technique of war today presents a new problem to civilized man. To the diplomat of the middle of the twentieth century, war is something that must be averted at almost any cost.

But technological development has altered the basis for diplomatic action also in another respect which should be just as obvious to everybody but seems sometimes to be forgotten. Just as the diplomat of today must rule out war as an instrument of policy, so he must recognize that in the new state of interdependence between nations war anywhere becomes the concern of all. The intricate web of relationships which now exist have as part of their basis the new means of communication which have overnight made our world so much smaller than it was in previous generations. We are all very conscious of the fact that it is now but a question of hours for military forces to reach distant parts of the globe and that the old considerations of strategy based on geographic separation no longer count for much.

News also reaches us from all corners of the globe almost as quickly as if we had been eye-witnesses. We are parties to an action practically at the very moment it is undertaken. The nerve signals from a wound are felt at once all through the body of mankind.

But in this rough mapping out of the diplomat's world of today we must go further and deeper. His relationship to his own people has also changed. This has come as a fruit of broader education, of a development of the democratic system and of the revolutionary growth of the mass media of communication. The diplomat may still confer behind closed doors, but he will be met by reporters and photographers when he comes out. His words will reach everybody by press and film and radio and television. His personality will be known to vast numbers for whom in other times he would have been only a name, or less than a name.

These last considerations lead me on to the final, least tangible, but perhaps most important new factor in diplomacy: mass public opinion as a living force in international affairs. Of course, this public opinion has as its background the new mass media of communication, but as a psychological phenomenon and a political factor it is not sufficiently explained by this background. It is the expression of a democratic mass civilization that is still in its infancy, giving to the man in the street and to group reactions a new significance in foreign policy.

Is it possible to envisage the making of foreign policy and the tasks and techniques of diplomacy in the same way for a situation such as the one just described as for previous stages in history? The reply must be *no*. The diplomat who works bilaterally on a national basis without the widest perspective, without recognition —and a proper handling—of the publicity aspect of his work, or without giving to public opinion its proper place in the picture, has little place in our world of today.

A first and major change in diplomatic techniques that is called for by developments, is the introduction of what might be described as the multilateral element. I do not mean to suggest that bilateral diplomatic contacts and negotiations have lost their old importance, only that they prove insufficient. In a world of interdependence means must be devised for a broadening of the approach so that the interests of a group of nations or of the community of nations are given their necessary weight.

Negotiations and conferences with several nations represented are, of course, as old as history, but what must be considered as new, in such a conference of today, is when the diplomatic representative speaks not only for his own country, but also shares responsibility for the interests of the other nations represented around the conference table. I have myself, before coming to the United Nations, seen such a development of community viewpoints at various conferences in Europe. On occasions which traditionally would have consisted simply of interlocking bilateral contacts and reactions, this development has added something essential to the picture, meeting a need of today and making the results transcend what would have come out of the conference, had everybody approached it in the traditional way.

A further element in the development of the multilateral approach may be found in the international Secretariat. The concept of an international civil service directly responsible to the whole community of nations was first developed in the League of Nations. It has been carried further in the United Nations, where the Secretariat has wider responsibility, negotiating rights, and powers of initiative, than in the League or in any previous international organization.

The much-debated independence of the international civil service being created in the United Nations Secretariat and in the secretariats of the specialized agencies and various regional organizations, has a vital significance here. If this independence should be jeopardized and national influences come to dominate the secretariats, this evolutionary development of the multilateral approach would receive a serious set-back and international organization would be gravely weakened in its capacity to meet the demands of interdependence upon the policies of all governments. I feel that the best defence for the independence of the administrations of the international organizations lies in a fuller understanding of the very special and new needs for such administrations in the kind of a world we live in today.

When I speak here, in the first instance, of the secretariats as representative of the multilateral element in international negotiations, I have done so because they demonstrate in the most obvious way what is new in the picture. However, it goes without saying that their status and their duties only reflect the tasks of international organization as such. Everybody working inside or with the United Nations also carries the responsibility for making it a multilateral diplomatic instrument transcending nationalism and bilateralism, in the approach to political problems.

This is well illustrated by the way in which the Security Council is entitled to go into questions concerning every single part of the world where a threat to peace and security is considered imminent or developing. Similarly, the General Assembly may discuss any question within the scope of the Charter and both the Council and Assembly appoint representatives of states far removed from an area of conflict to commissions charged with seeking peaceful settlements. Undoubtedly, there are some who still dislike the idea of a group of political representatives from countries far from the storm center passing judgment on the actors in the drama and making recommendations for a solution of conflicts. But is that not a true expression of a very real interdependence, where aggression in Korea may forebode dangers to a country at the other end of the globe ?

A characteristic of the new diplomacy, developing on the multilateral basis or with multilateral aims, is that it has to operate in daylight to an extent unknown in the diplomacy of a traditional type. The importance of publicity for good and for bad in international diplomacy may be studied with the greatest profit in the international organizations. It has been said that one should never forget that the United Nations operates in a glass house. I would add that in our world of today it could not operate properly under any other conditions; in fact, in my view, it should operate in a glass house in order to serve its purposes. Multilateral diplomacy is by its very nature such that the old secrecy has lost its place and justification.

But there should be no mistakes. Publicity is right and necessary in multilateral diplomacy. However, it also represents a danger. Open diplomacy may, as a prominent delegate to the United Nations recently pointed out, easily become frozen diplomacy. This comes about when open diplomacy is turned into diplomacy by public statements made merely to satisfy segments of domestic public opinion or to gain some propaganda advantage elsewhere.

Considerations of national prestige also enter into the picture. Legislators and members of parliaments in our democracies have long been used to the give and take of debate on state and national issues, to the compromises that are fashioned every day in the legislative process, to accepting defeat as well as victory in voting as part of the normal course of politics. Neither the diplomats who practice multilateral diplomacy on the public stage nor the governments they represent are yet fully acclimated to this new aspect of international relations. Nor, it must be said, is public opinion itself. Too often, any modification of national positions once taken publicly, or acceptance of sensible compromise, is shunned out of fear that it will be labelled appeasement or defeat.

At this point the diplomat of today has to face public opinion in its contemporary significance for international affairs. It may seem to him that this opinion, being more or less the master of his masters, is the most important single factor in his planning of the implementation of international policy. And, of course, it is a factor of singular importance. No diplomat can depart too far from what is accepted or acceptable to public opinion in those quarters which give weight to his arguments. But it does not follow from this that he should simply let himself be guided by anticipated reactions of the public. A diplomacy that gives full weight to recognized or anticipated public opinion may in a decisive way also give direction to this opinion.

In the modern world of mass media and publicity no diplomat trying to respond to the demands of the situations can be only a servant. He must to some extent and in some respects also be a leader by looking beyond the immediate future and going underneath the superficial reactions, be they expressed by ever so powerful news organs catering for what are believed to be the wishes of the broad masses—wishes which may in reality be as loosely attached to the man in the street as the suits which he decides to wear this year. It is part of the diplomat's responsibility not only to lead public opinion towards acceptance of the lasting consequences of the interdependence of our world. He must also help public opinion to become as accustomed to the necessity for give and take and for compromise in international politics as it has long been on questions of state and local concern.

I had promised to speak about diplomatic techniques. In fact, I have talked almost as much about the substance of modern diplomacy. The two things cannot be separated. The technique must be adjusted to the substance and to some extent it is the very substance of diplomacy. No diplomat is likely to play the multilateral game well unless he believes in the need for and value of a multilateral approach. No diplomat will adjust himself to the new type of publicity—which is unavoidable in all official activities but is of special importance in multilateral diplomacy—unless he has the courage of his own actions. No diplomat is likely to meet the demands of public opinion on him as a representative in international policy unless he understands this opinion and unless he respects it deeply enough to give it leadership when he feels that the opinion does not truly represent the deeper and finally decisive aspirations in the minds and hearts of the people.

The ultimate test of a diplomacy adequate to our world is its capacity to evoke this kind of response from the people and thus to rally public opinion behind what is wise and necessary for the peace and progress of the world.

AN INSTRUMENT OF FAITH

*Address before the Second Assembly of the World
Council of Churches, Evanston, Illinois,
20 August 1954.*

It is for me a privilege to be given this opportunity to address, as spokesman for the United Nations, the World Council of Churches. As a student I saw at close quarters the beginning of the great ecumenical movement, and I learned to admire one of its inspired leaders, Archbishop Nathan Söderblom. This makes it a special pleasure for me personally to be here with you at this important conference.

The Churches are guardians of and spokesmen for the deepest beliefs and the loftiest dreams of man. The United Nations, on the other hand, is an organization for continuous diplomatic negotiation concerning concrete political issues, providing also for international administrative action in the economic and social fields.

Yet, in spite of all differences in character and responsibility, the Churches and the United Nations have an aim in common and a field of action where they work side by side. I would like to talk to you this evening about a few aspects of the international situation as they appear to me in the light of what we have in common. However, before doing so, let me try to explain more fully how I view the task of the United Nations.

In a televised interview some time ago, a youngster of sixteen asked me with concern why there is no reference to God in the United Nations Charter. In my reply I drew his attention to the Preamble of the Charter where the nations express their 'faith in the dignity and worth of the human person' and pledge themselves 'to practice tolerance and live together in peace with one another as good neighbors'. I felt sure that he saw here an expression of what, in the faith which was his, was recognized as the will of God: that we should love our neighbors as ourselves. He could not expect a document which should serve as a basis for world cooperation to go further in the direction he had in mind. The United Nations must recognize and respect all the different creeds and attitudes represented by its Member nations.

The question and my reply emphasize some basic facts. The United Nations stands outside—necessarily outside—all confessions but it is, nevertheless, an instrument of faith. As such it is inspired by what unites and not by what divides the great religions of the world.

The keywords of this Conference are Faith and Order. These words could, with only a slight change of sense, serve as a motto also for the United Nations in its international activity. The Organization must be animated by and defend Faith in the dignity and worth of men, born equal. It must serve and strengthen Order as a guarantee for peace, giving to everyone a possibility to live a full life of freedom. In the Introduction to the Ecumenical Survey of International Affairs, prepared for this meeting of the Council of Churches, it is said that what is needed from Evanston is 'a renewed faith and determination, expressed throughout the world-wide fellowship in responsible action for peace and justice'. In the same spirit it may be said of the United Nations that what is required from the Organization—and from the governments and peoples therein represented—is a renewed faith, a faith renewed every day, expressed in a never abandoned, every day newly initiated, responsible action for peace.

Thus, in spite of their different roles in the life of the community and the peoples, the Organization and the Churches stand side by side as participants in the efforts of all men of good will, irrespective of their creed or form of worship, to establish peace on earth. Problems that worry us in the United Nations must worry you, and achievements which we may be permitted to make will be welcomed by you.

There is no need for me to describe or analyze the international situation of today in any detail. The facts are well known to all of you. Has there indeed been any time, when the troubles of all the world were brought so quickly and so fully into every home? Quickly and fully—but how rarely in a spirit of objectivity! How rarely in such a way as to make it possible for the common man to find what should be his proper reaction to world affairs in the light of his basic ideals!

It may be said that there is today—for the first time in how many years?—no open warfare anywhere in the world, but this does not mean that there is peace. Names that we find daily on the pages of our newspapers remind us of the major conflicts. Korea and Indochina. Palestine. Kashmir. The remaining problems are great, indeed, in all these places, although differing in scope and character.

To resolve them in a way which preserves peace and gives to the peoples concerned freedom and safety in a way of life of their own choice, is an aim never to be abandoned, but still far from being realized. Other names could be added, like Germany and Austria. Still others may in their turn come to dominate headlines telling about new threats of war.

Even if all these various conflicts and unresolved problems were but isolated cases they would be disturbing and deplorable indeed. They are alarming when, as is now the case, they must be viewed as expressions of trends and tensions, which make them all symptoms of one and the same sickness of our world.

Looking for explanations of the situation we are facing, we will find beneath the surface forces which are in themselves to a large extent both natural and constructive. However, permitted to develop outside a system of legal order which is inspired by a will to peace, these same forces threaten with destruction.

In broad terms, our time is characterized by two predominant trends, one in the direction of social and economic equality within the nations, the other one in the direction of equal rights and opportunities for all nations. I feel that we should welcome both trends as reflecting an urge for a world of greater justice—such justice as is necessary for lasting peace. But we should also recognize that, if no means are provided for an orderly development, these trends may lead to cataclysms like those which we have seen in the recent past.

In an effort to meet the demands which these trends make us face we must approach our task from two angles. There is, first of all, in the international field, a need for practical action, helping under-developed countries to achieve such economic progress as would give them their proper share in the wealth of the world, and there is a need for political arrangements, providing a framework for a development in peace towards independence and self-determination for peoples now experiencing a revival of national pride and achieving political maturity. But, on the other hand, there is also a need for inspiration, for the creation of a spirit among the leaders of the peoples which helps them to use the forces which they have to master, for peace and not for war, for evolution and not for revolution.

As a fruit of the developments which we thus find below the surface of world events, but also, in part, as an ideological inspiration behind those very developments, we meet basically different attitudes to the evolution of society and of the world community. Such differences are only too wide and too obvious even among those who share the same fundamental faith in the dignity and worth of men. Let us not overlook the ideological tensions, but, on the other hand, let us not exaggerate their significance. Especially, let us not get caught in the belief that divisions of our world between the righteous and the wrong-doers, between idealism and materialism, between freedom and slavery, coincide with national boundaries. The righteous are to be found everywhere—as are the wrong-doers. Those whose only ideal is material well-being meet us in every country—as those whose ideal is selfless service.

The conflicts behind the surface of international—and for that matter also of national—politics, are conflicts whose battlefield always has been, is and always will be the hearts of men. In a certain area, in a certain period, those in power may predominantly represent one or the other tendency. But we would lack in historical sense and psychological insight, if the experience we have gathered during our short span of time would lead us to believe that this or that people is to be considered as an enemy forever of our ideals, or if we were to believe that ideals which we feel should dominate our own society, will survive without an honest and continued fight for their supremacy in our own public life.

In the effort to build a world of justice and order the main task of the United Nations must primarily be one directly referring to the acute, concrete cases of conflict, where mediation, negotiation and reconciliation are time-honoured ways to establish peaceful conditions. But the United Nations can also serve the governments as a useful instrument in their attempts to direct the social and political forces behind the conflicts and to meet the widespread demands which these forces reflect. Thus, the United Nations is the main organ through which peoples under trusteeship, or the non-self-governing territories, may be helped to independence and self-determination. It is also a place where a nation, young in its political independence, can find a floor in the debate on world affairs. Through technical assistance and through pioneer action in the social field, the United Nations, however, can also be instrumental in lifting the living standards of peoples and in furthering their economic growth.

When we go beyond the great social and economic trends to the underlying ideological tensions, the contribution that the United

Nations can make is more limited. Faithful to its ideals, impartial in the clashes of interest, and with patience and perseverance, it can be one of the focal points for the hopes of all those who work honestly for peace. It can help to justify their patience. It can give encouragement to their own will to impartiality and to their respect for justice. But the very nature of the Organization makes it inadequate as a means of influencing those basic attitudes which are decisive in the battle for the hearts of men. The impact of its actions and attitudes can only be a very general one, and will always remain uncertain unless properly explained.

A war to be fought in the hearts of men can be waged only by those speaking directly to men. It is here that I see the great, the overwhelming task of the Churches and of all men of good will of every creed in the work for peace. Their vital contribution to this work is to fight for an ever wider recognition of their own ideals of justice and truth.

However, they also have the power to show men the strength— so necessary in our world of today—that follows from the courage to meet others with trust. We have seen how out of present-day conflicts and the underlying tensions has grown a widespread state of fear and frustration, of distrust and desperation. This is, as we all know, in itself a source of evil. It maintains an atmosphere in which unbalanced reactions may suddenly release the explosive power of the forces which we have to master. In the face of this development, we have reason to remember the truth that he who fears God will no longer fear men.

In speaking for justice, truth and trust in public affairs, the Churches may be a decisive force for good in international and national political life, without assuming a political role or trying directly to influence political decisions. Can or should the Churches go any further? In my view there is one thing they could do. They could help to explain how world affairs are run and what is the responsibility of every one of us. In doing so they could help to explain what an organization like the United Nations stands for: how its ideals run parallel to the very aims and beliefs of the common man who wishes to live in peace with his neighbors, with freedom to build his own little world in human dignity.

In explaining to the peoples the failures and achievements of the work for peace—whether it is the work of governments or churches, of an international organization, of private associations or of individuals—in order to win their understanding and their support for that work, there is one thought which I feel should be stressed.

In the Sermon on the Mount it is said that we should take no thought of the morrow—'for the morrow shall take thought for the things of itself. Sufficient unto the day is the evil thereof.' Can anything seem farther from the practical planning, the long-term considerations typical of political life? And yet—is this not the very expression of the kind of patience we must all learn to show in our work for peace and justice? Mustn't we learn to believe that when we give to this work, daily, what it is in our power to give, and when, daily, we meet the demands facing us to all the extent of our ability, this will ultimately lead to a world of greater justice and good will, even if nothing would seem to give us hope of success or even of progress in the right direction.

Certainly, the words about the evil of the day and the things of the morrow do not mean that our actions should not be guided by a thoughtful and responsible consideration of future consequences of what we do. But they do mean that our work for peace should be pursued with the patience of one who has no anxiety about results, acting in the calm self-surrender of faith.

For the Christian faith 'the Cross is that place at the center of the world's history . . . where all men and all nations without exception stand revealed as enemies of God . . . and yet where all men stand revealed as beloved of God, precious in God's sight.' (I quote from the Report on the Main Theme of this Assembly.) So understood, the Cross, although it is the unique fact on which the Christian Churches base their hope, should not separate those of Christian faith from others but should instead be that element in their lives which enables them to stretch out their hands to peoples of other creeds in the feeling of universal brotherhood which we hope one day to see reflected in a world of nations truly united.

ON MODERN ART

From Address at the Inauguration of the 25th Anni-versary of the Museum of Modern Art, New York, 19 October 1954. Dag Hammarskjöld was actively interested in the work of the Museum and paintings loaned by it were on the walls of his office suite and private dining room on the 38th floor of the Secretariat building.

. . . . In its search for the basic elements of the world surrounding us and in its fight for mastery of those elements, modern art has revealed to us also where lies the real victory of the great artists of the past. Without making us eclectics, it has helped us to understand —as far as that is possible without sharing the atmosphere of faith in which they were born—what has been achieved in the harmony of the best works of the past. Modern art has forged keys to a perfection which it has not itself reached. Shouldering courageously the problems of modern man, reflecting his situation in a world of conflicts born out of his own achievements, it has, thus, earned the recompense of being permitted also to illuminate the greatness of man in the high artistic achievements of the past.

Art gives more to life than it takes from it. True art does not depend on the reality about which it tells. Its message lies in the new reality which it creates by the way in which it reflects experience. In our minds, we, all of us, sometimes chisel beauty out of the stone of matter. If we had the courage and perseverance to push these experiences of a few moments to their extreme point, we would share in the effort of the modern artist to isolate beauty from the impurity of life, even if it has to be at the cost of dissolving the very forms of life. Why then, seeing modern art, should we feel estranged when we do not at the first glance recognize the familiar aspects of our every-day world?

Modern art teaches us to see by forcing us to use our senses, our intellect and our sensibility to follow it on its road of exploration. It makes us seers—seers like Ezra Pound when, in the first of his Pisan Cantos, he senses 'the enormous tragedy of the dream in the peasant's bent shoulders'. Seers—and explorers—these we must be if we are to prevail . . . .

HJALMAR HAMMARSKJÖLD

Inaugural Address upon taking his seat as a member of the Swedish Academy, Stockholm, 20 December 1954. While in Stockholm for this occasion the Secretary-General completed arrangements with the Ambassador of the People's Republic of China for his visit a few days later to Peking on behalf of the imprisoned American fliers.

Dag Hammarskjöld was elected to the seat left vacant by the death in 1953 of his father, Hjalmar Hammarskjöld, who served Sweden as Prime Minister from 1914 to 1917 as well as in many other capacities. A new member of the Academy gives an inaugural address on the life and work of his predecessor at a ceremonial meeting in the presence of the Royal Family and Government, but this was the first time that a son had succeeded to his father's seat. Although this speech and his later presidential address to the Academy on 'The Linnaeus Tradition and Our Time' (page 151) were delivered as a member of the Academy, not as Secretary-General of the United Nations, they have been included as relevant expressions of his philosophy, insights and style, as well as for their intrinsic interest. The Swedish Academy was founded in 1786 by King Gustav III, modeled on the French Academy and aimed at preserving and enriching Swedish language and literature. It is limited to 18 members, elected for life, who are generally authors and other leaders in the intellectual life of the country. Its most widely known responsibility is the annual award of the Nobel Prize in Literature.

[TRANSLATION FROM SWEDISH]

Last year, one day in October. On the desk was Anacreon. The empty chair was turned outward, toward Humlegården Park, where the swarms of jackdaws prepared to retire for the night into the autumn-reddened trees around the Royal Library—those swarms of jackdaws whose seemingly senseless fighting he had followed during his last years with ironical amusement as a picture of the rage of the heathen and the vain imaginings of the people. Those swarms of jackdaws which he had longed for more and more in his loneliness, and greeted, also, as messengers from the fields and the spires in the Upsala of his youth and manhood.

In the stillness around this final station on Hjalmar Hammarskjöld's path, far from the struggles of the day, the mind goes to its starting point, his childhood home in the Småland forests, on the border of Östergötland, more than ninety years ago. Hjalmar Hammarskjöld was one of those who are firm in their roots and firm in their faith, those whose changing fates may well deepen the convictions and directions of their early years, but not change them. They may be transported far from their original setting, but their roots are never cut off. In that sense, his life ended where it began.

What gave an inner unity to his life was that in the period of revolutionary development through which he lived, he remained faithful to his past, faithful also to *the* past. By easily discernible intermediate stages, this faithfulness bridged the span to a far earlier era, seventeenth-century Sweden, when the throne, the altar and the sword formed a terse triad in which a nation found its melody. Did that mean that he belonged to the past? Were his reactions to the problems of the day 'a cold and bitter gust from times gone by,' as an adversary whom he held in high esteem once said in a stormy political debate during the 1920's? Everyone must decide for himself what is the right answer, but fairness requires that it be based on knowledge. A man of firm convictions does not ask, and does not receive, understanding from those with whom he comes into conflict. In the synthesis which should be the task of posterity, it is necessary to disengage oneself from earlier conflicts to examine what he really stood for, and judge the power of survival of these things without projecting the conflicts of our day into the past.

To make such an examination is beyond my competence. Nor am I impartial. In recalling the main traits of Hjalmar Hammarskjöld's life I shall therefore only try to give a picture of the man I myself felt I discerned behind his work. May this be accepted as a personal contribution to the accumulation of data on which somebody else may sometime base an account fulfilling the requirements of scholarly completeness and perspective.

Hjalmar Hammarskjöld belonged to the generation which put its imprint on the 1890's with their newly awakened deep national sentiment—and their internationalism. Like Selma Lagerlöf and

Heidenstam* he was a child of the country estate. He often said that
the setting of his childhood might have given rise to a chronicle as
colourful—and probably also as proud in its poverty—as the one
Selma Lagerlöf wove from the tales of long winter evenings at
Mårbacka. But there was one decisive difference. The Värmland
of old sawmills and ironworks had its counterpart in a Småland
of old officer families. The family chronicle had a darker streak,
and the mood of the cavalier—where surroundings providing little
scope for extravagance would permit it at all—had back of it
generations of military and administrative service.

The way Selma Lagerlöf and Heidenstam depicted the Swedish
character was essentially romantic, and their epigones sometimes
added a trace of Cyrano bravura. For such an attitude there was no
basis in the Småland tradition. It may be profitable to consider
Hjalmar Hammarskjöld as a man of the '90's in Swedish public life,
but if so it should be done in the realization that, to him, Swedish
history was a living reality not as a cause for national conceit or
effusive sentiment, but as a reminder of the sacrifices by which
earlier generations gained what we received from them.

Between the nation in history and the individual, the family is
the primary tie. In Hjalmar Hammarskjöld there was an obvious
but subtle interdependence between national and family feelings. It
is tempting to speak of them as two phases of the same fundamental
reaction. But such a picture does less than justice to a situation in
which his feeling for his forebears gained strength from his feeling
for his country, and this in turn found support in his consciousness
of his origin.

His own family heritage was complex and offered ties to various
elements in Swedish cultural tradition and history. His father,
Knut Hammarskjöld, was a nephew on the maternal side of Leonard
Rääf, 'lagman'† and cultural historian, and on the paternal side of
Lorenzo Hammarskjöld, the author. In the generation before that,
he was descended from Carl Gustaf Hammarskjöld—himself for a
time a captain in the French regiment *Royal Suédois*—whose father
and grandfather had both taken part in Armfeldt's ill-fated retreat
from Trondheim in the days of Charles XII. A century earlier
knew the first bearer of the name, a stern gentleman of the school
of Charles IX.

* Verner von Heidenstam, Swedish author and poet, 1859–1940, winner of the Nobel
Prize for Literature, 1916.
† County-court judge

5

Life on his father's estate, Väderum, was strongly paternalistic in character. Class consciousness was there, but it was not reflected in the contacts of the youngsters with the farm hands. During Hjalmar Hammarskjöld's formative years, the difference in economic conditions does not seem to have been strongly felt. In Rääf's description of Ydre county, to which volume after volume was still being added as late as in his childhood, Hjalmar Hammarskjöld could read about trolls and woodsprites, pixies and elfins as beings one should not be surprised to meet in the neighborhood. He himself was raised in a spirit rooted in the faith of the Age of the Reformation. The old Wallin hymns remained his companions through the years.

At the age of ten he was sent to Upsala. As a schoolboy, a student and an academic teacher he was to remain in the city during this first period for more than twenty years. His second sojourn in Upsala, as Governor of the province of Uppland, spans twenty-three years. Even in an outward sense, Upsala thus was his home more than any other place. The city and the region also were home to him, inwardly. He felt in complete harmony with this world. Personal friends, men like Henrik Schück and Harald Hjärne, were part of it.

His recollections of six years in the Cathedral School included those of one teacher, Pontus Wikner, admired but also the object of the shy wonderment of his pupils. Once, when he wrote in the margin of a composition by Hjalmar Hammarskjöld that 'this boy may become a good stylist' in years to come, this created a pride which seemed traceable in the inflections of the narrator fully seventy years later.

His literary interests were intense. Walter Scott and Runeberg won an early place they were never to lose. Added later were Snoilsky, the Strindberg of *The Red Room* and the great Norwegians. One of the things Hjalmar Hammarskjöld remembered from his youth was how he used to queue up in the Lundequist bookshop in Upsala as soon as another work by Ibsen was expected in the mail. 'It was easy in those days,' he said once; 'you could have the ambition to read everything that was published in Scandinavia— and fulfill it.'

He felt most strongly attracted by the Latin and Greek authors. His interest was twofold, philological as well as literary. His future plans in those days clearly envisaged philology as a career, but to judge from his later development the starting-point was, to him, primarily an esthetic feeling for the language. He was as keen on the 'logic' of language as on what he called the 'plasticity' of the account. This attitude, and the self-discipline it led to, were mirrored in his judgment of literature.

He never had the practical use he had planned for the Latin and Greek studies to which he devoted his first years at the university. All the more enjoyable to him, in a personal sense, were the worlds these studies laid open. From farflung, uninterrupted forays into modern literature he always went back to the classics. He was also an assiduous composer of Latin inscriptions for medals in the various societies to which he belonged. In their economical style, these inscriptions often speak with the voice of their originator.

It is difficult to determine what made Hjalmar Hammarsjöld switch from philology to law. In letter after letter his mother, who was his close confidante, returned anxiously to the question whether he was sure of having made the right choice in abandoning a field for which he 'had shown such aptitude'. But his step brought him closer to the family tradition. He had a predecessor in the legal career in his cousin Carl Gustaf, twenty-four years his senior, who had been a professor at Upsala during Hjalmar Hammarskjöld's first years there and later became a member of the Supreme Court. Examples within his circle of friends may also have affected his decision. But probably practical considerations were the decisive ones. During his entire period as a student his economic position had been precarious. Difficulties mounted constantly, and it became increasingly clear that he had to face the necessity of assisting his parents and brothers. He failed in an attempt to obtain a language teaching appointment. The study of law then seemed a possible solution. But he immediately acquired a real interest in the subject and took his law degree quickly.

In 1884, a scholarship enabled him to pursue his legal studies through the winter and into the next summer at German universities, principally Strasburg and Freiburg. His experiences during this trip abroad, his first, had a far-reaching influence on his further growth.

In the late nineteenth century, the heyday of German academic life, the science of jurisprudence was not the least flourishing. Among eminent authorities whose teachings he followed, there is reason to single out for mention the law historian von Amira, who taught ancient Norse and German law. Amira, with whom Hjalmar

Hammarskjöld long maintained personal contact, and other scholars of similar stature whom he saw in this year of studies, rooted in him a feeling, typical of his generation, for the Germany of humanism and scholarship which he was never to abandon. The trip gave him the opportunity of deepening the acquaintanceship with German letters which had begun during his student years in Upsala. Notes and statements give an idea of his interests: Schiller's historical plays; of Goethe, for instance *Hermann und Dorothea*; Chamisso, Lenau, Heine and August von Platen—Platen perhaps most of all. As a youngster of nineteen, he translated Platen's sonnet 'O süsser Tod' with the concluding lines:

> 'Säll därför den som bad om döden blott,
> Hans längtan stillad blev och läkt hans smärta,
> Ty av en spade klyvs till sist vart hjärta,'

At ninety he could still recite from memory its counterpart, that other sonnet which begins:

> 'Wer wusste je das Leben recht zu fassen,
> Wer hat die Hälfte nicht davon verloren
> Im Traum, im Fieber, im Gespräch mit Toren.'

From these poets, admired during his student years, there is a clear line to those authors in German of a later period whom he treasured: Hofmannsthal, Rilke and Hesse.

But his studies at Strasburg also yielded experience of another kind. No matter how strong their feeling for national unity, the Rhinelanders always retained their ironical perspective of Wilhelminian Prussianism. In the Alsace, with its French orientation, that feeling had an accent of its own. What Hjalmar Hammarskjöld learned on this score was to produce, in later years, an echo in him in the form of cold irony at the *Herrenvolk* claims of the Third Reich. It was reflected also in the harshness with which he thought it necessary to proceed on the inner lines in various negotiations with Germany—'the only language they understand.'

A few years after his return from the trip to Germany he obtained his doctor's degree with a dissertation about the freight contract and its principal legal consequences. This first law work of his is typical of its author. The subject falls within civil law, but borders on administrative law and other disciplines of public law. In his further activity as a lawyer his concentration on public law grew gradually more pronounced, but its basis was always what may be called a civil law point of view.

Hjalmar Hammarskjöld's legal thinking reflects his schooling in an Upsala where theoretical traditions of idealistic philosophy still were dominant. Notes from his twenties yield the following typical statement: 'The fundamental fault with Nordling is that he didn't realize that a community of reason constitutes membership in a higher entity.' Translated into terms closer to our day and age, the idea seems to be that society is welded together by that higher 'reason,' common to us all, which is the bearer of justice.

Against this background we can understand his faith in a 'supranational' justice, through which may be created an international *Civitas Legum*. In attempting to interpret the internationalism represented by Hjalmar Hammarskjöld, this seems to me to be the key. *Civitas Dei* was a dream of the past. The present-day attempts to form an international organization with common executive organs had not yet been begun. Instead, there is a glimpse here of a world society, where national states live under the protection of an internationalism which gains its strength from the very logic of justice itself, not from dictates of power, and in which, therefore, the only international organs needed are of a judicial nature. Personally Hjalmar Hammarskjöld never developed his legal views in these terms. His disposition was pronouncedly deductive, but he distrusted abstract generalizations. In a book on neutrality law, of 1925, he restricted himself to a consistently descriptive account, in spite of the wider considerations the subject might have invited.

Of his legal works it may suffice to mention here the report of 1909 about the creation of a Supreme Administrative Court. This work, highly characteristic of its author, started an important evolution in administrative justice. He himself saw in it a lasting contribution, but thought that his ideas had been spoiled on one central point when his proposal was put into practice.

The work on the freight contract led to a teaching fellowship. After a term as a court practitioner, which helped break his academic isolation, he was appointed some years later to a new chair as professor of special civil law. But he did not remain a university teacher for long. In the early nineties he was brought into the commission of technical experts on legislation within the Department of Justice. This started a period of legislative and committee work, departmental chores and negotiations which removed him more and more from academic activities and finally led him into the world of politics. A hope to return to Upsala as a county judge was not fulfilled. Step by step, seemingly without any personal choice determined by his own interests, he reached the field of activity in which he was to make his main contribution, far from the life in philological research he had dreamed of in his youth.

But in this attempt at a portrait, I want to pay attention less to his working career than to a few events on a personal level.

After a period of financial difficulties, the family had lost its country estate. The road downward was typical of the times: unsuccessful timber speculations, and gaily optimistic engagements in a local railway venture, led to a crisis in the early 'eighties. Farm managers appear to have completed the damage. The event had extremely serious practical consequences. At one time, Hjalmar Hammarskjöld contemplated abandoning academic work completely and making use of his legal knowledge in service with a bank, which might open increased possibilities of financing the education of his brothers. It is safe to assume, though, that the blow hurt even deeper on a more personal level; the home of his ancestors had meant much to a man so much a part of his family, and inside his shield of pride there was much vulnerability. This crisis, and the poverty with which he had battled a long time but which now became heavy indeed, later lent color to his high appreciation of thrift and a sense of economy as social values.

In 1890, he founded a family of his own. In his wife he found a determined faithfulness to personal ideals on a par with his own. Otherwise, Agnes Almqvist was different from him in many respects. Her characteristics, which appear to me to reflect her family origin, had once emerged with particular clarity and with the somewhat frightening overtones of genius in the poet Carl Jonas Love Almqvist, a stepbrother of her father: a radically democratic view of fellow humans, 'evangelic' if you like, a childlike openness toward life, an anti-rationalism with warm under-currents of feeling. With these qualities, and the personal generosity toward both intimates and strangers to which it drove her, she introduced elements into Hjalmar Hammarskjöld's life which carry great weight in interpreting his subsequent development.

His first great political test was the difficult, almost hopeless task of presenting an electoral reform, as Minister of Justice in the von Otter Cabinet. His failure was complete. According to his own candid presentation of the proposal in the First Chamber, his view was that the decision of 1901 to introduce military conscription made it necessary to produce without delay a proposal for wider rights of voting, mirroring 'an increased public spirit in our nation.' At the same time, he had found it impossible to propose universal suffrage. The electoral reform, all the same, would have to be such as not to spoil the issue, but rather to start it on the right road, '*if* views later were stabilized in the direction of universal suffrage'. The misjudgment of which he was guilty seems principally to be explained by too theoretical an approach to the task, combined with a desire to proceed slowly. In his motives, he emerges not as a defender of privilege, but as a reformist of conservative disposition, who underestimated the strength of the forces driving ahead.

After a brief—and very happy—interlude as President of the Göta Court of Appeals, 1905 again found him in the Cabinet, now as Minister of Education in the Lundeberg government. Among his colleagues was one of his adversaries in the conflict over the electoral reform, Karl Staaff. Together with the Prime and Foreign Ministers, they both were delegates in the Karlstad negotiations about the dissolution of the union with Norway. It was a task for which Hjalmar Hammarskjöld had been prepared, *inter alia* as secretary to the Union Committee in the 'nineties. Though temperamentally uninclined to appeasement, he was a firm opponent of an adventurous policy in the union question.

This Cabinet period was also a short one. When the Government resigned in the autumn, he became minister to Copenhagen, a task of importance but one from which he longed to return to Sweden, actuated apparently in the first place by his desire to keep the children in their home during their school years. Two years later, he was appointed Governor at Upsala. In this first period, however, he was still called upon for many international tasks, primarily as Sweden's delegate to the second peace conference at the Hague, and later as an arbiter in various international disputes, among them the Casablanca conflict. During this period, he therefore never grew into his gubernatorial tasks in the way he did later.

In January of 1914, Hjalmar Hammarskjöld and Otto Printzsköld (the latter a high official of the Royal Court) went to St. Petersburg for negotiations. These were not concluded, when Printzsköld had to return temporarily to Stockholm. There was then no reason for Hjalmar Hammarskjöld to stay, and he accompanied Printzsköld home. It so happened that the two negotiators returned on the morning of 6 February. (That was the day on which advocates of strengthening Sweden's defenses made an appeal directly to the King, going over the head of the parliamentary government, by staging a 'Peasants' March' to the Royal Palace in Stockholm.) About what followed Hjalmar Hammarskjöld said in notes he prepared in 1950 for Sven Hedin, and which Hedin then published: 'Not until the following Monday (9 February), did it occur to Hammarskjöld that the crisis might have personal consequences for him. But when he learned, on Tuesday, that De Geer, at the request of the King, tried to form a Cabinet, he assumed that this attempt would succeed and made preparations to return to St. Petersburg.

'From Thursday afternoon, after De Geer had failed and Trygger had also turned down the task the King had then given to him, Hammarskjöld was subjected to increasingly intense pressures. On Saturday these led him to agree to form a Cabinet.'

Not until publication of the book by Hedin, in which these notes were reproduced, did Hjalmar Hammarskjöld learn who were the originators of the King's speech to the marching peasants from the palace courtyard (which caused the Prime Minister, Karl Staaff, to hand in the resignation of his Cabinet in protest against what he considered the extra-parliamentary action of the King in making commitments on defense policy). In forming his Cabinet, he arrived at a solution only haltingly. His wish was to assemble a group of men, prominent through their contributions in various fields but not too strongly engaged in a partisan sense. One candidate for the Ministry of Education was Henrik Schück.

How did Hjalmar Hammarskjöld view the crisis and the central part he assumed in trying to solve it? One thing is certain. His interest in a strong defense, coupled with a pessimistic appraisal of the international situation, played a decisive part. He has been represented as the last and most clear-cut advocate of the personal power of the King against the surge of parliamentary democracy. Such a view does not seem to do justice to the problem as it must have appeared to Hjalmar Hammarskjöld. It is overlooked that, with his strong sense of the independence of public administration and with his feeling about the duties accompanying the responsibilities of officials, he could feel bound to form a Cabinet without therefore taking sides concerning the principle involved in the current constitutional conflict, as represented by the opponents. He was convinced of the value of the monarchy as a form of government, but it was as an official that he assumed the task of forming a Cabinet. It is true that this brought him into conflict with the movement toward a fully developed parliamentarianism, but as representing a national interest of which he considered the administrative authorities as the bearers; he did not hesitate, on the other hand, to maintain the responsibility of the Cabinet also against attempts at the exercise of a personal royal power.

Hjalmar Hammarskjöld's own view of the crisis is elucidated from another point of view by the following extract from a statement in the spring of 1914, in which he recalled his cooperation during the Union crisis of 1905 with earlier adversaries, certainly in the first place with Karl Staaff: 'I understood very well, that once the present tasks had been solved, our paths would again be separated. But at the same time I trusted that those who have once worked unselfishly together for a high purpose, can never again become strangers to each other ... I have the same hope now. Common toil and struggle, common hopes, common memories, bright or dark, shall tie us lastingly one to the other. After all, everything is being done, borne or received in love of our fatherland, in humble endeavour to promote its welfare and stave off its misfortune or downfall.'

And when, in a parliamentary debate, he had been attacked for his interpretation of Staaff's attitude in the defense settlement of 1914, he replied: 'Karl Staaff's memory needs no protection against me. Staaff was—let me say it in one word—a political opponent exactly the way I want him.'

A different matter from his views on the questions here recalled was his stubbornly individualistic reaction to certain phenomena within political democracy. Two quotations may suffice to show this trait, which in combination with his political attitudes has often —and quite wrongly—been taken to express an anti-democratic position in the wider sense. In a speech in 1933 he said: 'To many, the name of freedom seems to be enough, while their most urgent concern is to exchange one tyranny, real or imaginary, against another one, preferably real and even more preferably many-headed.' In another context he said about a Swedish politician that 'he was too independent—and it might be added, too conscientious —to obey party signals, whether as leader or in the rank and file; he knew that the real task of the so-called party leader is only too often, as a classic French phrase has it, to follow, not to lead, to announce the course, not to determine it.'

Personally, he remained outside the parties all his life. Regardless of how close he was to conservatism, there was much in the views of this man with traditions of public service from the time before the industrial revolution in Sweden to set him apart from the twentieth-century views of the Conservative party.

In August war broke out, the war he had long feared and in the last few months expected with increasing certainty. His judgment of the future had proved realistic, so far. Now he was evidently influenced by a current view, according to which economic factors alone would of necessity put a severe limit to the time the war could last. He appears to have counted on a rather quick peace on the note of mutual exhaustion—without excluding, of course, the possibility of a strengthening of German power or, alternatively, the advancing of Russian positions in Europe. A long war, ending in a Western victory without Russia, was certainly an idea as foreign to him as to everybody else at that time.

The foreign policy for which he assumed responsibility, and the first manifestation of which was an unreserved declaration of neutrality, has been praised for its strong adherence to judicial principles, but on the same grounds it has been criticized just as frequently, or more frequently, sometimes by those who at the same time have advanced suspicions of a disguised partiality to German interests. He himself called his policy 'Swedish and nothing but Swedish', and this may serve as the starting-point of an interpretation of his motives, which regards the judicial arguments as means of achieving a national end and considers real or imaginary concessions to one party or the other from the same angle.

One thing seems certain, if the situation is appraised on the basis of what is otherwise known about his ideals and motives. In his inner deliberations the decisive objective was to keep the country out of the war, with the best possible protection of Swedish interests. But this was not all; when the work of developing an international order of law as a framework for Western life was later to be resumed, Sweden ought to be present as a participant who had not—without the excuses the belligerents were able to invoke—sacrificed its loyalty to such an order on the altar of opportunism. Sweden's defense forces, albeit inadequate, were one support for a policy with this goal in view. Another one—and this one, also, regrettably inadequate—was international law itself, which would, consistently applied, lend the country a weight in international debate it would otherwise have lacked.

In any case, the line Hjalmar Hammarskjöld represented was difficult to pursue. It became doubly difficult by the way in which leading political personalities from the outset of the war maintained contact with representatives of both belligerent camps. A conflict rooted in these circumstances came into the open when the German Minister, Reichenau, was recalled in the autumn of 1914. This was the result of a Swedish initiative which can be traced back to the Prime Minister.

In upholding, sharply and tenaciously, principles of international law—both as they were defined in extant treaties and as he thought they ought to be further developed in a new and unforeseen situation, the first rough outline of total war—Hjalmar Hammarskjöld indubitably was in part governed by ideological motives. In a joint Scandinavian note to the warring powers in the autumn of 1914 are the well-known words that after the war the belligerents would be satisfied to find inviolate some of the principles they themselves had earlier treasured. There is no doubt that this phrase was drafted by the Swedish Prime Minister. The political weight of the argument thus proffered can be confirmed by one who himself has had occasion to test it. But the maxim is more than an argument. It reflects the conviction of a man who wanted justice—wanted it in realization of how thin is the wall between culture and barbarism, presaging the bitter experience of later decades.

While Hjalmar Hammarskjöld unhesitatingly embraced the standpoint of justice he knew full well how incomplete and fluid were the rules in which the idea of justice was reflected in international intercourse. It was certainly not his view that a small country like Sweden had to strive to save them for a coming era of peace even at the cost of vital interests of her own; the point might be reached when compromises became as natural for a neutral state as for a belligerent, but until such a situation arose the neutral had particular obligations toward the future.

But it is necessary to pay attention to other views of international law than the ideological ones. What the critics have not realized, he said once, is that for a small country, international law, in the final analysis, is the only remaining argument, and that its defense is therefore worth sacrifices even in the egotistical interest of the country itself. It seems to me that this is the background against which it is necessary to view Hjalmar Hammarskjöld, when he invoked the 'obligations' of the neutrals as grounds for demanding considerate treatment by the belligerents, and when at the same time he found it necessary to widen the application of the principles of neutrality to trade policy.

The much-disputed positions here recalled were taken in a situation where the belligerent parties wanted to force Sweden at least indirectly to support their trade war. Sweden, it could be said, had the duty only to pursue her own interests and to protect her supply situation. In the very name of these interests, however, as Hjalmar Hammarskjöld saw the problem, Sweden had to avoid what one party might consider cooperation in the warlike actions of the other side. From this point of view, the obligation to safeguard one's own interests was widened to an obligation not to let oneself be used by either party. It was then natural—as natural as it was to appear to others at a later stage—to demand respect for our 'obligations' in negotiations with the belligerents, pointing out that deviations from these obligations could be invoked as the basis of warlike actions which would clash with our 'rights'.

A mature man is his own judge. In the end, his only form of support is being faithful to his own convictions. The advice of others may be welcome and valuable, but it does not free him from responsibility. Therefore, he may become very lonely. Therefore, too, he must run, with open eyes, the risk of being accused of obdurate self-sufficiency. As the war went on and difficulties increased, this was the fate of Hjalmar Hammarskjöld.

The autumn of 1916 brought a serious crisis. With urgent trade negotiations with Britain impending, the Prime Minister became isolated in resisting a line which he seems to have feared as the inception of a surrender of rights of uncertain scope and with uncontrollable consequences. In this situation, he obviously thought of resigning. What material has so far become available does not appear to me to permit final judgment of this episode or of his reactions in the complex interplay of conflicting forces during this turbulent autumn.

The Cabinet resigned in the spring of 1917 after a crisis fore-shadowed by the development just recalled. Further difficulties had been added. When Hjalmar Hammarskjöld relinquished the post of Prime Minister, he had also tried that responsibility which may be imposed on us by the confidence of friends. But still more, and to a degree rare in Sweden, he had experienced how sharply political passions may hit. He was to learn that the judgments of the moment may remain alive even decades later—surprised, however, only by the lack of political and diplomatic insight which in his view was sometimes illustrated by the manner in which historical data were treated.

His return to Upsala after the years in office opened the penultimate phase of his life, dominated by gubernatorial chores and enriched by the work on old interests to which he again found it possible to devote time with a good conscience. One basis for these activities was this Academy. In the classical spirit, he felt that the scholar, the orator and the legislator stood shoulder to shoulder with the poet and the narrator in their responsibility for the language as the voice of our spirit. He wanted to see his attitude to this Academy from that angle. Numerous remaining drafts show the unstinted care he devoted to the style of everything he wrote.

His work as Governor—a thousand and one administrative details, official opinions on a rich flow of proposals, agricultural bodies, school boards, road inspections, folk festivities—he was to fall in love with this life, seemingly without any yearning to return to national policy or international tasks. In the position and responsibility of Governor he found room for a patriarchal attitude which was natural to him. His administrative interests and strong sense of quality even in details made him engage vigorously even in things one might have expected him to regard with a certain indifference. Emotionally, the trips around the province apparently were what he found most rewarding. He found it easy to make contact with the peasants of Uppland, in whose company the country boy who once followed the work of the farmers in Småland seemed to gain life anew.

Parliamentary work and, somewhat later, the chairmanship of the League of Nations committee for the codification of international law and the post as delegate to the Disarmament Conference, round out the picture of his public activities.

Some time somebody will perhaps describe the Upsala of the 'twenties with the same loving care as has been devoted to the age of Geijer. The possibilities are there. The strange, brief idyll which burgeoned all over Europe between two crises and two wars had a reflection all its own in Upsala. The church policy of Söderblom in this period made the city an international center. Söderblom and Hjalmar Hammarskjöld joyfully shared the burden of the ceremonial tasks which accompanied this development. Both had a strong sense of academic pomp and circumstance.

The way things developed, Hjalmar Hammarskjöld got an opportunity to pursue his literary interests, long relegated to the background. Increasingly, he paid attention to Spanish, Portuguese and South American poetry. As a pastime to begin with, later with earnest consistency, he began using his spare hours, or his regular solitary holidays at Storlien, in translating folk songs from these areas. Leafing through the extensive notes, one is struck by the Heine-like inflection of light raillery in his selections. But sometimes the words fall heavily, and the personal engagement of the translator becomes apparent.

In 1930 he left his post as Governor. The final period of his life thus begun was as long as the whole of his gubernatorial term. It covers the upsurge of Nazism, the second World War and the Cold War. In spite of further public tasks, and in spite of an intense interest in what happened throughout the period, he was a man placed entirely aside. Sometimes he reflected resignedly on the extravagance of life, which constantly shoves aside the experience built over long years, finally to let it be destroyed by senescence and death.

His last interest in tasks to which he had earlier devoted his time concerned this Academy.

In looking back to find a situation reflecting the essential core of Hjalmar Hammarskjöld's personality, I pause before this recollection.

It is late in the day, the third day of the defense debate of 1925. In the First Chamber, the discussion has largely been colored by echoes from the great battles of 1914. Hjalmar Hammarskjöld, who has sharply fought for his views from his position outside the parties, has become a personal target. In this situation he takes the floor for the last time. He ends with these words: 'It was said here before the recess that large circles realized that in the question of defense they could follow no poorer counsellor than I. To the extent that this is true, I would ask you gentlemen all to forget, and forget completely, that I am a friend of strong defenses, so as to prevent this from being an obstacle to a good decision. *Who takes the initiative, who exerts influence, is so utterly indifferent compared to the one great question: to make our country secure for the future.'*

To the nineteen-year-old listener in the gallery, these words epitomized a life of faith in justice and of self-effacing service under a responsibility which unites us all.

INTERNATIONAL SERVICE

Address at Johns Hopkins University Commencement Exercises, Baltimore, Maryland, 14 June 1955. This address and the two which follow immediately were prepared as a series at the time of the Commemoration in San Francisco of the 10th anniversary of the founding of the United Nations.

At this time of great ideological conflicts and violent clashes of interests, technological and economic developments have, as never before, brought us together as members of one human family, unified beyond race or creed on a shrinking globe, in face of dangers of our own making. In such a situation many ethical problems take on a new significance and our need to give sense to our lives exceeds the inherited standards. True, our duties to our families, our neighbors, our countries, our creeds have not changed. But something has been added. This is a duty to what I shall call international service, with a claim on our lives equal to that of the duty to serve within those smaller units whose walls are now breaking down. The international service of which I speak is not the special obligation, nor the privilege, of those working in international economic corporations, in the field of diplomacy, or in international political organizations. It has become today the obligation, as well as the privilege, of all.

Is it not, you might ask, paradoxical to strive for truly international service in a divided world? Is it not even more than paradoxical—is it not impossible? It is said that nobody can serve two masters. How is it then possible that anybody can serve—or even should serve—a world community that is split in fractions, demanding loyalty to divergent ideas and warring interests? In such a situation, will not international service require abject self-surrender, leaving us empty of personal convictions? Will it not emasculate our will and strength to fight for ideals and interests which we hold dear and to which we are bounden?

My reply to these sceptical questions is a 'no'. International service requires of all of us first and foremost the courage to be ourselves. In other words, it requires that we should be true to none other than our ideals and interests—but these should be such as we can fully endorse after having opened our minds, with great honesty, to the many voices of the world. The greatest contribution to international life that any one can render—be it as a private citizen or as one professionally engaged in international work—is to represent frankly and consistently what survives or emerges as one's own after such a test. Far from demanding that we abandon or desert ideals and interests basic to our personality, international service thus puts us under the obligation to let those ideals and interests reach maturity and fruition in a universal climate.

If this is the essence of international service, such service will expose us to conflicts. It will not permit us to live lazily under the protection of inherited and conventional ideas. Intellectually and morally, international service therefore requires courage to admit that you, and those you represent, are wrong, when you find them to be wrong, even in the face of a weaker adversary, and courage to defend what is your conviction even when you are facing the threats of powerful opponents. But while such an outlook exposes us to conflicts, it also provides us with a source of inner security; for it will give us 'self-respect for our shelter'. This is, as you may remember, the privileged position which Epictetus grants to the Cynic when he, true to his ideals, sacrifices all outward protection.

In the flourishing literature on the art of life there is much talk about that rare quality: maturity of mind. It is easy to circumscribe such maturity in negative terms. In positive terms it is difficult to define it, although we all recognize it when we have the privilege of seeing its fruits. It is reflected in an absence of fear, in recognition of the fact that fate is what we make it. It finds expression in an absence of attempts to be anything more than we are, or different from what we are, in recognition of the fact that we are on solid ground only when we accept giving to our fellow men neither more nor less than what is really ours. You yourselves can complete the picture. Maturity of mind seems to me to be the very basis for that attitude which I have described here as the essence of international service. It is by striving for such maturity that we may grow into good international servants.

We are now ready to return to the question whether international service is possible without split loyalties in a divided world. The problem as posed here is to my mind unreal. We are true to this or that ideal, and this or that interest, because we have in openness and responsibility recognized it as an ideal and an interest true to us. We embrace ideals and interests in their own right, not because

6

they are those of our environment or of this or that group. Our relations to our fellow men do not determine our attitude to ideals, but are determined by our ideals. If our attitude is consistent, we shall be consistent in our loyalties. If our attitude is confused, then our loyalties will also be divided.

In the world of today there is an urge to conformism which sometimes makes people complain of a lack of loyalty in those who criticize the attitudes prevalent in their environment. May I ask: who shows true loyalty to that environment, one who before his conscience has arrived at the conclusion that something is wrong and in all sincerity gives voice to his criticism, or the one who in self-protection closes his eyes to what is objectionable and shuts his lips on his criticism? The concept of loyalty is distorted when it is understood to mean blind acceptance. It is correctly interpreted when it is assumed to cover honest criticism.

The question to which I have just referred has attracted special attention in discussions concerning the attitude of those who work in international organizations, the policies in which in some cases may conflict with that of their home countries. Again I would say that the problem is unreal. The international civil servant who works for an organization with members of different ideologies and interests remains under the obligation that applies to all of us—to be faithful to truth as he understands it. In doing so he is loyal—both in relation to the organization and to his country. In doing so, he must, of course, subordinate himself to rules of good order, as all of us should do. Nobody should use his position in an international organization for attacks on his own country or its policies, however strongly he may feel that he is right. Nor should anybody, as a national, attack the international organization for which he is working, and thereby place himself outside the discipline and the procedure established for the maintenance of that organization. But it is equally true that nobody should suffer, either as a national, or in his position in the international organization, for faithfulness to ideals of truth and justice, provided he observes the laws of his country as well as of the organization which he serves. There cannot be, and there should not be, any real conflict between international service and international civil service, between the way of life we have been considering and the duties of someone engaged in professional work for the international community.

It may seem to you that this problem of loyalties is one of limited interest, relevant only to those who have chosen an international career. That is not so. I have brought it up here in relation to international organizations because those organizations present the problem in a clear-cut form which has attracted some public attention. However, the problem is common to us all in all walks of life, and of significance especially to those who, like you, are engaged in intellectual activities or are planning for a future which will bring you in contact with the civilizations, traditions and interests of many countries. In fact, it is a national problem, and a problem within whatever group of friends and associates you may be working, just as much as it is an international problem. The essence of international service, and the problem of loyalty as it presents itself in the light of such service, is the essence of all service to fellow men, and it is the problem of loyalty as we face it everywhere.

The attitude and the way of life which I have tried to describe as being the very essence of international service is more than a mere pattern of behavior. Implied in it is a positive ideal. We hear much about freedom and the blessings of freedom. We hear less about the obligations of freedom and the ideals by which freedom must be guided. Every individual prefers freedom from constraint and freedom from intervention in his personal pursuit of happiness. But, as we all recognize, such freedom is possible in a world of order only when the individual replaces outward limitations on his freedom of action by self-imposed laws which may be, and frequently are, no less severe. An individualism carried to the extreme where you neither accept restraint imposed on you by society, or by your fellow men, nor submit yourself to the laws of a mature conscience, would lead to anarchy. This is true no less of international life than of life within your own country.

The attitude basic to international service places the pursuit of happiness under laws of conscience which alone can justify freedom. In accepting such a way of life we recognize the moral sovereignty of the responsible individual. In the fight for freedom which puts its stamp so strongly on present-day life, the final issue is what dignity we are willing to give to man. It is part of the American creed, part of the inherited ideology of all Western civilization, that each man is an end in himself, of infinite value as an individual. To pay lip-service to this view or to invoke it in favor of our actions is easy. But what is in fact the central tenet of this ideology becomes a reality only when we, ourselves, follow a way of life, individually and as members of a group, which entitles us personally to the freedom of a mature individual, living under the rules of his conscience. And it becomes the key to our dealings with others only when inspired by a faith which in truth and spirit gives to them the value which is theirs according to what we profess to be our creed.

In a stirring and provocative book recently published in this country its author, a man of intelligence and great moral integrity, raises the question whether we can justify our faith in freedom in a world of materialistic thinking unless we are willing to depart from standards of value which measure success primarily in terms of outward achievement.* He never got a chance to elaborate his reply, as his work was interrupted by death. But from what he had already written, it is apparent what he wanted to say: that the dignity of man, as a justification for our faith in freedom, can be part of our living creed only if we revert to a view of life where maturity of mind counts for more than outward success and where happiness is no longer to be measured in quantitative terms. I doubt whether the author, had he been given the chance to complete his work, would ever have found it possible to go far beyond this point, because the final reply is not one that can be given in writing, but only in terms of life. There is no formula to teach us how to arrive at maturity and there is no grammar for the language of inner life. His study, like the effort of every single individual, finally led him to the doorstep where the rest is silence because the rest is something that has to be resolved between a man and himself. The rest is silence—but the results of the inner dialogue are evident to all, evident as independence, courage and fairness in dealing with others, evident in true international service.

You may be surprised by an approach to international service and to the problems raised by present-day developments in international life which, like mine today, is concerned mainly with problems of personal ethics. The so-called realists may regard what I have tried to say as just so many fine words, only tenuously related to everyday life and political action. I would challenge this criticism. The thoughts I have shared with you about international service are conclusions from a most practical experience. Politics and diplomacy

---

* *The Dignity of Man*, by Russell W. Davenport, published by Harper & Bros., Inc. 1955.

are no play of will and skill where results are independent of the character of those engaging in the game. Results are determined not by superficial ability but by the consistency of the actors in their efforts and by the validity of their ideals. Contrary to what seems to be popular belief there is no intellectual activity which more ruthlessly tests the solidity of a man than politics. Apparently easy successes with the public are possible for a juggler, but lasting results are achieved only by the patient builder.

What is true in a life of action, like that of a politician or a diplomat, is true also in intellectual activities. Even a genius never achieves a lasting result in science without patience and hard work, just as in politics the results of the work of the most brilliant mind will ultimately find their value determined by character. Those who are called to be teachers or leaders may profit from intelligence but can only justify their position by integrity.

THE WORLD AND THE NATION

Commencement Address at Stanford University,
Palo Alto, California, 19 June 1955.

Nationalism—internationalism. These abstract words, so often abused, so often misunderstood, cover high ideals and strong emotions, reflect modes of thought and action which shape our world.

We often see the word 'nationalism' used in a derogatory sense. The same is true of the word 'internationalism'. When nationalism connotes, for example, a 'go-it-alone' isolationism, and internationalism an outlook which belittles the significance of national life and of nations as centers of political action and spiritual tradition, the words become contradictory and the attitudes they describe irreconcilable. From such interpretations of the words comes the tendency to think of nationalism as in fundamental conflict with an internationalist attitude.

But other interpretations lead to a quite different result. Nationalism and internationalism, when understood as meaning recognition of the value and the rights of the nation, and of the dependence of the nation on the world, represent essential parts of the mental and spiritual equipment of all responsible men in our time. Everybody today, with part of his being, belongs to one country, with its specific traditions and problems, while with another part he has become a citizen of a world which no longer permits national isolation. Seen in this light there could not be any conflict between nationalism and internationalism, between the nation and the world.

The German poet and philosopher Friedrich von Schiller, conscious of the importance of his message of freedom and brotherhood, said that he would find it a miserable idea to write only for one nation. A philosopher could not limit himself to but a fraction of mankind. This nation or that national event could inspire him only in so far as it was of importance to all mankind. In his biography of Schiller, Thomas Carlyle criticized this attitude. He feared that a feeling which extended to all mankind would be too diffuse to operate as it should for individual life. The world idea would not provide the necessary guidance for personal conduct and might lead to anarchy. Schiller's own enthusiasm, he felt, would move us more strongly if he had directed himself to a narrower field.

86

In a speech on the 150th anniversary of Schiller's death last spring Thomas Mann dealt with this conflict between the idea of the world and the idea of the nation as represented respectively by Schiller and Carlyle. He felt that in our time the narrow field, the nation, was sinking back into the past. Everyone should realize that no problem, be it political or spiritual, could any longer be resolved on the basis of Carlyle's approach. Our world of today in his view required a universal vision—indeed, our anguished hearts demanded it. Mankind as an ideal was not too weak a guide for our conduct. It was necessary, more necessary than ever, to seek in it an inspiration for all our actions.

We may well feel that there is truth both in the attitude of Schiller and Mann and in the attitude of Carlyle, but that these great authors in their own personalities reveal that the concepts of the nation and of the world to which they have given expression, are, each one, incomplete and one-sided. Are they not firmly rooted in a national tradition, and yet, do they not belong to all mankind? Are they not internationalists in truth and spirit, and in being so, have they not served their own peoples? The question is not either the nation *or* the world. It is, rather, how to serve the world by service to our nation, and how to serve the nation by service to the world.

The dilemma is as old as mankind. There has always been the problem of how to harmonize loyalty to the smaller group, inside which we are working, with loyalty to the larger unit to which this group belongs. However, in our time this problem has taken on new proportions and a new significance. It has also developed aspects unknown to previous generations.

For vast multitudes this is an era when, for the first time, they have fully sensed the rights and responsibilities of free peoples and sovereign nations. It is also the era when freedom and sovereignty for the first time have been actually within their reach. Parallel with great social and economic revolutions within many countries, we witness now a world revolution from which peoples, long dependent on others, begin to emerge as strong, dynamic national states.

In the pride of self-realization natural to these new states we should welcome the constructive element—a self-assertion like that of a young man coming of age, conscious of his powers, eager to find his own way, to make his voice heard and to render his contribution to progress. We should meet this new enthusiasm with understanding, in full appreciation of the rich gifts it may bring to a world of many nations and peoples in friendly competition. In world affairs such an attitude, which is in line with the great traditions of this country, may be regarded as an expression of true democracy in international life.

I have spoken about the positive aspect of the nationalism of a young state. Let us not forget that these positive elements can be turned into an explosive force if repressed or unguided. It is a sign of true statesmanship, both in the new countries and in older nations, so to direct national policies as to avoid collisions developing out of unwise reactions to the new forces. History places a burden on our shoulders. The creative urges of the emergent nations are tinged with strong emotions from the past. It is for all of us, denying neither the good nor the ills of that past, to look ahead and not to permit old conflicts to envenom the spirit of the creative work before us.

We have to face also another kind of new nationalism, which is a strong force in every state. It is a commonplace that recent technological changes have created a new kind of interdependence among nations and brought all peoples much closer to each other. For reasons which lie outside the political sphere, practically all mankind today must be regarded as a unit in important economic, technical and political respects. Economic changes tend to sweep over all the world. New inventions influence quickly the life of all peoples. Because it is more difficult to limit wars to a single area, all wars are of concern to all nations. Not only construction, but also destruction may today be global.

It is natural that this new situation should provoke a resistance, inspired by the fear that our own country and our own private world might find itself submerged in some global development. And so we find people trying to find ways to isolate themselves from general trends and to build up closed, protected units. We can understand or even sympathize with such a reaction, but we must recognize that if it represents a resistance to change, it is doomed to failure. Such self-sought isolation may persevere for some time. It will not endure forever, and the longer the change is resisted and adjustment shirked, the more violent will be the final reaction when the walls collapse.

The reply to nationalists who wish to remain aloof in such vain efforts at self-protection is that the way to safeguard what they rightly want to defend is not isolation. The way is a vigorous and self-confident development, in free contact with the world, of the special qualities and assets of their nation and their people—a development which should give them their just weight in the international balance. Giving thus to the world what is specifically ours, we could manifest and protect our national character, while accepting change and opening our minds to the influences of the world.

It has been said that in our world of today, united in an outward sense by technical developments, international organization has ceased to be a utopian idea and has become a practical necessity. But what do we mean by international organization? The term seems to cover a vast range, from agreed cooperation, freely entered into by all nations or by a group of nations, to various kinds of federal arrangements involving varying degrees of surrender of sovereignty.

We undoubtedly need world organization, but we are far from ripe for world government. Indeed, even modest attempts at regional 'integration' have met with considerable difficulties, not because of any superstitious respect for national sovereignty, but because the peoples want to know in whose hands they put their fate, if they are to surrender part of their self-determination as nations. Further: how often have we not seen those who most eagerly plead for integration among other countries themselves shrink back from even the slightest discipline of their own sovereign rights?

Discussion about international integration, world organization and world government throws much light on the problem of the nation versus the world. I would not regard the widespread and often vocal resistance to anything which might be construed as tending to limit national sovereignty as a new upsurge of nationalism. It should rather be regarded as a symptom of how heavily faith in national self-determination weighs in the scales in every effort to reconcile the nation and the world. Such expression of national feelings is both an asset and a liability. It is an asset to the extent that it reflects the determination to shape one's own fate and to take the responsibility for it. It is an asset as a brake on immature experiments in international integration. But it is a liability when it blinds our eyes to the necessity of that degree of international organization which has become necessary to national life.

So far we have considered the question of the nation and the world in what I may call pragmatic and practical terms. The problem has also an ideological aspect. Every nation has its heroes, its martyrs and its saints. The world also has its heroes and saints. One who long ago spoke among a small, oppressed people for the brother-hood of all men, was sacrificed as a danger to the safety of his own nation. Western civilization has aspired for nearly 2,000 years to follow the life and teachings of this apostle of peace. But all through those 2,000 years nationalism in the narrow and dangerous sense of the word has remained a major force. In the light of history, one might well ascribe to mankind the words of Milton's Lucifer: 'For only in destroying I find ease to my relentless thoughts.'

The cynic may well ask: where in the political and national histories of this period do we see a reflection of the creed professed by sovereigns and peoples alike? The cynic may also say that as the past has been, so will the future be. It is my belief that he is wrong on both scores. Whatever doubts history may cast, I believe that the hope for a world of peace and order, inspired by respect for man, has never ceased to agitate the minds of men. I believe that it accounts for the great and noble human spirit behind the ravaged exterior of a history whose self-inflicted wounds have become more and more atrocious. And I believe that at the point we have now reached in our technical development, our creed may gain new possibilities to shape history. A faith like that which has inspired the spiritual life of the West could seem only a dream to the leader of the people of a powerful nation which can dominate others, or considers itself untouched by their actions. There is a new situation the day you have to recognize that you cannot dictate to other nations and that you are not independent of the actions of other nations. It is more difficult to see your brother in a slave or a master. It is easier to see him in somebody with whom you have to live without giving or taking orders. Looking back into the past we see how peoples have been oppressed—and how peoples have accepted oppression—in the name of God. May we not be approaching a time when in His name they will instead be giving and accepting freedom?

This week we will celebrate here on the West coast and all over the world the 10th anniversary of the signing of the United Nations Charter. It will be an occasion for fresh thinking about the problems and the challenge of our world. The United Nations is an expression of our will to find a synthesis between the nation and the world, overcoming the one-sidedness reflected in the words of Schiller and Carlyle. It is an attempt to provide us with a framework inside which it is possible to serve the world by serving our nation, and to serve our nation by serving the world. Whatever may be the past shortcomings of this experiment in world organization, it gives sense and direction to the efforts of all men who are striving towards a better world. The Organization was born out of the cataclysms of the second World War. It should justify the sacrifices of all fighters for freedom and justice in that war. I remember the bitter lines of a great Anglo-American poet who writes in an 'Epitaph on an Unknown Soldier':

'To save your world, you asked this man to die,
Would this man, could he see you now, ask why?'*

It is our duty to the past, and it is our duty to the future, so to serve both our nations and the world as to be able to give a reply to that anguished question.

* W. H. Auden.

INTERNATIONAL COOPERATION
WITHIN THE UNITED NATIONS

Address at University of California United Nations
Convocation, Berkeley, California, 25 June 1955.

In this week of commemoration, the representatives of governments have renewed the pledge of their nations to support the joint efforts of the Member States to develop, through the United Nations, international cooperation for the purposes common to all peoples, which we find stated in the Charter.

On this occasion, now that we have listened to the pronouncements of national spokesmen, it may perhaps be appropriate for me, as spokesman for those who work in the Secretariat of the Organization, to tell you about its problems, as they present themselves to the international civil servant: not political questions, but current operations inside the United Nations which are somewhat obscured from public view, but are as essential to the life and well-being of an international organism as the pulsation of the blood to the living body.

When a new social organism is created, we give it a constitution. Inside the framework of that constitution, the first vital urges begin to stir, but as its life develops towards fullness the constitution is adjusted, so to say from within, to new and changing needs which even the wisest legislator and statesman could only partly foresee. In this process, which gives life and substance to the written word, a point is sooner or later reached when legislators find that they should take stock of the situation. They develop theories, which in turn influence our actions and lead, perhaps, finally to a review or revision of the written constitution. In national life and in the life of communities, of corporations and associations, we all know this sequence of events. A similar development is also taking place inside the United Nations. It must be so if the Organization is to remain a living and growing organism.

Western constitutional thinking has developed the theory that a balance of power must be maintained between the executive, the judicial and the legislative functions of government. This theory provides us with a kind of rule of thumb in analyzing the specific character of a national constitution. But it also has an important influence on our whole concept of government and on political action. You all know how it is reflected in the constitution of this country.

In the United Nations, as set up by the Charter, you also find the problem of maintaining balance of power between organs which bear resemblance, although but superficially, to the executive, judiciary and legislature of a government. Instead of a parliament we have the General Assembly; in place of the judiciary, the International Court of Justice; in place of the executive, the three Councils and the Secretariat under the Secretary-General. There is a resemblance between this system and a national constitution—for example, of this country—but there are also fundamental differences. The General Assembly is not a legislature. It cannot pass laws binding on its members. The international judiciary is likewise limited in its competence to a far greater degree than a national judiciary, and we find equally strict and significant limitations circumscribing the authority of the executive organs.

The explanation of these restrictions is, of course, that the United Nations is an organization for cooperation between *sovereign* states. This reserves for them the basic rights of sovereign states, which are normally exercised by the chief organs of a nation. Thus, the United Nations permits binding decisions only in a few cases, and under conditions which today are not likely to be fulfilled.

I have reminded you of these elementary facts because they provide the framework inside which we in the United Nations Secretariat have to work for the purposes common to all Member nations.

It has rightly been said that the United Nations is what the Member nations make it. But it may likewise be said that, within the limits set by government action and government cooperation, much depends on what the Secretariat makes it. That is our pride in the Secretariat and that is the challenge we have to face.

I have already compared the silent Secretariat activities inside the Organization with the pulsation of the blood-stream inside the living body. The first and fundamental function of the Secretariat is service to the governments as members of the General Assembly, of the Councils and of the committees and commissions which are set up by those organs. That is an unspectacular, but vital work, like the carrying of nourishment through all the tissues of the body. The members of the Secretariat may feel—to make another comparison—that they are wheels in a big machine with which all the peoples of the world have to work—wheels, however, which are not dead mechanical things but set in motion by individual will, and the smooth operation of which must be guaranteed by professional skill and great devotion to the work.

Because the Secretariat is a living thing—and its individual members, with their own convictions and hopes, their own idealism, are independent of orders from any government—it is, however, something more than a ticking mechanism. It has creative capacity. It can introduce new ideas. It can in proper forms take initiatives. It can put before the Member governments new findings which will influence their actions. Thus, the Secretariat in its independence represents an organ not only necessary for the life and proper functioning of the body, but of importance also for its growth.

It is natural that in the close contact between the Secretariat and the Member governments, which develops in the daily work, and with the opportunity given to the Secretariat to provide information and ideas, the Secretary-General can to some extent exert influence on the frame within which it is his duty to accept responsibility for a sound development of the United Nations. He and the Secretariat can do so, without pleading its case, by creating confidence in its truly international spirit, in its loyalty and its judgment.

In a certain sense the Secretariat represents the United Nations and the ideals of the Organization in relation to nations within or outside it. The Charter requires of the Secretariat that it should act without taking or seeking advice from Member governments. It follows that the assistance that the Secretariat can give must be inspired only by the principles and aims of the Organization, independent of the special interests of any individual Members. This duty to represent the collective ideal is a heavy responsibility, but also an essential one if the Organization is to function vitally. It has found its recognition in the Charter in the well-known provision which entitles the Secretary-General to take initiatives in the Security Council when he considers that peace and security are seriously threatened.

Even this last function of the Secretariat—and by necessity especially of the Secretary-General personally—is and should be unspectacular. The very rules of the game, and the specific position of the Secretariat inside the system, force the Secretariat in its activities as representative of the Organization as a whole to apply what is now often called quiet diplomacy. Such an activity, in fact, comes very close to that of a Foreign Office, working along classical lines as a servant of the Government and of the people— with a discretion and integrity rendered necessary by the fact that none of the interests it is there to safeguard and none of the confidences that it may be privileged to enjoy, is its own property but something entrusted to it by its master, the people.

In the General Assembly, as well as in the Councils, open debate is the rule. The public and the press are admitted to practically all meetings and are able to follow the development of arguments, the evolution of conflicts and the arrival at solutions. The debates cover a ground which in earlier times was mostly reserved for negotiation behind closed doors. They have introduced a new instrument of negotiation, that of conference diplomacy. This instrument has many advantages. It can serve to form public opinion. It can subject national policies and proposals to the sharp tests of world-wide appraisal, thus revealing the strength, or weakness, of a cause that might otherwise have remained hidden. It can activate the sound instincts of the common man in favour of righteous causes. It can educate and guide. But it has, also, weaknesses. There is the temptation to play to the gallery at the expense of solid construction. And there is the risk that positions once taken publicly become frozen, making compromise more difficult.

Thus we find introduced in conference diplomacy an aspect of propaganda and an element of rigidity which may be harmful to sound negotiation. In these circumstances it is natural, and it has been increasingly felt, that the balance to be struck within the United Nations between conference diplomacy and quiet diplomacy —whether directly between representatives of Member governments or in contacts between the Secretary-General and Member governments—has to be carefully measured and maintained. This balance should obviously be established in such a way as to render the Organization as valuable an instrument as possible for the achievement of progress towards peace. It is my feeling that there now is a broader recognition than before of the value of quiet diplomacy within the framework of the Organization as a complement to the conference diplomacy of the public debates. My belief is that a further development in that direction is warranted and would in no way reduce the value of conference diplomacy.

It is a fact, sometimes overlooked, that within the framework of the Charter, as within the framework of a national constitution, infinite variation of practices is possible, and that new and useful forms of operation may come into being which, although entirely consonant with its philosophy, were not written out in the constitution. The United Nations is still at a very early stage in that development of constitutional life inside the framework of the written word which we regard as normal in the life of nations. It is my hope that, by methods of trial and error, cautious but firm progress can be made inside the United Nations in the development of new forms of contact, new methods of deliberation, new techniques for reconciliation.

The Charter prescribes certain forms for settlement of disputes in and by the organs of the United Nations. When those organs are used, the prescribed forms should, of course, be observed. But half-way between the formal procedures of the organs established in the Charter and the methods of quiet diplomacy that may be employed by Member nations and the Secretariat there are many possibilities so far untried. Several great problems have been discussed outside the Organization and in forms other than those foreseen in the Charter. With only slight adjustments of the conventional mould, in ways that are appropriate, such discussions could often be fitted into the general framework of the United Nations, thus adding to the strength and prestige of the Organization, as well as drawing strength and prestige from it. Let us hope that such possibilities will be explored with confidence and with imagination and in full recognition of the need to give the United Nations a chance to develop its potentialities to the full.

So far I have—to use the general constitutional terminology—looked at the work of the United Nations from the angle of the executive and legislative organs. When I now turn to the judiciary, today represented here by President Hackworth of the International Court of Justice, I wish to emphasize that my mentioning of the judiciary last does not in any way imply that it is of lesser importance than the other organs. On the contrary, I feel that the United Nations will never grow and prosper in the way we hope for, unless the central role of the judiciary comes to be recognized in the international sphere as fully as it is in national life.

Between sovereign nations conflicts arise to a large extent in a political context. But the substance of the disputes is also often in fact a question of law. While it is natural that the conflicts tend to be treated in forms adequate to political problems, it is also true that they could be resolved on a basis of law much more frequently than is now the case. If the position of the judiciary inside the international constitutional system so far is weak, in practice, this may be explained primarily by the fact that it often seems most safe for a sovereign state to tackle a problem as a matter for political reconciliation. The system of international law is still fairly undeveloped and there are wide margins of uncertainty. Why, one may ask, run the risk of a possibly less favourable outcome reached on the basis of law instead of a more advantageous one that might be achieved by skillful negotiation and under the pressure of political arguments. Why? Is not the reason obvious? First of all, is it not in the interest of sound development to restrict as much as possible the arena where strength is an argument and to put as much as possible under the rule of law? But there is a further consideration. If we regret the undeveloped state of international law, should we not use all possibilities to develop an international common law by submitting our conflicts to jurisdiction wherever that is possible? I apologize for having gone into these matters, so ably and with such competence covered here by Judge Hackworth. I have done so only because it appears to me on the basis of daily experience that the world of order and justice for which we are striving will never be ours unless we are willing to give it the broadest possible and the firmest possible foundation in law.

Summing up what I have said you will see that our experience in the Secretariat has led us to believe that we should try to give a wider scope to quiet diplomacy—which in practice means that we should rely more heavily on unspectacular negotiation and on the service of the executive organs than we have done so far—and, further, that we should attempt to give our judiciary a stronger position inside the international constitutional system.

My starting point was the constitution set up by the Charter and its development in practice as a guide for the daily work of the Secretariat. I have told you how we in the Secretariat dream that one could improve the working of the Organization we serve, which to us is very precious. However, whatever changes in the balance between the main constitutional organs may take place, the Secretariat will be happy in its role. It is for us a privilege to serve the community of nations. We do not ask for wider powers, but we are ready to accept fully all the responsibilities that the Member governments may entrust to us. We are willing to risk *our* personal peace and security and welfare if this can help world peace, world security and world welfare.

The motto of one of the old ruling houses in Europe was: 'I serve.' This must be the guiding principle, and also the inspiration and the challenge, for all those who have to carry the responsibility of office for any community. Is it not natural that this motto should be felt with special faith, sincerity and loyalty by those who assist in the greatest venture in international cooperation on which mankind has ever embarked?

At the induction in my present office I quoted these lines by a Swedish poet: 'The greatest prayer of man is not for victory, but for peace.' Let this be the end of my words today also.

FROM THE INTRODUCTION TO THE
ANNUAL REPORT 1954–1955

8 July 1955

———◆———

THE STRENGTHENING OF
INTERNATIONAL LAW

... If the system of international law remains insufficiently developed, there are many ways in which this situation may be progressively corrected. The beginnings of a 'common law' of the United Nations, based on the Charter, are now apparent; its steady growth will contribute to stability and orderliness. Advisory opinions of the International Court of Justice have added substantially to the law of the United Nations; their more frequent use should be encouraged. In appropriate cases, arbitral proceedings may usefully be employed in connection with controversies on legal points; the use of such proceedings would tend both to facilitate immediate solutions and to further the long-range goal of strengthening the authority of law. The systematic examination within the United Nations of the practice of States can bring to light areas of agreement and divergence in the law and stimulate efforts to seek a reconciliation of opposing views.

To some extent, this process is taking place through the work of the International Law Commission and through the adoption of conventions by the Economic and Social Council and the General Assembly. It is apparent, however, that the resources devoted to these purposes have been far from adequate, and it is important that Member States and the United Nations as a whole should give renewed consideration to the task. It may well be that each Government should constitute a specialized group of highly qualified jurists, either within or outside the Government, to carry on the work on a national level, and thus to facilitate well-informed and considered decisions by the responsible governmental authorities. Within the United Nations, similarly, there is room for making better use of the machinery and improving the procedures for the development of international law.

The more frequent submission by the Member States of their legal disputes to the International Court of Justice is essential to progress in this direction. It is apparent that there are a number of controversies between governments which continue to be sources of tension but which are suitable, in whole or in part, for judicial settlement through the Court. Only half the Member States have so far accepted the compulsory jurisdiction of the Court, under Article 36, paragraph 2, of the Statute. To those States which have not yet accepted the compulsory jurisdiction of the Court, I draw attention to the resolution of the General Assembly of 1947 calling for such acceptance, and propose again that these States should give favorable consideration to this recommendation. The Court has fully demonstrated that it merits their confidence. . . .

THE POLITICAL SIGNIFICANCE OF THE ATOMS FOR PEACE CONFERENCE

Extract from Statement at the opening of the International Scientific Conference on the peaceful uses of atomic energy in Geneva, 8 August 1955. This Conference was the first important step in a United Nations program for international cooperation in developing the peaceful uses of atomic energy that grew out of proposals first made by President Eisenhower to the General Assembly on 8 December 1953. A second Conference took place in 1958. Thousands of scientists and engineers from both sides in the Cold War and elsewhere in the world participated. The organization of both conferences was entrusted by the General Assembly to the Secretary-General, working with a Scientific Advisory Committee on which the principal nuclear Powers were represented. Another result of this program of cooperation was the establishment in 1957 of the International Atomic Energy Agency as a member of the United Nations family of international institutions, with headquarters in Vienna.

. . . One is often asked whether this Conference has any political significance. In its conception, its purposes and its approach, this Conference is as non-political as a conference of this nature should be. The personalities that we see around us are not concerned with expediency, with strategy or with tactics of any kind, but with the search for truth and with the idea of brotherhood based on the concept that all knowledge is universal. Nevertheless, since their deliberations are bound to affect human life in all its aspects, it would not be correct to say that they have no political significance. I am sure that their cooperation will ease tensions. I am sure that their exchange of scientific data will inspire confidence and I am sure that the trend of their discussions will turn men's thoughts away from war to peace. We all should render our thanks to the scientists who, by moving in this direction, will expiate, on behalf of all of us, that feeling of guilt which has so universally been felt, that man in his folly should have thought of no better use of a great discovery than to manufacture with its help the deadliest instruments of annihilation.

We have a long road ahead of us to traverse before nations can hope to eliminate the threat of atomic destruction. But we cannot hope to travel at all unless we begin to take down the barriers to understanding and friendship and begin to work together in growing confidence. . . .

THE INTERNATIONAL SIGNIFICANCE
OF THE BILL OF RIGHTS

Address at Celebration of the 180th Anniversary of the
Virginia Declaration of Rights 1776–1956,
Williamsburg, Virginia, 14 May 1956

The Virginia Declaration of Rights may be considered to mark the beginning of a series of declarations of human rights leading up to the Universal Declaration proclaimed in 1948 by the General Assembly of the United Nations. The United Nations Declaration is the most comprehensive in the whole long line of such attempts to crystallize our faith in the dignity of man. It reflects what has been acknowledged as one of the main purposes of the United Nations.

Who can trace the first sources of a great idea? Such ideas are brought to our awareness when they break through the inertia of human minds and of social institutions, but their antecedents, we find, generally go far back into the past. Early American political philosophy and American liberties were rooted in European theory and in British traditions that dated back in outward expressions to the Great Revolution of 1688. But behind those European theories and behind the British traditions, we find the same ideas, and the prophets for those ideas, in the distant past of our civilization.

Although justice requires that we recognize the heritage, it would, however, be unjust to belittle the significance of the act through which ideas break through the barriers and become an active factor in the life of the community. The Virginia Declaration of Rights is older by thirteen years than the French Declaration of the Rights of Man and of the Citizen of 1789. Your country can take just pride in being the one where this historically significant affirmation of human rights was given.

What was new in the Virginia Declaration of Rights was the formal recognition of human rights as part of written constitutional law. This recognition introduced a technique for the protection of the people not only against the tyranny of monarchs, but also against the intolerance and tyranny of majorities.

There is an intellectual freshness and clarity of thought about the period in American political history to which this day draws our attention, that cannot fail to attract everybody interested in a sound development of modern society. The Virginia Declaration bears testimony to this constructive state of mind.

In every society there is a tendency, as time passes, to lose dynamism and to seek protection behind time-honored formulae, protection against the law of change which is basic to all growth. 'Whenever any government,' the Virginia Declaration says, 'shall be found inadequate or contrary to those purposes, the majority hath an indubitable, inalienable and indefeasible right to reform, alter or abolish it.' This is the voice of self-confidence. This is the voice of trust. This is the voice which should always speak in favor of evolution in the interest of man.

The questions about the relationship of the individual to the state as they presented themselves in the eighteenth century, seem to us still to be within human perspective. There was at that time a kind of balance in the relationship of the individual to organized society. If a man were dissatisfied, he still had plenty of ways in which he might, as an individual, expect to influence the course of events.

Today, on the 180th anniversary of the Virginia Declaration, the perspective is different. The development of society is such that, in the very interest of the individual, the organized collectivity can no longer give the same scope to individual action and influences as was possible in a smaller and less developed community. Modern man seldom acts alone. He is integrated in a series of collectivities which together form our society. In almost every phase of his life and work he feels the necessity of organizing his activities in common with others, whether through trade unions, cooperatives, other economic organizations or public associations or enterprises. Over and above these various collectivities, the individual meets the state, which is their general framework, and beyond the state there is the international community of nations with its necessarily ever-widening influence.

It would take me too far to raise here the very important issues of principle, philosophy and law involved. I cannot do so without getting deep into questions which are at the very root of the major conflicts of our time and which should not be discussed on this occasion. What I have said should suffice as an indication of the setting in which we, children of the twentieth century, have to keep alive and to apply the old ideas based on the recognition of the dignity of the human being which found a first constitutional expression in the Virginia Declaration of Rights.

The series of declarations of rights, from the Virginia Declaration to the Universal Declaration proclaimed by the United Nations, reflects indirectly the change of setting to which I have referred. At one end of the chain we have a declaration by a group of far-sighted men, framing the life of a new small community. At the other end of the chain we have a statement by the first international organization that can claim to speak for the world.

An optimist might be led to believe that this same development reflects not only the growth of society from the small national unit to the organized collectivity of nations, but also a growth of the recognition of human rights. Such an optimist would be right in the sense that ideas which seemed revolutionary, when crystallized in legal form a couple of hundred years ago, today are so generally recognized as to make it seem improper to question them. But he would be wrong if he meant that the forces against which human rights have to be defended are less strong or less complicated than at earlier times. On the contrary, the complications have grown in manifold ways, while the resistance which arises from certain tendencies in the behavior of both the individual and the masses has certainly not lessened. We need only to remember what circumstances forced on the United Nations the problem of human rights, to understand that my pessimistic words about human nature are not unfounded. What happened in the 'forties may happen again. And the complications we are meeting in the 'fifties will still be there in the 'sixties.

The Charter of the United Nations calls for international cooperation in 'promoting and encouraging respect for human rights and for fundamental freedoms for all without distinction as to race, sex, language or religion.' At the San Francisco Conference eleven years ago, a determined effort was made to incorporate a Bill of Rights in the Charter. However, it was realized that the task was beyond the capacity of a relatively short conference. It was therefore decided that it would not be done until the international organization had been established.

Three years later the Universal Declaration of Human Rights was a fact. This Declaration enunciates not only all the traditional political rights and civil liberties, but also economic, social and cultural rights. It is an international synthesis of the thinking of our generation on these questions. Unlike the Virginia Declaration, which was drawn up by George Mason, there is no one person who can be identified as the principal draftsman of the Universal Declaration. The Declaration is anonymous in its character, and back of it we find literally thousands of people who directly and indirectly participated actively in its drafting. Also for that reason it may be called the universal expression in the field of human rights of the aims of our world of today, a world where the memory is still fresh of some of the worst infringements of human rights ever experienced in history, and a world which is also facing the problem of human rights in new and increasingly complicated forms.

The Universal Declaration is not, of course, a treaty and has, in itself, no force in law. But, as 'a common standard of achievement for all peoples and all nations,' it not only crystallizes the political thought of our times on these matters, but it has also influenced the thinking of legislators all over the world. It is in this sense a worthy successor to the long line of affirmations of human liberties which began here in Williamsburg, though it is not and cannot be the final word in these questions, which by their very nature are as dynamic as life itself.

The relationship of man to society is a relationship for which every generation must seek to find the proper form. But, just as ideas far back in the past gave direction to the efforts for the best in former times, so this declaration should give direction to those who now carry the responsibility for a sound development of society.

As it stands, the Universal Declaration of Human Rights is both a symbol of the magnitude of the problem of human rights in our century and a measure of the concern with the problem which is shared by the governments and peoples represented in the United Nations. But it is also, in words for our time, a reminder of what must be the goal for the individual as well as for governments; the recognition in action of the dignity of man and of the sanctity of those freedoms which follow from such recognition.

Some days ago I returned from an assignment in the Middle East. I had to negotiate questions connected with the implementation of the Armistice Agreements between Israel and her Arab neighbor states. In their first articles those Armistice Agreements establish the right of each party 'to its security and freedom from fear of attack.' In a political context of the utmost significance, this clause recognizes a human right which, in a broad sense, may be said to sum up the whole philosophy of human rights.

What is the right to security? Is it not the right to the free development of individual and national life within the limits set by the right of other parties to the same security? What is the right of freedom from attack? Is it not the right to freedom from fear?

Thus we see how close the links are between the philosophy reflected in the recognition of the rights of individuals and the basic principles which may decide the issue of war and peace.

We all know how, when moved by fear, people may act against what others see as their own best interest. We know how, when people are afraid, they may act even against their own fundamental will. We have seen how, when influenced by such actions, the course of events may take on aspects of inexorable fatality up to the point where, out of sheer weariness, no resistance to the gravitation into open conflict any longer seems possible. This is a constantly repeated pattern of tragedy.

Why is war and fear of war in the headlines of every daily paper, if not because man fears man and nation nation? Could there be a more eloquent sign of how far we are from recognition of the philosophy behind the principles of human rights on which alone peace can be built? Can there be a greater challenge for us to work for such a recognition of the dignity of man as would eliminate the fear which is eating our world like a cancer?

I have moved on from talking about the principles of human rights to touch upon the spirit behind those principles. That brings me to the point where our concern is no longer with social philosophy, or with political action, but with individual life. If, at long last, the recognition of human dignity means to give others freedom from fear, then that recognition cannot be simply a question of passive acceptance. It is a question of the positive action that must be taken in order to kill fear.

This is not a question of abstract ethical principles. I state conclusions from some very concrete recent experiences. It is when we all play safe that we create a world of the utmost insecurity. It is when we all play safe that fatality will lead us to our doom. It is 'in the dark shade of courage'* alone, that the spell can be broken.

* From Ezra Pound: 'Canto XC.'

WOODROW WILSON AND THE UNITED NATIONS

Address at New York University Hall of Fame cere-
mony of the unveiling of the Bust and Tablet for
Woodrow Wilson, 20 May 1956, the centennial
year of his birth.

May I first of all thank you for inviting me to join in this ceremony. An occasion such as this in the Hall of Fame for Great Americans belongs in a very special way to the American people. This is a national shrine. The men who are honored here have helped to make the history which is your national heritage. They are bone of your bones and flesh of your flesh.

In asking an international official—the Secretary-General of the United Nations—to speak on this occasion, you have, I am told, broken a precedent of long standing. I am deeply grateful for the generous thought which prompted your invitation. You have done so because of Woodrow Wilson's pioneering leadership in the struggle to achieve a just and peaceful international order.

Woodrow Wilson came to that leadership as an authentic and eloquent spokesman to the world of the spirit of American idealism. That spirit, expressed anew from generation to generation, is deeply rooted in your own national culture. But because it also reflects and shares ideals that are universal, it has often been an inspiring and enriching influence for all mankind.

This is the case with the great idealists of any age and culture. This was the case with Woodrow Wilson's advocacy of world organization. From the very first, he spoke in terms of universal ideals and of the common interest. His first public commitment to the idea of a League of Nations was made just forty years ago this month. It was made when he spoke on 27 May, 1916, to a meeting of a group of world-minded Americans who had banded together as The League to Enforce Peace.

Why was an association of nations needed? Because, he said, 'the peace of the world must henceforth depend upon a new and more wholesome diplomacy'; because 'the principle of public right must henceforth take precedence over the individual interests of particular nations'; because 'the nations of the world must in some way band themselves together to see that that right prevails as against any sort of selfish aggression'; because 'there must be a common agreement for a common object' and 'at the heart of that common object must lie the inviolable rights of peoples and of mankind'.

In this same speech he defined some of these rights: the right of every people 'to choose the sovereignty under which they shall live'; the right of small States 'to enjoy the same respect for their sovereignty and territorial integrity as the great nations' and the right to be free from every disturbance of the peace 'that has its origin in aggression and disregard of the rights of peoples and nations'.

These statements of the reasons for, and purposes of, world organization are as much to the point today as when they were made forty years ago. In his stress upon the precedence of 'public right' over 'the individual interests of particular nations' and upon 'common agreement for a common object'—that is for the rights of peoples—Woodrow Wilson went to the heart of the matter.

As he so clearly understood, the international interest had to be institutionalized if it were to have a reasonable hope of prevailing in the course of time. No matter how solemn the engagement to common purposes and universal aims, whether expressed in a Covenant for a League of Nations or in a Charter for the United Nations, institutions functioning continuously in the service of these purposes would be needed to give them effect. When he opened discussion of plans for a League of Nations at the Paris Peace Conference in January 1919, Wilson called for the creation of an organization that should, he stressed, be 'not merely a formal thing, not an occasional thing, not a thing sometimes called into life to meet an exigency' but that should have a 'vital continuity' of function. He summed it up in these expressive words: 'It should be the eye of the nations to keep watch upon the common interest, an eye that does not slumber, an eye that is everywhere watchful and attentive.'

Forty years after Woodrow Wilson first uttered these words, the idea of world organization is far more firmly established than it ever was in the years of the League of Nations. The mere fact that the United Nations, unlike the League, has never lost a Member state, and now, with seventy-six Members, seems to be moving inexorably towards true universality, speaks for this. But we are still seeking ways to make our international institutions fulfill more effectively

the fundamental purpose expressed in Woodrow Wilson's words—
'to be the eye of the nations to keep watch upon the common
interest'.

I have no doubt that forty years from now we shall also be engaged
in the same pursuit. How could we expect otherwise? World
organization is still a new adventure in human history. It needs much
perfecting in the crucible of experience and there is no substitute
for time in that respect.

Two of our most common human failings, indeed, seem to be
our disrespect for the slow processes of time and our tendency to
shift responsibility from ourselves to our institutions. It is too often
our habit to see the goal, to declare it and, in declaring it, to assume
that we shall automatically achieve it. This leads us to confuse ends
with means, to label as failure what is in fact an historic step forward,
and in general to mistake the lesser for the greater thing.

Thus Woodrow Wilson, in the years between the wars, was
commonly considered to have failed because the United States
refused to join the League of Nations. Yet, in fact, he had made
history, great history, by being the principal founder of the first
world organization.

The League itself was labelled a failure because its existence did
did not prevent a second World War. Yet the failure lay not in the
League, but in the nations which failed to live up to their pledged
word and also failed to infuse into the League as an institution the
vitality and strength that Wilson had pleaded for in 1919.

In our day too, we often hear it said that the United Nations has
succeeded here, or has failed there. What do we mean? Do we refer
to the purposes of the Charter? They are expressions of universally
shared ideals which cannot fail us, though we, alas, often fail them.
Or do we think of the institutions of the United Nations? They are
our tools. We fashioned them. We use them. It is our responsibility
to remedy any flaws there may be in them. It is our responsibility
to correct any failures in our use of them. And we must expect the
responsibility for remedying the flaws and correcting the failures to
go on and on, as long as human beings are imperfect and human
institutions likewise.

This is a difficult lesson for both idealists and realists, though
for different reasons. I suppose that, just as the first temptation of
the realist is the illusion of cynicism, so the first temptation of the
idealist is the illusion of Utopia. As an idealist, it was natural that

Woodrow Wilson also did not entirely escape this temptation, any more than have most of the idealists of history. In his valiant fight for the cause of the League of Nations, he went beyond the concept of an institution acting for the common interest of the peoples of the world. He visualized the establishment of the League as ending the old system of the balance of power and substituting what he called a 'community of power'.

The creation of a true community of power to serve the common interest is, indeed, the goal—now as it was in Woodrow Wilson's day. But the establishment of the League of Nations did not, and could not, of itself bring such a community of power into being. It did not, nor could it, end at one stroke the system of the balance of power in international affairs.

The League was an association of sovereign nation-States, just as the United Nations is today. In such an association, the play of the balance of power is inevitable. And it should be said that one of the most serious remaining obstacles in the way of public understanding of the true role of the United Nations today results from a similar tendency to picture the United Nations of 1945 as establishing collective security for the world.

Now, as then, it is important for all of us to understand that true collective security, in the sense of an international police power engaged to defend the peace of the world, is to be found at the end, not at the beginning, of the effort to create and use world institutions that are effective in the service of the common interest.

The spirit and practice of world community must first gain in strength and custom by processes of organic growth. It is to the helping along of these processes of growth that we should devote all our ingenuity and our effort. To the extent that we are able to increase the weight of the common interest as against the weight of special interests, and therefore of the power of the whole community to guide the course of events, we shall be approaching that much much nearer to the goal.

This is, in fact, the most essential message of the career of Woodrow Wilson for the present day, whether we think of him as educator, as President of the United States, or as the pioneer of world organization.

Throughout his life he was the eloquent spokesman and dedicated champion of the general welfare both within his nation and among the nations of the world. Though his hopes for the enforcement of peace through collective security were ahead of the times, he also saw that international organization should rely primarily upon moral force, because— in his words—it was 'intended as a constitution of peace, not as a league of war.'

He understood very well what was at the root of the difficulty with making world organization work more effectively in the common interest, and he expressed it in words that we would do well to turn into the first person plural and repeat to ourselves in our own times: 'They have thought too much of the interests that were near them and they have not listened to the voices of their neighbors.'

Woodrow Wilson could denounce such selfishness, as powerfully as he could evoke a vision of 'pastures of quietness and peace such as the world never dreamed of before.' He could also give movingly human expressions to his deep-seated faith in the processes of democracy. Just before he died in 1924, he told a friend: 'I am not sorry I broke down. As it is coming now, the American people are thinking their way through and reaching their own decision, and that is the better way for it to come.'

It is not only the American people, of course, but the peoples of many nations who have been thinking their way through and reaching their own decision since Woodrow Wilson first showed the way. The United Nations stands as evidence of the direction of their thinking and of their decision.

How would Woodrow Wilson have reacted to the present developments in the life of the United Nations?

Would he not have hailed the atomic conference at Geneva last summer as evidence of the possibilities of cooperation even in a divided world, when a major interest common to all is at stake? Would he not have been happy that this cooperation developed within the framework of an organization owing so much to his original conceptions?

Would he not have hailed the development of the membership, which shows the vitality of the concept of universality at the present juncture in the growth of internationalism?

And, although he certainly would have been deeply worried by the underlying problems, would he not have been happy to see how in the Middle East the United Nations machinery could help Member governments in crystallizing their wish to re-establish order?

I think he would, but I think he also would have found reason for criticism. He would have been surprised to see how far we have yet failed to bring international conflicts effectively under the rule of law.

Although the spokesman for 'open covenants openly arrived at' —for democracy in international negotiation—he would also, I think, not have approved all of the applications given to that sound principle. Knowing too well the ways of man to believe in his ability to resist selfish or short-sighted public pressures, he would certainly have found it appropriate to plead for a combination of the new methods of diplomacy, of which he was in favor, with such of those time-honored political techniques as would give us the result best serving the interests of peace.

It is a true measure of the leadership and idealism of Woodrow Wilson that it is not a vain pastime in this way to give some thought to the question of how he would have looked at our endeavors, our failures and our successes, in the fields to which he devoted the best of his life. He is not only the first and foremost spokesman for true international organization. He is one of those who helped to create an international conscience which is, and will remain, a living force in all attempts to build a world of order.

AN INTERNATIONAL
ADMINISTRATIVE SERVICE

From an address to the International Law Association at McGill University, Montreal, 30 May 1956. In this address Dag Hammarskjöld first proposed a new departure in the forms of expert assistance which international organization might render to the new and less economically developed countries, most of which suffer from a severe shortage of administrators and civil servants with the training and experience needed to carry out their development programs. The concept of a career service under which international officials would, in effect, be seconded to serve inside national administrations in an executive capacity rather than as technical advisors for specific projects, was a new and imaginative one. It took some time to win full acceptance, both from the industrialized nations and from a few of the under-developed countries fearing a 'neo-colonialist' development, but it is now an established United Nations program under the somewhat unhappy name of OPEX (Operational and Executive Personnel), though still on a very modest scale that is far short of the needs.

... I have linked the question of assistance for economic development, as a tiding-over operation pending a more normal solution, to the parallel problem of the emergence—or re-emergence—into self-determination of a great number of peoples and nations. To a large extent, although not fully, the two problems cover basically the same regions of the world. Apart from the mutual relationship which exists between the two problems, they have one factor in common to which we should give special attention. This is a factor which, in my view, presents the greatest difficulty, though so far it is the least discussed and least recognized aspect.

Nations emerging from long foreign rule generally lack an independent administrative tradition and a social structure within which it is easy to build up a class of national administrators. This is a major problem not only for such nations, but also for many other

countries which seek to achieve a major economic and social reconstruction and to use international economic assistance in the best
possible way for this end.

It may be said that this question of administration, linked as it
is to the related question of the social structure, constitutes the
main bottle-neck which must be broken in any soundly conceived
policy aimed at solving the problems of self-determination and
economic balance.

Nearly all the nations whose independence as modern states is of
recent date are to be found in the economically under-developed
areas of Asia and Africa. Their social organization and, in many
cases, their administrative arrangements and the available trained
personnel fall far short of their needs. No one who has spent even
a short time in any of those lands can fail to have been impressed by
the magnitude of the task with which the new leaders are grappling,
or by the truly heroic character of the effort which some of them
are making to establish more secure foundations for their country.

While the need for an expansion of economic aid is now generally
recognized and the debate has, by and large, turned from questions
of principle to a discussion of ways and means, insufficient attention
has, I think, been given to this administrative difficulty in the path
of economic development. The capacity of a country to absorb
large-scale economic assistance or to make the best use of its
domestic resources is in no small measure determined by its administrative arrangements. It is significant, for example, that in every one
of the reports of the economic survey missions sent out by the United
Nations and the International Bank, some reference has been made
to the handicap imposed by poorly developed public administration
and the shortage of competent officials. It is no disparagement of
any of the countries concerned to note that the existing governmental organization is insufficient to carry out the greatly expanded
public investment and development programs that are needed.
Most of these countries have had only a short period to replace the
arrangements of the former administering power with their own
organization and to create a public service at once efficient and
responsive to their will.

It is true that in some of the countries concerned, the former
administering authority has bequeathed a valuable legacy in the
form of an efficient administrative apparatus and sizeable cadres of
experienced local officials at many levels. But this is by no means

generally so. Even where it is, it does not meet the needs of peoples whose awakening has stirred far deeper feelings of hope and endeavor than were felt under the most enlightened colonial regime. Great economic development programs have been planned which are held back more by lack of men to direct them than by lack of capital. Great national programs of social welfare are failing to move forward primarily for lack of experienced officials to undertake the manifold administrative tasks which they entail.

In the long run national training programs for officials and workers will doubtless meet the needs of the new nations for administration of their development plans. But the long run may be very long and the need is urgent. It is for this reason that I welcome the suggestion of the Canadian Secretary of State for External Affairs, Mr. Pearson, that we should consider establishing what he describes as 'an international professional and technical civil service of the United Nations with experts especially trained for work in the under-developed areas.' This far-sighted proposal stands, I feel, side by side in importance with the proposal recently made by the French Foreign Minister, M. Pineau, who has called for the establishment of a new United Nations agency for world economic development.

Mr. Pearson's proposal might seem, at first glance, to call for no more than an extension of existing technical assistance activities of the United Nations. To my mind, however, it should, in the light of the immensity of the problems we are facing, imply a new departure along lines rather different from those we have hitherto followed. An essential feature of a new international service adequate for the task would be this: It would be a career service under international responsibility for qualified men and women of any nationality, who were prepared to devote a significant part of their lives to work in the less-developed countries of the world as public officials integrated in the national administrations of these countries while maintaining their international status. (In fact, such an arrangement was foreshadowed as early as 1951 in the Report of the United Nations Technical Assistance Mission to Bolivia, where it was proposed that 'the United Nations assist the Bolivian Government in obtaining the services of a number of experienced and competent administrative officials of unquestioned integrity drawn from a variety of countries, and that the Bolivian Government appoint these officials on a temporary basis to positions of influence and authority as integral members of the Bolivian civil service.')

The highest standard of selection would rightly be demanded for such a service with special emphasis on quality of character and social outlook as well as upon intellectual background. Can it be imagined, though, that there would be any lack of candidates, well qualified and eager to take part in such an absorbing, so worthwhile a venture?

Before an international service of this kind on anything like the scale needed could be established, it would be necessary to clarify the principles which would govern its operation and to examine a number of legal and practical considerations to which such a program would give rise. Above all, it would be essential to remove any latent ambiguities in the relationships which will come into being between such officials enjoying the special responsibilities and status of an international official and the governments to which their loyal and devoted service would be due. . . .

In the present world situation, we have had a tendency to give much attention to the need for a wider movement of capital to areas in need of economic development. We are right in doing so. The needs are enormous. But even more important than the money are the skills. The greatest contribution to the creation of the world we want to see come into being is to put at the disposal of the less developed countries our own human resources. Fundamentally, man is the key to our problems, not money. Funds are valuable only when used by trained, experienced and devoted men and women. Such people, on the other hand, can work miracles even with small resources and draw wealth out of a barren land.

ON THE UPSALA TRADITION

Remarks at Upsala College Commencement Exercises, East Orange, New Jersey, 4 June 1956.

The name of this college carries with it a responsibility—not because the name is shared with the great sister institution in Sweden, but because of what the name symbolizes of human endeavor, of ideals and of their realization. The name carries with it memories from what is known to us as the first religious shrine in the North to which people from all over Scandinavia found their way. It carries memories of the birth of the national State we today call Sweden. It reminds us of great Roman Catholic archbishops and later of the Reformation and the Thirty Years' War. Its history as a center of learning is marked by names such as Rudbeck and Linné.

A name with such traditions is a challenge. But it can rightly be for us also a source of pride only when we, in our own efforts, live up to the standard it sets for us.

The Upsala tradition reflects, within its limited sphere, a heritage which I feel has something to give to our world of today. It may therefore be justified to say a few words about what this heritage means. In doing so I am not referring to any country or people but to a spiritual legacy beyond such boundaries.

At their best the representatives of this legacy show the quiet self-assurance of people firmly rooted in their own world, but they are, at the same time and for that very reason, able to accept and develop a true world citizenship. At their best they are not afraid to like the man in their enemy and they know that such liking gives an insight which is a source of strength. They have learned patience in dealings with mightier powers. They know that their only hope is that justice will prevail and for that reason they like to speak for justice. However, they also know the dangers and temptations of somebody speaking for justice without humility. They have learned that they can stand strong only if faithful to their own ideals, and they have shown the courage to follow the guidance of those ideals to ends which sometimes, temporarily, have been very bitter. And, finally, their spirit is one of peace.

FROM THE INTRODUCTION TO THE
ANNUAL REPORT 1955-1956

4 October 1956

------◆------

UNIVERSALITY AND ITS CONSEQUENCES

... In the period under review the most important development bearing upon the future role of the United Nations in world affairs is the decisive step that has been taken toward universality of membership.

When the General Assembly convenes next month, sixteen new Member States will be represented and the Assembly will have before it the unanimous recommendation of the Security Council for the admission of three additional new Members. Thus, after many years of deadlock, the United Nations will have increased its membership within a single year by approximately one-third. Furthermore, important additions have been made to the membership of the Specialized Agencies. The whole United Nations system, therefore, enters its second decade far closer than before to becoming, in fact, a system fully representative of the diversity of the world community.

The new Members of the United Nations will be welcomed in their own right. Their admission, and the admission of other nations which may be expected to follow in due course, will also be welcomed because of the opportunities for more effective service to the purposes of the Charter that the wider membership will give to the Organization.

We live in a period of fundamental and rapid changes in the relationship of nations and peoples having differing cultures and social systems. The new age that is emerging is an age of promise. It could also become one of disaster. We are seeking to cope with world issues of great difficulty but equally of high challenge. The hope of finding peaceful, just and constructive solutions of these issues rests upon our ability to foster the growth of understanding, cooperation and mutual accommodation of interests among all the nations.

Because its Charter is a world Charter, the United Nations is a unifying force in a divided world. Because its institutions are world institutions, they are fitted to determine the common interest and enlarge the area of common grounds. This applies in full measure, I believe, to three great challenges of our times. These are: first, the relationship of the peoples of Asia and Africa with the peoples of Western traditions; second, economic development for that majority of mankind which has so far shared so little in the fruits of the industrial age; third, the unresolved conflict between the ideologies that divide the world. Because the United Nations is now becoming more widely representative, its capacity to serve as an influence for peace and constructive progress in meeting these great challenges has been increased.

To make good use of this increased capacity for service presents, in itself, a challenge of considerable difficulty. The admission of many new Members creates new constitutional, political and organizational problems for the United Nations. There are such constitutional questions as those raised by proposals to enlarge the membership of the Security Council and of the Economic and Social Council. There are problems of political adjustment to the fact that changes in world relationships will henceforth be more fully reflected in the debates and decisions of the United Nations. There are procedural problems relating to the orderly, responsible and expeditious conduct of business which increased membership inevitably brings and there are, for the Secretariat, organizational and administrative problems.... These problems are, however, far outweighed by the opportunity to build a more effective world organization.

The United Nations can grow in real strength only to the extent that ways are found to use the Organization to full advantage for the purposes it was created to serve. The events of the past year have in some respects given encouraging evidence of such growth.

THE ROLE OF THE UNITED NATIONS
IN A CHANGING WORLD

Article 1 of the United Nations Charter states that one of the main purposes of the United Nations is 'to develop friendly relations among nations based on respect for the principle of equal rights and self-determination of peoples.' This recognition of the principle of self-determination as a basis for friendly relations among nations means that democratic ideals, which have carried many peoples to new heights, are given a world-wide application. The governments signatories to the Charter have formulated here a policy which, in the light of history, may well come to be regarded as one of the most significant landmarks of our times.

The United Nations, of course, is not the cause of the great change through which more than half of mankind, for centuries voiceless, has grown into or is now moving towards membership of the world community as citizens of independent national States. But the Organization is inevitably a focal point for the efforts so to guide the difficult and delicate development that this progress may be achieved in peace and become a means to reinforce peace.

To say this is not to overlook that, in many cases, other procedures than those created by the Charter may provide possibilities of working out fundamental elements of the new relationship. The Charter itself foresees negotiations between parties as an initial step in the solution of conflicts which are unavoidable during a period of fundamental change. But I believe that such negotiations gain by being conducted against the background of the purposes and principles of the Charter and that the results can usefully be brought within the framework of the United Nations. If the negotiations prove unsuccessful, they should then be followed up on the basis laid down and in the forms prescribed by the Charter.

It is important to remember that the Charter endorses self-determination as a basis for friendly relations among nations. Both unrealistic impatience in the movement towards self-determination and wasteful resistance to it would contradict this philosophy of the Charter by leading to conflicts which might threaten peace. Under the Charter, the nations concerned are therefore called upon to further the movement toward self-determination in such a manner as to strengthen the bonds of world community instead of weakening them.

Forces that stimulate this movement have also led to the emergence of a new nationalism. This nationalism can be a constructive element, raising the dignity and stature of peoples and mobilizing their best moral resources. But, in a period of severe emotional strains, it may also find expressions which are in fact hostile to the steady growth of the very national life it aims to serve. The United Nations may help in avoiding such a self-defeating development.

Within the community of nations, so great a change in the political relationships must arouse deep emotions on all sides. Positions long vital to great nations are involved. And on the other side the intensity of aspirations for equal status creates pressures for extreme action. I am convinced that in this situation the United Nations could be a source of greater assistance to governments than it has so far been. The give and take of public debate has been firmly established within the Organization and plays a valuable role in the determination of the common interest, but the resources for reconciliation, which the Organization can also provide, have not received equal recognition. The tensions of our time are too severe to permit us to neglect these resources and should impel us to use the United Nations in such a manner as to widen the possibilities for constructive negotiation which are inherent in the nature of the Organization.

We should, I believe, seek a development which would give greater emphasis to the United Nations as an instrument for negotiation of settlements, as distinct from the mere debate of issues. The Charter does not envisage settlements imposed by force. But the obligation of States to settle their disputes by peaceful methods does not mean that principles of justice and international law may be disregarded. The Charter reconciles the obligation of peaceful settlement with the objective of justice and equity through its emphasis on peaceful negotiation in which the full weight of the world community, as organized in the United Nations under the principles of the Charter, is brought to bear on the issue at stake. . . .

STATEMENTS AT THE TIME OF THE SUEZ AND HUNGARIAN CRISES ON THE DUTIES OF THE SECRETARY-GENERAL, BEFORE THE SECURITY COUNCIL

The first of the following statements was made at the beginning of the meeting of the Security Council on the afternoon of 31 October 1956. On 29 October Israeli forces had begun an invasion of Egypt. On 30 October the United Kingdom and France had vetoed United States and USSR resolutions for the immediate withdrawal of Israeli forces and calling upon all Member States to refrain from intervening with the use or threat of force. On the morning of 31 October British and French forces had begun landings in the Suez Canal zone. It was at this meeting that the Security Council voted to call an emergency special session of the General Assembly, since exercise of the veto had prevented it from fulfilling its responsibility for the maintenance of peace.

The second statement was made at a meeting of the Council called at 3 a.m. on 4 November, after reports had been received during the night of renewed attacks by Soviet troops in Hungary instead of the negotiations for their withdrawal that had been reported to the Council on 3 November. At this meeting the USSR vetoed a resolution calling for the withdrawal of its forces and the Council voted to convene an emergency special session of the General Assembly for the same reason as in the case of the invasion of Egypt.

I. SUEZ, 31 OCTOBER 1956

Yesterday morning—on the basis of the information then available —I would have used my right to call for an immediate meeting of the Security Council, had not the United States Government in the course of the night taken the initiative.

Yesterday afternoon—on the basis of reports of the Anglo-French ultimatum to Egypt—I would have acted likewise, had not the substance of the matter already been under consideration as one, new aspect of the item proposed by the United States.

This morning, under my special mandate from the Security Council which still is formally valid, I would have directed an appeal to the governments of Israel and Egypt to the effect of the second draft resolution of yesterday, had not the most recent developments rendered my mandate and such an initiative pointless.

This afternoon I wish to make the following declaration: The principles of the Charter are, by far, greater than the Organization in which they are embodied, and the aims which they are to safeguard are holier than the policies of any single nation or people. As a servant of the Organization the Secretary-General has the duty to maintain his usefulness by avoiding public stands on conflicts between Member nations unless and until such an action might help to resolve the conflict. However, the discretion and impartiality thus imposed on the Secretary-General by the character of his immediate task, may not degenerate into a policy of expediency. He must also be a servant of the principles of the Charter, and its aims must ultimately determine what for him is right and wrong. For that he must stand. A Secretary-General cannot serve on any other assumption than that—within the necessary limits of human frailty and honest differences of opinion—all Member nations honor their pledge to observe all articles of the Charter. He should also be able to assume that those organs which are charged with the task of upholding the Charter, will be in a position to fulfill their task.

The bearing of what I have just said must be obvious to all without any elaboration from my side. Were the Members to consider that another view of the duties of the Secretary-General than the one here stated would better serve the interests of the Organization, it is their obvious right to act accordingly.

In the course of the meeting the representatives of the Great Powers including France, the United Kingdom and the USSR as well as the United States and other members indicated their acceptance of this statement of the right and duty of the Secretary-General to speak and act in support of the principles of the Charter in such circumstances.

II. HUNGARY, 4 NOVEMBER 1956

Last Wednesday I had the honor to make before this Council the declaration concerning the views I hold on the duties of the Secretary-General and my understanding of the stands that he has to take. It is certainly not necessary, but all the same I would like to put on record that the observations I made on that occasion obviously apply also to the present situation.

HUMAN RIGHTS AND THE WORK
FOR PEACE

*Address at the Fiftieth Anniversary Dinner of the
American Jewish Committee—New York,
10 April 1957.*

Four years ago today, I was inducted into my present office, to
which I had been catapulted without previous soundings, indeed,
without any pre-warning. I felt that it was my duty to accept it, not
because of any feeling of confidence in my personal capacity to overcome the difficulties which might arise, but because, under the
conditions then prevailing, the one to whom the call had come
seemed to me in duty bound to respond.

The situation that faced me at the very outset has proved not to
be unique. It has been repeated several times in the past few years,
most recently in relation to problems of the Middle East. The other
day, returning from the latest visit to that area on a UN mission, I
read a book by Arthur Waley—certainly well known to many of
you as one of the great interpreters of Chinese thought and literature
and as one of those great Jewish students of humane letters who
have so splendidly enriched our cultural tradition. In his work
Waley quotes what an early Chinese historian had to say about the
philosopher Sung Tzu and his followers, some 350 years B.C. To
one who works in the United Nations, the quotation strikes a
familiar note. It runs as follows:

> 'Constantly rebuffed but never discouraged, they went round
> from State to State helping people to settle their differences,
> arguing against wanton attack and pleading for the suppression
> of arms, that the age in which they lived might be saved from
> its state of continual war. To this end they interviewed princes
> and lectured the common people, nowhere meeting with any
> great success, but obstinately persisting in their task, till kings
> and commoners alike grew weary of listening to them. Yet
> undeterred they continued to force themselves on people's
> attention.'

Is this a description of a quixotic group, whose efforts are doomed
to failure? The wording, with its tone of frustration, may lead us to

think so. However, I believe that this interpretation would be wrong. The historian tells us about a group engaged in a struggle he considers very much worth while and one which will have to go on until success is achieved.

The half-ironical, half-sad note which he strikes indicates only his knowledge of the difficulties which human nature puts in the way of such work for peace. His pessimism is tempered by the mild sense of humor and the strong sense of proportion of a man seeing his own time in the long perspective of history. We can learn from his attitude, both in our efforts to move towards peace and in our work for universal recognition of human rights.

We know that the question of peace and the question of human rights are closely related. Without recognition of human rights we shall never have peace, and it is only within the framework of peace that human rights can be fully developed.

In fact, the work for peace is basically a work for the most elementary of human rights: the right of everyone to security and to freedom from fear. We, therefore, recognize it as one of the first duties of a government to take measures in order to safeguard for its citizens this very right. But we also recognize it as an obligation for the emerging world community to assist governments in safeguarding this elementary human right without having to lock themselves in behind the wall of arms.

The dilemma of our age, with its infinite possibilities of self-destruction, is how to grow out of the world of armaments into a world of international security, based on law. We are only at the very beginning of such a change. The natural distrust in the possibility of progress is nourished by unavoidable set-backs and, when distrust is thus strengthened, this in turn increases our difficulties.

The effort may seem hopeless. It will prove hopeless unless we, all of us, show the persistence of Sung Tzu and his followers, and unless peoples and governments alike are willing to take smaller immediate risks in order to have a better chance to avoid the final disaster threatening us if we do not manage to turn the course of developments in a new direction.

The United Nations finds itself in a difficult stage of its development. It is still too weak to provide the security desired by all, while being strong enough and alive enough effectively to point out the direction in which the solution must be sought. In its present phase the Organization may look to many like a preacher who cannot impose the law he states or realize the gospel he interprets. It is understandable if those who have this impression turn away in distrust or with cynical criticism, forgetting that set-backs in efforts to implement an ideal do not prove that the ideal is wrong, and overlooking also that at the beginning of great changes in human society there must always be a stage of such frailty or seeming inconsistency. It is easy to say that it is pointless to state the law if it cannot be enforced. However, to do so is to forget that if the law is the inescapable law of the future, it would be treason to the future not to state the law simply because of the difficulties of the present. Indeed, how could it ever become a living reality if those who are responsible for its development were to succumb to the immediate difficulties arising when it is still a revolutionary element in the life of society? The history of the Jewish people offers some of the most magnificent examples of how ideals and law may be brought to victory through courageous assertion of new universal principles which the wise call folly when they are first introduced in a society shaped on a different pattern.

The thoughts I have tried to express apply to practically the whole field of United Nations activities, but in particular to the work of the Organization for the implementation of the principles of the Charter in the fields of international security and disarmament and in the field of fundamental human rights. They apply likewise to the United Nations itself as an experiment in international organization.

But is not an experiment something tentative and passing? And should not the United Nations be regarded as something definite and lasting? I think it is important to be clear on this point. Certainly the experiences and achievements of the United Nations as it is today are helping us to build the future. The United Nations is something definite also in the sense that the concepts and ideals it represents, like the needs it tries to meet, will remain an ineluctable element of the world picture. However, that does not mean that the present embodiment of the groping efforts of mankind towards an organized world community represents a definite shape for all time. The United Nations is, and should be, a living, evolving, experimental institution. If it should ever cease to be so it should be revolutionized or swept aside for a new approach.

The growth of social institutions is always one where, step by step, the form which adequately meets the need is shaped through selection, or out of experience. Thus an effort that has not yielded all the results hoped for has not failed if it has provided positive experience on which a new approach can be based. An attempt which has proved the possibility of progress has served the cause of progress even if it has had to be renewed again and again, and in new forms or settings in order to yield full success.

When we look back over the experiences in the United Nations over the past few months, we may differ amongst ourselves as to the wisdom of this or that particular stand and we may have doubts about the end result of this or that step. But I think we all can agree on the value and historical importance of certain developments.

First of all, it proved possible in an emergency to create for the first time a truly international force. This Force, although modest in size and, for constitutional reasons, also modest in aim, broke new ground which inevitably will count in future efforts to preserve peace and promote justice.

I think we can likewise agree that the fact that the United Nations could undertake and carry through a major field operation like the clearance of the Suez Canal, where no government was in a position to accomplish the task, indicated possibilities for international organization which, once proven, cannot in future be disregarded.

Finally, deeply regrettable though the conflicts of views and interests were, it should not be forgotten that those who now feel they had to sacrifice for the maintenance of a principle, in a different situation may be the first to profit from the fact that the principle was maintained. As individuals we know that the law which restrains us likewise protects us. The same holds true in international life.

Some moments ago I referred to the fact that lasting peace is not possible without recognition of fundamental human rights and that human rights cannot reach their full development unless there is peace. The United Nations cannot lay down the law for the life within any national community. Those laws have to be established in accordance with the will of the people as expressed in the forms indicated by their chosen constitution. But just as the United Nations can promote peace, so it can, in joint deliberations, define the goals of human rights which should be the laws of the future in each nation. Whatever the distance between these goals and the everyday reality we meet all around the world, it is not vain thus to set the targets as they present themselves to the most mature political thinking of our age. . . .

9

You have put 'the pursuit of equality at home and abroad' as a motto of your anniversary. Interpreted in a broad sense these words reflect a basic human right, equal in significance to the right to security and freedom from fear.

I had, last year, the privilege of visiting a couple of kibbutzim in Israel and of talking to people coming from many lands, who were devoting their lives to these courageous experiments in practical and total democracy. I looked upon them as fellow workers in an 'experiment in progress'. Through such experiments alone can progress be achieved.

I also remember experiences of experiments in community development in India. There I met the same enthusiasm, the same devotion, the same idealism as in the kibbutzim. Yet, how different a situation it was! In one case there were people, stepping out of their Western societies of highly organized and specialized industrial life in order to create new collectives, pioneering in the building up of a strong economic life on a barren soil. In the other case, communities which, although living in a rich land, so far had remained poor for the lack of the revolutionary development carried to fruition by Western individualism, but the members of which now devoted all their energy towards taking the giant step into the economic and social world of today.

In both cases we meet a realization in practice of basic human rights. The difference, however, indicates the diversity of the problem and this calls for great flexibility in our approach and in the choice of the ways in which the various societies may become integrated into a world community.

The underlying problems now making the Middle East such a troubled area, should be understood partly in the terms of which these two experiments in community development may serve as illustrations. They lend special weight to the undertaking of the Member nations in the Charter 'to practice tolerance'.

The words just quoted from the Charter are among those which link its text to a great ethical tradition. They are often overlooked, sometimes brushed aside as empty ornaments without political significance, sometimes honored by lip-service. However, they represent an element without which the Charter and the system it creates would disintegrate. Both the work for peace and the work for human rights must be anchored in and inspired by a general approach which gives balance and substance to the results. Peace cannot be enforced for selfish reasons, equality cannot be imposed as an abstract concept. In fact, attempts to do so account for some of the darkest episodes in history.

The work for peace must be animated by tolerance and the work for human rights by respect for the individual. A student of the growth of human rights through the ages will recognize its close relationship to the development of tolerance inspired by intellectual liberalism or, perhaps more often, by ethical concepts of religious origin. Attempts are made to link the development of human rights exclusively to the liberal ideas which broke through to predominance in the Age of Enlightenment. However, to do so means to me to overlook the historical background of those ideas. It means also cutting our ties to a source of strength that we need in order to carry the work for human rights to fruition and to give to those rights, when established, their fitting spiritual content.

To some, the word 'tolerance' may sound strange in a time of 'Cold War' and of negotiations 'from positions of strength'; it may have an overtone of meekness or appeasement. And yet, have we reason to believe that what was true in the past is no longer true? It is not the weak but the strong who practice tolerance, and the strong do not weaken their position in showing tolerance. On the contrary, only through tolerance can they justify their strength in the face of those counteracting forces that their own strength automatically sets in motion.

I am sure that this holds true of all those in the present world situation who may be, or may consider themselves to be 'strong', be it the industrialized West in relation to the under-developed countries, be it the Powers whose military resources give them key positions, be it those who have achieved a state of democracy and of recognition of human rights towards which others are still groping.

I remember in this context words from another translation by Arthur Waley—this time from Tao Te Ching. Its paradoxical form and mystical background should not lead us to overlook its realism: 'Heaven arms with pity those whom it would not see destroyed.'

Over the ages and over the continents, these words join with those of the Psalmist: 'There is mercy with Thee; therefore shalt Thou be feared.'

PRESS CONFERENCE COMMENTS

Extracts from verbatim transcripts, 1955–1957

———◆———

THE POLITICAL VALUE OF DISARMAMENT
NEGOTIATIONS

From transcript, 19 May 1955

QUESTION: Some of my colleagues and some of yours take a very cynical attitude regarding the possibilities of disarmament. The opinion that I get from them is that it is a road show put on by the diplomats because the customers expect it, but that no one really believes, after the experience of the 'twenties, that disarmament is possible; that the political problems must be solved first and then disarmament will take care of itself. I wonder what your attitude is on the problem of the realistic possibilities of disarmament.

THE SECRETARY-GENERAL: I would say that I react very strongly against pessimism couched in those cynical terms. I think it is even irresponsible, to use a strong word. There have been no precedents or experiences which entitle us not to try again. It is quite true that there is an interplay between political factors—the political atmosphere—on the one side, and disarmament on the other. But, when people say, in those simple terms, that if the political situation improves, disarmament will follow and that, for that reason, it does not make sense to discuss disarmament, they overlook one essential factor: that the very study of disarmament may be the vehicle for progress towards greater international political understanding. That is to say, disarmament is never the result only of the political situation; it is also partly instrumental in creating the political situation.

THE UNITED NATIONS
AND PREVENTIVE ACTION

From transcript, 27 February 1956

QUESTION: Would you mind telling us exactly what kind of preventive action the United Nations might be able to take in an area where war threatens or is right on the verge of breaking out?

THE SECRETARY-GENERAL: If we take the acute situation in the Middle East, I think that we all know that the threat, if threat there is, is on two levels, so to speak. First of all, we have the current incidents along the border. I am thinking not of the major incidents, of the Tiberias or El Auja or Gaza type, but of the current incidents —raids, shooting between patrols and so forth. An obviously necessary preventive action is to take all possible steps to stop such developments, to eliminate the source of continuous friction on this simple level. This is the real purpose of the work of the Chief of Staff and his collaborators in the field (The United Nations Truce Supervision Organization). I think that up to a point we have been successful, although not as successful as I should like. I feel that more can be done and more should be done, and I am certainly trying to do what I can to improve that situation.

The second level on which you may have a 'threat'—I put that word in quotes—is, of course, one on which there are very basic differences of interest, territorial or otherwise. In such a case, I think that the preventive action is mainly what I might call midwifery. It is not a case of open mediation; I do not believe that the United Nations is a very good tool for open mediation in a situation such as that. It is not a case of imposing the United Nations' will. There may be situations in which that is possible, but I would not consider this to be one of them. It is a matter of continuous and intense study of the problems on both sides, of canalizing the tension and always of finding the greatest common denominator. I personally believe that, just as negotiation keeps people from shooting, in the same way reasonable progress towards a goal keeps people from rushing into a conflict because they cannot get everything at once or cannot get it in just the form that they would like.

In other words, the two lines of preventive action which I think are obviously indicated are, first, to stabilize the situation in the field on a day-to-day basis and to avoid the incidents which may lead to major frictions, and, secondly, to be—you will excuse me for using the word—*quietly* helpful by being a third party with which the two conflicting parties can discuss matters and which may help them to bridge the gulf not by formal mediation but by working out a maximum of understanding, an understanding which,

I think, will increase as time goes on if the operation is wisely run.

ASIAN AND WESTERN ATTITUDES
TOWARDS THE UN

*From transcript, Canadian Broadcasting Corporation
Television Press Conference, 7 March 1956.*

QUESTION: During your press conference last week, sir, you told us about the very high standing that the United Nations enjoys in Asia, and you spoke of the man in the street, who sometimes considers the United Nations as a bulwark against tyranny and exploitation. Is there any way that this feeling which you gathered during your trip could be conveyed to the developed nations of the world, where sometimes, as we all know, the United Nations is thought of as a poor relation?

THE SECRETARY-GENERAL: I think we must look at this in the light of historical developments, and I should like to put my answer in a somewhat paradoxical way. It is natural for old and well-established countries to see in the United Nations a limitation on their sovereignty. It is just as natural that a young country, a country emerging on the world stage, should find in the United Nations an addition to its sovereignty, an added means of speaking to the world. That difference between the two approaches is basic and is easily explained, I think, by historical circumstances and present political problems.

You complain indirectly of the somewhat high-handed way in which, perhaps, the United Nations is sometimes treated and discussed in some countries. I would not complain about it, because I think it is perfectly natural—just as I regard the reaction of many countries in the East as being natural. But I think that to whatever extent Asian people and, to some degree, I myself, as a kind of indirect spokesman for Asian people, can make it clearer to the Western countries that the United Nations comes into the picture in this way in a very great part of the world, to that extent we will smooth out this curious difference and at the same time bring about a realistic appraisal of the United Nations in political terms, so that you will reach your result in the long run. But I would not like to preach to the Western countries that you are criticizing. I would just like to bring home to them the natural difference of view which is represented by the Asian countries.

ON POLICIES OF NON-ALIGNMENT

*From transcript, Canadian Broadcasting Corporation
Television Press Conference, 7 March 1956.*

QUESTION: As a result of your trip to India, do you have the feeling that India and countries with a position like hers are right and sensible in following a policy of non-involvement in the ideological war of East and West?

THE SECRETARY-GENERAL: I do not think that primarily it is a question of right and wrong, because right and wrong, of course, are to be considered mainly in the light of one's own interests in the political field. I think it is much more a question of seeing what is a natural reaction in the light of the historical situation and political balance. From that point of view, I think we should recognize that the great ideological conflict which is splitting our world is a conflict which is a little bit extraneous from the point of view of the many Asian countries. It is really a conflict between two big groups in the West. The East has a tradition of its own. If, for that reason, they look at these ideological developments from some distance and find it natural, first of all, to develop their own approach, whatever it may be, I consider that to be a political fact about which it does not make much sense to say that it is right or that it is wrong. It is a political fact which I think we simply have to recognize, and with which we have to live, and which we have to take into account also in discussing the problems of the historical West, including the Soviet Union and its collaborating countries.

You talked about freedom from alignments. Of course, in a peculiar sense, that is the specific problem also of the Secretary-General. Whatever my personal ideology may be, I have certain obligations in relation to all the Member nations, and one primary obligation, of course, is to understand—without approval or disapproval—what the facts are and how they fit into the picture.

It is in that light that I give these comments on the developments in Asia—very much the same kind of light in which I would comment on something said or done in the historical West.

PROBLEMS OF THE
SECRETARY-GENERAL AS NEGOTIATOR

From transcript, 4 April 1957

QUESTION: I would like to ask two questions. You said before that the position of Secretary-General does not correspond to that of a government. I wonder whether, on your visits to various capitals, you found that it was difficult for you to negotiate since you had no point to refer back to? Have you given any thought to setting up a political department so that they can refer back to you?

THE SECRETARY-GENERAL: To my mind, the first question you raised is a rather interesting one. It is partly insufficiently understood and partly insufficiently explored. I would say this: that the Secretary-General does not suffer from the fact that he has nobody to refer back to provided that the main organs of the United Nations, the Security Council or the General Assembly, have taken clear decisions on general terms of reference, short of which, of course, the Secretary-General is forced to undertake a kind of policy-making which from the point of view of Member governments I feel may be considered unsound, or at least not in line with the kind of procedure we should have here.

On the other hand he finds himself in a situation where he lacks not means of pressure, but the kind of weight which every government necessarily has because it is part of the world picture, part of the whole pattern of trade, policy-making and so on and so forth. That is partly compensated for by one fact. Because he has no pressure group behind him, no territory and no parliament in the ordinary sense of the word, he can talk with much greater freedom, much greater frankness and much greater simplicity in approaching governments than any government representative can do. In summing up, I would say that the lack of a superior body to which to refer does not matter if there is a clear-cut policy line laid down by the main bodies here. The lack of means of 'pressure'—if the word is not misunderstood—is in a certain sense a weakness which, however, is compensated for, by the freedom of action, the freedom of expression, which the Secretary-General can grant himself and which, I am happy to note, governments do grant him. . . .

You talk about the possibility of some kind of policy-making body, a political division. I do not remember exactly what you called it. In a sense, you have it, in the Middle Eastern question at present as regards the UNEF, in the Advisory Committee. The Advisory Committee has proved to be an extremely useful body to which I owe a great debt of gratitude for the assistance they have given to me, in a free exchange of views which has clarified both the reactions of the General Assembly and my own thinking, and for the support they have given to me in practice—also in other respects. It may be that such an Advisory Committee system in particularly crucial questions may prove an avenue towards a more balanced cooperation in fields like this one between the Secretary-General and the policy-making bodies, in the first place, of course, the General Assembly.

FROM THE INTRODUCTION TO THE
ANNUAL REPORT 1956-1957

22 August 1957

.... During the past year, the United Nations was confronted with some of the most difficult situations it has been called upon to meet since 1945.

In the establishment of the United Nations Emergency Force and the clearance of the Suez Canal, the United Nations also assumed responsibilities previously untried by world organization. On another level and in another direction the investigation made by the Special Committee on the problem of Hungary was a new departure.

The chapters on 'Questions concerning the Middle East' and 'The Hungarian question' in the twelfth annual report which I submitted last month give an historical account of these important developments up to 15 June 1957. It may now be useful to offer certain observations arising from the experiences of the past year that bear upon the present situation and possible future courses of development.

THE PALESTINE QUESTION

As this is written the United Nations Emergency Force is completing its sixth month of deployment on the Egyptian side of the Armistice Demarcation Line with Israel. It has, I believe, been a pre-condition for the maintenance of general quiet in the area of its deployment, just as in earlier months it played an essential part during the withdrawal of foreign troops from Egyptian territory. Indeed, the Commander and members of the Force have fully earned the admiration and gratitude of the United Nations for the manner in which they have served and continue to serve the cause of peace in the Middle East in a pioneering role accompanied by many difficulties and endowed with limited authority. Equally, thanks should be expressed to the States which have supplied the units composing the Force and given it logistical support.

The present situation in the area is, of course, based on the interplay of many influences. The presence of UNEF, incomplete though its present deployment and other arrangements may be, is an important element. However, the policies of governments and the atmosphere of opinion promoted by governments underlie and influence most decisively the course of development. In this respect the comparative quiet that has prevailed is a welcome symptom. At the same time there have been few, if any, signs of further progress.

The quiet maintained in recent months helps towards creating a favourable setting for future progress towards those basic solutions which are so necessary to the security and well-being of all the nations of the area. Now, as always, progress towards such solutions depends primarily upon attitudes and initiatives of the governments themselves. The United Nations can help by lending its influence, its presence, and the processes of diplomacy which are available to world organization. It can also help by providing an objective judgment of the rights and interests involved.

In the Palestine question the United Nations has two special responsibilities. One of these is in regard to the Armistice Agreements endorsed by the Security Council. The other is the humanitarian responsibility for the Palestine refugees, who have been under United Nations care for nine years now as homeless victims of events outside their control, while the problems of repatriation or resettlement have remained unsolved by the governments upon whom rests their hope for a life more consonant with human dignity.

To work towards a restoration of the Armistice Agreements, primarily in their spirit but, in consequence, also in their letter, and to give constructive help to the refugees, are obligations of first priority resting upon the Organization and its Member governments.

There continues to exist, I am convinced, a basic will to peace in the area despite whatever signs there may have been to the contrary. I would be the last to minimize the very great difficulties that lie in the way of steps by governments which are necessary in order to translate this will to peace into concrete progress towards peaceful solutions. These difficulties must nevertheless be surmounted. The United Nations cannot, and of course should not, attempt to do this alone. The governments concerned, with whom the power of decision rests, may not be able to do it alone. But the governments, strengthened by the help available from and within the United Nations, can, and I hope will, decide to lead their people step by step upon this road towards a more secure and promising future for them all.

THE UNITED NATIONS EMERGENCY FORCE

The United Nations Emergency Force is the first of its kind. It was created in a few days under emergency conditions without benefit of precedents. It is a temporary force with a limited mandate and designed to meet a special situation. But the value of such a force in situations like that in the Middle East has, I believe, been fully demonstrated and this value should be preserved for the future.

There is need for careful analysis and study of the UNEF experience in all its aspects in order to give the United Nations a sound foundation, should the Organization wish to build an agreed standby plan for a United Nations peace force that could be activated on short notice in future emergencies to serve in similar ways. Steps have been taken for such a study to be undertaken in the Secretariat.

The indispensable services performed by the UNEF Advisory Committee established by the General Assembly should be noted. In the execution of future mandates of this kind that may be entrusted to the Secretary-General or some other agent of the United Nations I believe that the appointment of such 'select committees' composed of representatives of Member States would often be of value and would represent a desirable development in the practices of the Organization.

THE SUEZ CANAL

During the past year the United Nations has been concerned with the Suez Canal in two respects. There were the differences over the regime of the Canal which arose after Egypt's nationalization of the Universal Suez Canal Company, some of which are still pending. There was also the responsibility assumed by the United Nations, at the request of the General Assembly and on the invitation of the Government of Egypt, to assist in reopening the Canal after it had been blocked early last November.

Like UNEF, the international clearance operation under the United Nations flag was the first undertaking of its kind attempted by a world organization. The vital importance of the Suez Canal to the economies of many nations made this a grave responsibility.

The Canal was reopened to full traffic a little more than three

months after the United Nations salvage fleet began its work. This
was well ahead of schedule. The cost is estimated at about 8,600,000
dollars.

An account of the operation is given in the chapter on the Middle
East in the annual report of the Secretary-General. A special report
will be presented to the General Assembly later. I am sure that the
Member governments would wish to join me in paying tribute to
all those who collaborated in carrying this task to a successful and
speedy conclusion.

Since April, Suez Canal traffic has returned to the normal flow
of recent years. However, various questions regarding the regime of
the Canal, following nationalization, have still not found solutions
which are generally accepted. It should also be noted that the six-
year-old question of Israeli shipping remains in dispute.

Members will recall that a number of such questions and doubts
concerning the Declaration registered by Egypt with the United
Nations as an international instrument were left pending at the
conclusion of the Security Council's meetings last spring. The
President of the Council then stated that most members had
qualified their acquiescence in the Egyptian Declaration as provisional and that, pending concrete steps the Egyptian Government
might wish to take to remove the doubts that had arisen, the
Council would remain seized of the question.

Since then, in accordance with the intention expressed in its
Declaration, the Government of Egypt has deposited its acceptance
of the compulsory jurisdiction of the International Court of Justice
in legal disputes arising between the parties to the Constantinople
Convention of 1888 in respect of the interpretation or applicability
of its provisions. On other questions which arose at the Security
Council meetings the Secretary-General has continued his efforts
through informal contacts with the parties without as yet being in
a position to report further progress.*

THE HUNGARIAN QUESTION

The Hungarian question will come once more before the General
Assembly when the Assembly takes up the report of the investigation made by its Special Committee a few days after this

* See *Private Diplomacy in the Suez Settlement*, page 175.

communication reaches the hands of the Member governments. A full account of the United Nations' concern since last October with the Hungarian problem, as well as with relief to the people in Hungary and assistance to Hungarian refugees, has already been transmitted to the Members in my annual report and the detailed findings of the Special Committee on the Problem of Hungary were circulated in its report last June.

In view of the wide interest taken in the constitutional issues that were involved for the United Nations in both the Hungarian and Middle Eastern situations, and the discussions to which they have given rise, it may be useful to review here the manner in which the General Assembly met these constitutional issues.

There was, first, the matter of pronouncing judgment as to the facts and recommending remedial action. In the case of Hungary, just as in the Middle East crisis, there was a difference of opinion between a majority and a minority. In each case, the majority acted in a manner consistent with its interpretation of the applicability of the provisions of the Charter and of the powers granted to the General Assembly by the Charter. In both cases, it should be noted, the majorities were very large.

There was, second, the matter of compliance by the Member States toward whom the Assembly's resolutions were directed. There were varying degrees of compliance at first in the withdrawal of troops from Egyptian territory and eventually full compliance as to withdrawal, though not with respect to some of the other recommendations of the Assembly. In the case of Hungary there was no compliance with the Assembly's political recommendations, a position based from the constitutional side on the minority's view of the applicability of the domestic jurisdiction clause of the Charter. In these circumstances, the question arose as to the means which the General Assembly might use to secure compliance.

The Assembly may recommend, it may investigate, it may pronounce judgment, but it does not have the power to compel compliance with its decisions. Under the Charter, only the Security Council has the power to order the use of force, and then only to maintain or restore international peace and security. In the 'Uniting for Peace' resolution, the General Assembly adopted a plan under which it might make appropriate recommendations to Member States 'for collective measures, including in the case of a breach of the peace or act of aggression the use of armed force when necessary to maintain or restore international peace and security'.* Thus, the General Assembly may recommend that Member States give aid, including economic sanctions and military aid, to the victim of an armed attack in the circumstances envisaged under Article 51 of the Charter. In such a case the power of decision on action implementing the recommendations would rest, as it constitutionally must under the Charter, with the respective Member governments.

At one stage, when there was delay in compliance with the General Assembly's resolutions calling for withdrawal of foreign troops from Egypt, the possibility of recommending sanctions arose but no formal proposal to that effect was presented in the Assembly. Likewise, in the case of Hungary, when compliance was refused, no delegation formally proposed a recommendation by the General Assembly to the Member States that they apply sanctions or use force to secure the withdrawal of foreign troops. The judgment of the majority of Member States as to the course to pursue in this latter case was, instead, reflected in the General Assembly's resolution of condemnation and decision to order an investigation. Both of these measures were appropriate to the General Assembly's own constitutional authority.

THE ROLE OF THE UNITED NATIONS

The events of the past year have, I believe, cast a clearer light upon the role of the United Nations in these times. The Charter, read as a whole, does not endow the United Nations with any of the attributes of a super-State or of a body active outside the framework of decisions of Member governments. The United Nations is, rather, an instrument for negotiation among, and to some extent for, governments. It is also an instrument added to the time-honoured means of diplomacy for concerting action by governments in support of the goals of the Charter. This is the role the Organization has played, sometimes successfully, sometimes with disappointing set-backs, throughout its life.

From time to time complaints are heard about the limitations

* This resolution was adopted in 1950 during the Korean conflict and was popularly known as the 'Acheson Plan' after its originator, the then Secretary of State of the United States, Dean Acheson. The resolution established procedures by which the General Assembly could take up within 24 hours a question concerning peace and security whenever a veto by one of the Great Powers prevented a decision in the Security Council. These procedures were invoked in the Suez, Hungarian, Lebanon and Congo cases.

upon the Organization's power. It has even been suggested that, unless these limitations are corrected, the usefulness of the United Nations is so questionable that the main effort of the governments in the search for peace should be concentrated in other directions.

This view does less than justice to the contributions of the United Nations in its short life. Especially, it fails to take into account that the real limitations upon action by the Organization do not derive from the provisions of the Charter. They result from facts of international life in our age which are not likely to be by-passed by a different approach or surmounted by attempts at merely constitutional reform.

To turn aside from the United Nations now because it cannot be transformed into a world authority enforcing the law upon the nations would be to erase all the steady, though slow and painful, advances that have been made and to close the door to hopes for the future of world society, towards which present efforts and experiences should be at least a modest stepping stone.

We should, rather, recognize the United Nations for what it is— an admittedly imperfect but indispensable instrument of nations in working for a peaceful evolution towards a more just and secure world order. The dynamic forces at work in this stage of human history have made world organization necessary. The balance of these forces has also set the limits within which the power of world organization can develop at each step and beyond which progress, when the balance of forces so permits, will be possible only by processes of organic growth in the system of custom and law prevailing in the society of nations.

These processes of adjustment take time. Systems of alliance, maintained side by side with the United Nations in recognition of the prevailing balance of forces, may serve a useful purpose during the period through which we are passing. However, most of us agree that such systems of alliance, like other traditional means of diplomacy and defense of the national interest, are limited in their value as safeguards of the present and future security and welfare of our countries. Nations and groups of nations will never again be able to live and to arrogate judgment unto themselves in international affairs in ways which once were a matter of course.

The greatest need today is to blunt the edges of conflict among the nations, not to sharpen them. If properly used, the United Nations can serve a diplomacy of reconciliation better than other instruments available to the Member States. All the varied interests and aspirations of the world meet in its precincts upon the common ground of the Charter. Conflicts may persist for long periods without an agreed solution and groups of States may actively defend special and regional interests. Nevertheless, and in spite of temporary developments in the opposite direction under the influence of acute tension, the tendency in the United Nations is to wear away, or break down, differences, thus helping toward solutions which approach the common interest and application of the principles of the Charter.

I believe that the criticism of the system of one vote for one nation, irrespective of size or strength, as constituting an obstacle to arriving at just and representative solutions tends to exaggerate the problem. The General Assembly is not a parliament of elected individual members; it is a diplomatic meeting in which the delegates of Member States represent governmental policies, and these policies are subject to all the influences that would prevail in international life in any case. Smaller nations are not in the habit of banding together against the larger nations whose power to affect international security and well-being is so much greater than their own. Nor do I see justification for talk about the responsible and the irresponsible among the nations. Finally, the two-thirds rule applied to all major decisions in the General Assembly should serve as a reasonable assurance to those who may not fully share the views that have been here expressed.

In this connection, it is worth recalling that the 'Uniting for Peace' resolution, in establishing a procedure intended to safeguard the application of the relevant provisions of the Charter—Articles 10, 11, 12 and 51—in support of the maintenance of peace, did not constitutionally transfer to the General Assembly any of the enforcement powers reserved to the Security Council by the Charter. Enforcement action by the United Nations under Chapter VII continues to be reserved to the Security Council. The relative role and significance of the Assembly and the Council, in practice, reflect general political conditions playing within the constitutional framework which, thus, was maintained in line with the basic concepts of the Charter.

With its increase in membership, the United Nations more fully mirrors the realities of the present world situation than ever before, although necessarily the picture given in the debates and votes in the United Nations can be truly evaluated only after a careful analysis. The United Nations reflects, but is in no sense a cause of, the renaissance of Asia. The awakening of Africa, and the other great changes that are under way in the balance of power and relationships of the peoples, are likewise part of the dynamics of history itself. As always, they bring with them many grave problems of adjustment. These all too easily may become the occasion for arousing passion, fear and hatred, and lead in turn to violent upheavals and to the ultimate disaster of war in this atomic age.

The functions of debate and vote are an essential part of the processes by which the United Nations can assist the governments in avoiding these dangers and in guiding the development in constructive and peaceful directions. But if it is accepted that the primary value of the United Nations is to serve as an instrument for negotiation among governments and for concerting action by governments in support of the goals of the Charter, it is also necessary, I believe, to use the legislative procedures of the United Nations consistently in ways which will promote these ends. In an organization of sovereign States, voting victories are likely to be illusory unless they are steps in the direction of winning lasting consent to a peaceful and just settlement of the questions at issue.

Full weight should also be given to the fact that the processes of adjustment and negotiation which the institutions of the United Nations make available to the Member governments embrace much more than the public proceedings of its Councils and Assembly. In the diplomacy of world organization the quiet work of preparing the ground, of accommodation of interest and viewpoint, of conciliation and mediation, all that goes into the winning of consent to agreed solutions and common programmes, this forms a basis upon which the United Nations can become an increasingly influential and effective force to aid the governments in pursuit of the goals of the Charter.

There are, I believe, promising and practical opportunities for improving the practices and strengthening the institutions of the United Nations in this area of multilateral diplomacy. Especially in the past two years we have begun to explore these opportunities in a number of ways with generally positive results. I hope this evolution of emphasis and practice will be pursued and broadened in the future. This seems to be a more urgent task than to attempt formal constitutional changes, the consideration of which the Committee of the whole Assembly, charged with studying the problem of time and place for a Charter review conference, at all events unanimously wished to postpone until a later stage. . . .

STATEMENT ON HIS RE-ELECTION TO A SECOND TERM, BEFORE THE GENERAL ASSEMBLY, 26 SEPTEMBER 1957

In this statement the Secretary-General re-affirmed the understanding of the responsibilities of his Office which he had given to the Security Council at the time of the Suez and Hungarian crises eleven months before and defined these responsibilities in terms which clearly included scope for his independent action in support of peace on the basis of the principles of the Charter. This statement was followed by pledges of support by delegates from all sides reflecting the unanimity of the vote by which he had been re-elected.

It is with a deep awareness of the significance of the responsibility which your decision imposes on me that I accept the appointment as Secretary-General of the United Nations for a second term.

When, in the spring of 1953, I was elected to my present office, I felt that it was my duty to respond to the unexpected call. What I could hope to do was to serve the aims of the United Nations to the limits of my capacity. My only claim now is to have tried to do so. Whether my service has met the needs of this difficult period in the life of the Organization and, indeed, the world, is for others to decide. Whether the direction I have tried to give to the development of the Office of the Secretary-General is the best one, will have to be judged in the perspective of time. Your decision is in these respects an encouragement for the future and a highly valued expression of confidence.

Nobody, I think, can accept the position of Secretary-General of the United Nations, knowing what it means, except from a sense of duty. Nobody, however, can serve in that capacity without a sense of gratitude for a task as deeply rewarding as it is exacting, as perennially inspiring as, sometimes, it may seem discouraging.

There are many reasons for such gratitude. Let me mention first the privilege of working, on terms of mutual confidence, with all the governments and their representatives in order to find ways through the many problems arising in international cooperation.

Let me mention also the gratitude a Secretary-General owes to his collaborators in the Secretariat from the third basement to the 38th floor. He is fortunate to profit in his work from a team-spirit which renders him unfailing support. He can count on dedication, often to thankless jobs, necessary for the success of the joint effort. He can trust that a challenge will be met with a deep sense of responsibility, broad knowledge and a truly international spirit.

The significance of what this Organization stands for, as a venture in progress towards an international community living in peace under the laws of justice, transforms work for its aims from a duty into a privilege.

Political factors, yet to be overcome or outgrown, may put narrow limits on the progress possible at a particular juncture. We may believe that the United Nations needs basic reforms. We may even share the view held by some that its task ultimately will have to be taken over by a body with a different structure. However, we cannot doubt that the main direction of the work of the United Nations, as determined by the purposes and principles of the Charter, indicates the path which the world must follow in order to preserve the achievements of the past and to lay a basis for a happier future.

Therefore, service of the United Nations guided by those principles is profoundly meaningful—whether it bears immediate fruit or not. If it paves one more inch of the road ahead, one is more than rewarded by what is achieved. This is true whatever setbacks may follow: If a mountain wall is once climbed, later failures do not undo the fact that it has been shown that it *can* be climbed. In this sense, every step forward in the pioneer effort of this Organization inevitably widens the scope for the fight for peace.

I have tried to present my views on the role of the United Nations in the Introduction to this year's Report to the General Assembly. Last year I explained in the Security Council how I feel that I should interpret the responsibilities of the Secretary-General. I have little to add here, and nothing to change.

In the multi-dimensional world of diplomacy, the Euclidean definition of the straight line as the shortest way between two points may not always hold true. For the Secretary-General, however, it is the only possible one. This line, as traced by principles which are the law for him, might at times cross other lines in the intricate pattern of international political action. He must then be able to feel secure that, whatever the difficulties, they will not impair the trust of Member governments in his Office.

I do not believe that the Secretary-General should be asked to act, by the Member States, if no guidance for his action is to be found either in the Charter or in the decisions of the main organs of the United Nations; within the limits thus set, however, I believe it to be his duty to use his office and, indeed, the machinery of the Organization to its utmost capacity and to the full extent permitted at each stage by practical circumstances.

On the other hand, I believe that it is in keeping with the philosophy of the Charter that the Secretary-General should be expected to act also without such guidance, should this appear to him necessary in order to help in filling any vacuum that may appear in the systems which the Charter and traditional diplomacy provide for the safeguarding of peace and security.

The many who, together, form this Organization—peoples, governments and individuals—share one great responsibility. Future generations may come to say of us that we never achieved what we set out to do. May they never be entitled to say that we failed because we lacked faith or permitted narrow self-interest to distort our efforts.

THE LINNAEUS TRADITION
AND OUR TIME

Presidential Address at the Annual Meeting in Stockholm of the Swedish Academy, 20 December 1957.

[TRANSLATION FROM SWEDISH]

The plain lay green with Ceres, the sky was clear and the lark whirred in the air on that May morning when Carl Linnaeus, '25 years old but for one night' rode from Upsala on his journey to Lapland 'in order to illustrate the same in 3 Regna Naturae.'

The November night in Tistedalen, fourteen years earlier,* was far away. A conquest of the homeland had started, in art and in science. A conquest of the homeland—but also the conquest, in the world of intellectual culture, of a position which genius, courage and effort cannot alone create in the political world.

A nation seeks its image in fiction and in history. Seeks and forms. Finds and forms itself accordingly—or rejects. The man on the bier in Tistedalen, and the student who rode out on the long trail through the three realms of nature, have both been simplified in popular imagination and fiction, and turned into figures embodying what we have wished to view as essential features of Swedish character. But, to the present generation, one of them and his times have increasingly receded into a past obscured by 'the shadows which have converged in their wake.' The other has come ever closer to us: a shining prince of the land of summer—although his mind, also, was to turn toward brooding and to get chilled by the needling winds whistling through the small-town streets; a Swede whose disciples were sent to the four corners of the earth and returned with their findings to the master who was—and knew that he was—one of the foremost figures of European culture.

This year, 250 years after his birth, our nation has paid homage in many forms to the memory of Linnaeus. Here, some thought may be devoted to his contribution towards the development of values which it is the task of this Academy to safeguard.

Linnaeus wrote to inform. 'The style is very simple,' and 'I have presented things quite briefly,' he wrote about himself as an author. But freshness and precision, enthusiasm without lyricism, an

---

* Refers to the death of Charles XII in 1718, which marked the end of Sweden's position as a Great Power in Europe.

instinctive eye for meaning and causality, raised the great travel accounts and his other writings in Swedish far above criticism from those 'Nightingales of Pliny' whose disapproval he foresaw. Matter-of-fact poetry—this term of Almqvist's for a faithful realism in the Strindberg manner, ennobled into song—is a phrase which comes to mind in characterizing Linnaeus as a portrayer of the Swedish land. From his own points of departure, he found his tune and his language. Thus he became both a pioneer and a paragon. As an observer and a name-giver, Linnaeus taught us to see with insight, but freely, as when 'it is 10 in the morning in head and heart.' With the creative power of the poet, he showed us how better to capture and hold the elusive experience of the moment in the net of language. Along the lines which were Linnaeus', our literature has been enriched by values as essential to our emotions as the nature they mirror.

In his diaries, the botanist, physician and economist amassed useful and 'curious' notes, which as a whole gave a detailed and vivid picture of the country. In all this, he remained one of those for whom 'nature rejoices.'

His scenery 'resounded like a paradise of birds.' 'Everywhere in the forest, there was the laughter of the grouse.' 'Picus played a creaking bass in the tall dry trees. The black grouse cooed far away; the thrushes chirped in the trees and the other little birds twittered each in its own manner.' With keener senses, he felt how 'the forest, wide, received the tepid rain.'

It was also a world of colour. The most magnificent is the famous description of Scania (Skåne). 'Brown with sorrel lie the fallow fields. Brightest blue *Echium* covers the slopes, as brilliant as you can imagine. Yellow and shining, *Chrysanthemum* adorns the plowed fields.—Red as blood with *Viscaria*, the hills. Snow-white with fragrant *Dianthus*, the sandy expanses. Multicoloured are the rims of the roads with *Echium*, *Cichorium*, *Anchusa Malva*.'

Deep down, it was a world full of meaning. In Linnaeus, a glimpse appears of that 'conspectus of varied sounds, of forms and garb' which Fröding considered the attribute of God, not of man. A great naturalist guided the author, but a great poet permitted the scholar to peer into the secret council chamber of God. The totality of his works, in this respect, is more eloquent than the fragments one may select as samples. It may be permitted, however, to recall one of many which come to mind.

'The spruce were now in full bloom and gave off a strong dust in the strongest heat as soon as the trees moved; their infinity of male flowers, once strawberry-like and vivid in colour, were now pale and spent; the female flowers were few, of a bright red, reclining with opened hollow scales as if to spoon up the male pollen and lead it to the red lancet-like pistils.'

In this experience of *sponsalia plantarum* on a dusty summer's day in the forest on the road from Norrköping, Linnaeus gives us a key to the secret of his view of nature. Here, man is no longer the centre of the world, only a witness, but a witness who is also a partner in the silent life of nature, bound by secret affinities to the trees whose wedding celebration he is allowed to observe. In this way, to Linnaeus, the forest ceases to be just a scenic decoration around the adventure of man, a romantic sounding board for dreams and fears, or a material asset to use or abuse. In its own right, it is moved by him into Swedish poetry, given domicile there in all its opulence and with a life of its own, along with the meadow and the roadside, the arctic heath and the moor, the seashore and the plain.

Linnaeus' humility as an observer and a researcher did not exclude a strong self-confidence. In a less generous general setting his reactions sometimes would have had a petty ring. Until dignity became a burden and melancholy caught up with him, he was saved by his lively eye for those amusing features which are rarely lacking in even the most sombre situation. A little impressed himself—and perhaps not free of the desire to impress others—but at the same time with irony, he told of his tribulations in the high mountains, when he fell 'one musket shot' and 'almost ended the comedy'. His description of an old Lapp woman whom he once met on the moors is a caricature, cruel in a way, in its seeming lack of feeling for the fate underneath the surface, but its point is turned also against the narrator and his pathetic position. The irony which he showed towards pretentious know-alls and the numerous charlatans of his day found expressions which did not conceal his sense of superiority, but conveyed a picture of retained perspective and freedom from professorial self-sufficiency. Before the eye under which he felt the whole of God's creation was living, everybody was, after all, to the Linnaeus of the travel accounts, both a wise man and a fool.

In his Journey in Dalecarlia he described how the cattle, chased by the innumerable gadflies of summer, 'would rather let a rickety skeleton dance over hill and dale' than expose themselves to these tormentors. That was a facet of his drastic imagination which for a moment brightened a situation where, on reflection, he would look at the other side of the picture. To suppress this smile would have been hypocrisy, a tribute his seriousness was too genuine to exact or permit. Linnaeus' feeling for the right, certain word has often been attested to. He had access to a rich treasury of dialect, without caring about the restrictions imposed in those days on an author. Nevertheless, his style would hardly have found its freshness had he not been guided by his sense for the striking and for the unexpected associations of humor. Thus, in his accounts he often relied on meaningful but unexpected similes where his choice of words, leaping between different impressions and ideas, was capable of giving to his style a spontaneous richness comparable to what later poets have achieved in endeavours undertaken with that very purpose in mind.

Wonderment at nature's proof of the Lord's omnipotence had made young Linnaeus write this comment on his first experience of the midnight sun: 'Oh Lord, Thy verdicts are incomprehensible.' Later, when his eye, guided by sombre experiences, was directed towards the world of men, this wonderment was turned into fatalistic mysticism. A parallel has sometimes been drawn with Strindberg: against the summer of the senses in the travel books or in *Hemsöborna*, there stands 'Nemesis' and the wintry world of the Powers. Similar comparisons could be made with others. One may seem to discern a pattern. But why labour similarities which after all cannot do justice to the personality and its development? Suffice it to say that Linnaeus, even in the darker reaches of his being, can carry out the role as one of those in whom the people of Nifelhem have wished to see their features reflected with particular clarity.

Even the notes on Nemesis, now all too inaccessible, belong to our living literature. Crime and retribution, misfortune breeding misfortune, the vanity of mundane aspirations—thus fate is linked to fate in this dance of death, where the style has the economy and dry precision of a woodcut. Linnaeus' introductory words, addressed to his only son, provide the motif of these pictures of life. 'There was a time when I doubted that God cared about me; many years have taught me what I leave to you. Everyone wants to be happy, but few are able to be.' Besides this, however, there is a poem where brooding finally gives way to the trust of a grown-up child.

'Thou sawest my happiness
when I was still lying
in darkness.
Thou settest my clock,
Thou cuttest my bread.
So why, almighty Hero,
shouldst Thou forget me now?
My house I have built
by the grace of God.
Therefore, I sleep unafraid.'

These lines reverberate with the happy humility before the mystery which from the outset gave his accounts their paean note. Life, to Linnaeus, became a *mysterium tremendum*. It remained, till the end, a *mysterium numinosum*.

Linnaeus' Swedish works have always been read, and are perhaps read to an increasing extent, even outside the circle of experts. Their position is certainly explained in part by the personality behind the works and its continuing appeal to interest and imagination. The fact that, for instance, the *Öland Journey* has been able to find readers in low-priced editions demonstrates, however, that it responds to a need, determined by the direction developed by the Swedish feeling for nature.

The relationship of a nation—and a generation—to older literature tells something about the continuity of spiritual life. It can also give an idea about the conditions of writing and of the writer: what is the reader seeking, and why?

Outside the limits of belles-lettres, the works of Linnaeus occupy a place of their own with us. Other books which still have much to offer are resting in oblivion on the shelves of libraries, or reach only the few in new editions. Among them are, for example, the account of Linnaeus' pupil Pehr Kalm of his voyage to America, and Petrus Laestadius' *Journal* with its experiences of years as a missionary in Lapland.

The situation is hardly surprising, if we consider how short our memory has been even when it comes to the greatest innovators of earlier periods. The poetry of a man like Bellman has remained the property of the people thanks to the music. But the baroque paintings of a poet like Stiernhielm, where the blood pulsates and imaginative language is flowering without crowding out even the purest lyricism, appear as dead museum pieces in the nebulous perspective of school-day reminiscences. The history of literature has done its share. Perhaps it is now up to the writers themselves to go exploring, more than they have done, with their eye and their dexterity trained in what last year's Bellman Prize winner called 'the difficult school'. Might they not count on finding an audience for their counsel and interest in their findings among the readers whom, happily, this school has attracted? Perhaps this might also narrow the gap to the immediately preceding generation of writers, a gap which, now as always, is threatening because of the illusion that the old order is dead as all is renewed.

There is one possible reason for the estrangement from the past that is disquieting. In a mass culture, where publicity, working in the interest of sales, is constantly harping on the idea that the latest must be the best, the book, in the view of many, becomes relegated to the ranks of disposable and rapidly aging consumer goods. This may lead to an industrialization of literature, which pays attention to the indications about public taste in the best-seller lists in preference to that which is essential and therefore vital. In a situation which for such reasons, and perhaps also for other and deeper ones, is characterized by the quest for novelty and by conformism, a weakening of the position of older literature would be natural. The risk is enhanced if at the same time the position of the written word as such is becoming more precarious.

The book now has to compete with the press, and jointly they must hold their own against new forms of expression and communication: the films, radio and television. The need for personal contact with literature of quality reflects an acquired taste. A form of expression requiring less activity on the part of the recipient is favoured by that law of least resistance which prevails in this as in other fields.

In the end, we are faced here by the question of the intellectual climate and what determines it. It would be presumptuous to try, here and now, to contribute to this discussion. It is a banality which need not be further developed in this connection, to say that the present has given unusual weight to material progress, and that this means that it has deflected interest from spiritual exercises and found ways of satisfying it by a thousand and one new inventions. Nor is it an original view—whatever importance it may have—that new generations in the Western world have broken out of the sets of problems to which *une littérature engagée* seeks the answers. Observers of the international currents of today may be tempted to name another tendency, although so far it has not made a very deep imprint in our country. It may be that the cult of amorphous spontaneity in art and of a philosophy of absurdity which is calling the tune in some quarters these days, will prove to be a transitory phenomenon. No matter what new paths it may open for creative writing, it contains risks of a growing estrangement from readers whose interest is a prerequisite for the continued life of a work of art.

Eliot has spoken of our era as one when wisdom has been forgotten for knowledge and knowledge for information. May we escape a situation where these words become more than an expression of frustration, and where beside an esoteric poetry—which will probably always have its practitioners—there is produced nothing but literature where realism has been changed into reporting aimed at filling the mental vacuum of increasing leisure without worry or effort for the reader.

In such a situation the dead writers would become definitely forgotten. To keep their works alive is also a means of making room for new, creative writing which, like that of their precursors, is begotten in earnest and often born in pain.

The mental climate here referred to is also influenced, and perhaps not least, by political factors. One of these deserves mention here. This generation has seen Europe lose much of the powerful position it occupied for centuries, and a wave of nationalism has swept the continents. The revolutionary events we witness have led many into a defeatism which, although unspoken, is revealed by its inseparable companions: fatigue, bitterness and sterile self-assertion. In this development, there are traces of the life of nations in earlier periods of upsetting social change—however difficult it may sometimes be to recognize in the coexistence of nations the principles for which one has once fought in one's own country.

There are good reasons, and good chances, to offer resistance to such a situation. The old is not so rotten, nor the new so immature as many seem to think.

Only those who do not want to see can deny that we are moving these days in the direction of a new community of nations, however far we may be from its full realization, however often we may seem to have chosen the wrong path, however numerous the setbacks and disappointments have been. Could it be otherwise, when no other road appears open out of the dangers a new era has created? That democracy of human rights, with equality for nations irrespective of race and history, which has come nearer with the rebirth of Asia and Africa and must form the framework of the international community of the future, may open the door for new spiritual contacts, impulses and problems. To give it reality, much must be jeopardized and perhaps sacrificed, but this is the price of an evolution, the main direction of which we can agree with. It would be a sign of spiritual senescence if such a situation gave rise to destructive despair.

But we can feel the pressure of other forces of the times as a threat to the life we find worth living. If we were to falter in our resistance on these fronts, we should have cause for despair. Then the shadow would fall heavily over the future, be it that of humanity, of the West—or of literature. Then our sacrifices for the development of a community of nations, formed by faith in the value of every human being, would lose all their meaning.

In spite of the changes in its external position, Europe is certainly able, in these various contexts, to keep a place worthy of its traditions. What has been lost in power can be made up by leadership. One condition is that Europe understands how to develop and maintain the values which are the foundation of her spiritual greatness. In this, every nation has its role to play. This Academy has part of the responsibility for the way in which Sweden meets the demands placed on her.

When Linnaeus, after his years abroad, was tempted by most favourable offers to remain there, he declined them because 'a higher urge pulled him towards his Fatherland'. Sweden to Linnaeus was the country where he wished to round out his life's work. It was done as he willed it. The scholar, however, knew no national frontiers. He was a European and, as a European, a citizen of the world. Much has changed, but it is still possible to balance and reconcile home and world, heritage and task in this manner. This can provide an answer to even larger problems than those of the individual.

Linnaeus rode out of Upsala one morning in May. Many years later, on an evening in August, he returned over the plain.

'Ever since Fällingsbro, autumn had steadily appeared before our eyes. The forest, 'tis true, was green, but more severe than in summer. The pastures and the meadows, 'tis true, were green; but without flowers, for the cattle had gone over the former and the scythe over the latter. The plowed fields were full of yellow sheaves, and the yellowish stubble after the harvest was mixed with green weeds. The ditches were full of water after the wet summer, and the multitude of Bur Marigold made them yellow, the rims of the road were covered with *Persicaria acri*, which now began to redden and hang its ears. Everywhere, the farmers were out working: some of them were cutting the grain with the scythe, while their women-folk, heads and arms all white, sheaved it, some carted home their rye, some threshed, some crushed the clods with the sledge, some evened the field with the iron harrow, some sowed winter rye, some harrowed down the seed, some evened the field with the roller, while cow-herding children sang and blew their horns for the cattle in the pastures, until the bleak evening wind began to whistle, and the bright sun sank below the horizon as we entered the Garden of Upsala.'

May this timeless picture of man's work and nature's rest form the tail-piece of these thoughts on the Linnaeus anniversary.

A ROOM OF QUIET

———◆———

THE UNITED NATIONS MEDITATION ROOM

*Dag Hammarskjöld personally planned and super-
vised in every detail the creation of the United
Nations Meditation Room as it exists today. It is
located off the public lobby of the General Assembly
Hall. He wrote the following text of the leaflet which
is given to the thousands who visit this room, in
1957, when the room was reopened to the public.
The fresco on the front wall to which he refers is the
work of the noted Swedish artist and his friend,
Bo Beskow. The block of iron ore in the middle
of the room is also Swedish.*

We all have within us a center of stillness surrounded by silence.

This house, dedicated to work and debate in the service of peace,
should have one room dedicated to silence in the outward sense and
stillness in the inner sense.

It has been the aim to create in this small room a place where
the doors may be open to the infinite lands of thought and prayer.

People of many faiths will meet here, and for that reason none of
the symbols to which we are accustomed in our meditation could
be used.

However, there are simple things which speak to us all with the
same language. We have sought for such things and we believe that
we have found them in the shaft of light striking the shimmering
surface of solid rock.

So, in the middle of the room we see a symbol of how, daily, the
light of the skies gives life to the earth on which we stand, a symbol
to many of us of how the light of the spirit gives life to matter.

But the stone in the middle of the room has more to tell us. We
may see it as an altar, empty not because there is no God, not
because it is an altar to an unknown god, but because it is dedicated
to the God whom man worships under many names and in many
forms.

The stone in the middle of the room reminds us also of the firm and permanent in a world of movement and change. The block of iron ore has the weight and solidity of the everlasting. It is a reminder of that cornerstone of endurance and faith on which all human endeavor must be based.

The material of the stone leads our thoughts to the necessity for choice between destruction and construction, between war and peace. Of iron man has forged his swords, of iron he has also made his ploughshares. Of iron he has constructed tanks, but of iron he has likewise built homes for man. The block of iron ore is part of the wealth we have inherited on this earth of ours. How are we to use it?

The shaft of light strikes the stone in a room of utter simplicity. There are no other symbols, there is nothing to distract our attention or to break in on the stillness within ourselves. When our eyes travel from these symbols to the front wall they meet a simple pattern opening up the room to the harmony, freedom and balance of space.

There is an ancient saying that the sense of a vessel is not in its shell but in the void. So it is with this room. It is for those who come here to fill the void with what they find in their center of stillness.

PART II
1958–1961

THE BEGINNING OF THE
SECOND TERM

Although he was elected to his second term as Secretary-General on 26 September 1957, his second term of office began 10 April 1958.

———————◆———————

I

From transcript of extemporaneous remarks at the UN Correspondents Association Luncheon in his honor, 9 April 1958.

... There is a Swedish poem which I'll have to translate to you. It is very, very good in my own language; it will probably be a fairly poor translation, but I can at least get across the idea. It was in fact written at whatever hundredth anniversary of the University of Upsala by a close friend of mine who is now dead. He wrote at one point that: 'The past is always with us and to the coming days we are those who carry the past centuries and also our own few days.'* I think that is really the way we must look at all our various efforts in the realm of international peace, of the movement towards a world of order and justice.

We have back of us the responsibility created by, in fact, centuries of development. We have in front of us millennia. And in between those centuries and those millennia there are a few years which we might measure in days and weeks and years and five-year terms of office of the Secretary-General, if I look at it from my angle, and those days are really nothing in comparison to what is back of us, and what is in front of us. But they get their sense from what is back of us, and they get their sense in what they mean for the future; that is to say, what we can hand over after our time of work is not just what we have managed to add to the heritage, it is the whole heritage with the little we have managed to add.

It is a confession to a kind of conservatism, a confession to a belief in the continuity of human history, of the history of society, of the

* Gunnar Mascoll Silfverstolpe (1893-1942), member of the Swedish Academy, in 'Cantata on the 450th anniversary of Upsala University', 15 September, 1927.

history of human endeavour. It is also a belief in the steady growth of human endeavour in a sound direction. I cannot belong to or join those who believe in our movement towards catastrophe. I believe in growth, a growth to which we have a responsibility to add our few fractions of an inch.

It is not the facile faith of generations before us, who thought that everything was arranged for the best in the best of worlds or that physical and psychological development necessarily worked out towards something they called progress. It is in a sense a much harder belief—the belief and the faith that the future will be all right because there will always be enough people to fight for a decent future.

I do not think that there is anything automatic in progress. I do not think that there is anything we get for nothing in success. But I do believe firmly that here in this room, around this Organization, in this city, in this country, in the world, there are enough people who are solidly engaged in this fight and who are strong enough and dedicated enough to guarantee its success. It is in a sense a switch from the atmosphere of pre-1914 to what I believe is the atmosphere of our generation in this time—a switch from the, so to say, mechanical optimism of previous generations to what I might call the fighting optimism of this present generation. We have learned it the hard way, and we will certainly have to learn it again and again and again. . . .

II

From transcript of extemporaneous remarks at a
Special Meeting of the UN Staff,
10 April 1958.

The surprise you have given me—because this is a surprise, I heard about it only late yesterday night—is really a kind of 'increased remuneration' of the type which makes me very happy. There are possibilities of remuneration and promotion also for the Secretary-General, and here today you as the staff have in a sense given him increased remuneration and promotion, and I thank you for it.

I was standing here in this very place five years ago this very day, and in fact this very hour. I was facing a rather unknown kind of journey. I knew only one thing and that is that nobody can do more than is in his power, and I had only one intention and that was to do that much. I had only one simple rule, which may sound terribly selfish, but that rule is a fairly valid rule. I felt that this kind of job—and it is true not only of my post but of very many of the jobs held here—is a job which carries with it very considerable risks. There is very much you can lose on them. But I knew one thing: that there is one thing that nobody ever needs to lose, and that is his self-respect. And if I had any promise which I had in mind and which I gave to myself five years ago, it was just this one: Whatever happens, stick to your guns, so that you can feel satisfaction with what you have done, whatever the outcome.

I knew, however, that it would be vain indeed and very selfish if I felt that that depended on personal efforts, personal contributions alone. I knew only too well that every real achievement, in whatever field it is, is always the work of many. I knew for that reason that, for me to meet in any way the demands put upon me in this job, it was necessary to build on the work of every single colleague in the staff, on the Organization and the staff as it had been built up over the years. For that reason, I also felt that the first duty of the Secretary-General must be to give to the staff and to staff problems their proper priority in the efforts. How can you possibly go into the field of political activity, try your efforts in the diplomatic sphere, if you have a feeling that the very basis on which these efforts have to be developed is a weak one—not in the professional sense, but in the sense of human satisfaction in the job, human feeling of belonging to the joint effort?

For that reason, as you may remember, in a way which caused some surprise in some quarters, during my first term here I felt that the staff problems should indeed have the first claim on me and that, without pushing political and diplomatic duties out of view, I should regard them as things that had to follow once we, so to say, had gotten together in the right way and felt that we had this whole operation, as colleagues in a joint effort, on the rails.

To what extent that has succeeded, I do not know. But I know that personally, after, let me say, a couple of years, I felt that at least we were moving in the right direction. If that was so, it was very largely due to the way in which you had supported those very efforts, the way in which you had responded, and a kind of cooperation which was built up and growing between your representatives

and yourselves on the one side and the Secretary-General representing that curious abstraction, the Organization, on the other
side.

It would therefore be but proper for me on this occasion, looking
back over the five years, to thank you and to thank you most sincerely for all the support and encouragement you have given me,
both directly as man to man, and indirectly by your own devotion
to your own work. It is also the right time for me to thank your
representatives, those now acting and those whom you have had in
previous years, for, so to say, understanding my side of the problem.
There are not two sides, but after all there are different aspects of
the problem and we have to represent those different aspects. And
my own feeling is that this kind of understanding, which is a two-
way traffic, also has been growing over the years and is now as solid
as it ever was, if not more solid, and providing very great encouragement for the future development of staff relations within this
building.

I would say this much, and I say it with the greatest sincerity: I
am both happy and proud to be one of you.

I previously used the phrase 'to belong'. It is all right talking about
teamwork, but teamwork may easily mean simply that people work
for the same purpose, that we are, so to speak, formally tied together
by the very fact that we are on the same payroll, that we are under
the same rules, and so forth, and that we have the same general
objectives. From my point of view, that is not enough. We are not
what we should be, we have not reached the full strength of our
possible contribution, until we have managed to develop within
ourselves, and in our relations with others, the sense of belonging.
We are no Vatican, we are no republic, we are not outside the world
—we are very much in the world. But, even within the world,
there can be this kind of sense of belonging, this deeper sense of
unity. I hope that we are on our road to that sense. I feel that we
have moved in that direction and, to the extent that it depends upon
me, I can give you one assurance: Whatever I can do for that
purpose, I will do.

In that connection, I should like to tell you about a decision that
I really took quite some time ago. From your point of view, it may
seem unnecessary, perhaps even sentimental. But why not? I think
it is the right time for me to repeat a very fine and very encouraging
experience I had when I came here. So I hope, within the next

fortnight, to be able to go around the house—all over it again—and meet with you all again personally.

Our friends here were singing a Swedish song, the melody of which I think is very beautiful. The words are perhaps a little bit on the sad side. If I may translate the first line of the song, it runs like this: 'Will the flowers of joy ever grow?' Those words, in fact, were taken up later by a Swedish poet, who developed the theme in a way which I would like to mention today as a kind of background for what I would like to say in conclusion. The poem culminates in the words: 'Will the day ever come when joy is great and sorrow is small?'*

Looking at it in terms of humanity, looking at it in terms of the development of human society, it can be said, of course, that what we are trying to do here is to make our small contribution, during our short time, to a development which will finally lead us to the day 'when joy is great and sorrow is small'.

However, you can also look at those words in a much more personal and intimate sense. I think it is possible to interpret them superficially but it is also possible to interpret them in a sense which goes to the very heart of our way of settling our relation to life. And then I would say that, on the day we feel that we are living with a duty, well fulfilled and worth our while, on that day joy is great and we can look on sorrow as being small. . . .

* Gunnar Ekelöf (b. 1907), member of the Swedish Academy, in the poem 'Prästkrage säg.' The song is an old Swedish folk-song and was a favorite of Dag Hammarskjöld's.

THE USES OF
PRIVATE DIPLOMACY

From Address to a Meeting of Members of both Houses of Parliament under the auspices of the British Group of the Inter-Parliamentary Union, London, 2 April 1958.

. . . . Criticism has been directed against the great emphasis which I have in recent years put upon the adaptation of private diplomacy to the multilateral framework of the World Organization in pursuit of the goals of the Charter. But, whether you call it private diplomacy, or quiet diplomacy or something else, I believe it is in the interests of the Member States that we move in this direction.

I would not for a moment suggest that the functions of debate and vote do not have their essential place in world affairs today. Nor would I suggest that any step be taken that would retard the development of an increasingly influential role for a well-informed public opinion in the making of foreign policy. But the United Nations is subject to the same principles as apply to diplomacy in all its forms. Long experience has shown that negotiation in public alone does not produce results. If the United Nations is to serve as an increasingly effective instrument of negotiation, the principles and methods of traditional diplomacy need to be applied more fully alongside its public procedures.

There are many opportunities for the greater use of private diplomacy in the United Nations in conjunction with its parliamentary procedures. Let me give you a few examples drawn from the experience of recent years. Some of them have a direct relevance to the relationship of the West with the Communist countries, some with the relationship of the West with the Middle East. All of them have served the aims of UN and have been used to reduce the tensions and dangers of conflict.

The first example is the follow-up to the Atoms-for-Peace plan adopted by the General Assembly in 1954. One part of that plan was to bring the atomic scientists and engineers of the world together for an exchange of information on the peaceful uses of atomic energy, as distinct from its military applications. To help in planning the first such scientific conference, the General Assembly created an

Advisory Committee on Atomic Energy to advise the Secretary-General. On this Committee of seven, outstanding nuclear scientists like Sir John Cockcroft have served as governmental representatives of the three major atomic powers, the United Kingdom, the United States of America and the Union of Soviet Socialist Republics.

This Committee, which always sits in private, contributed a great deal to the success of the first Geneva Conference in 1955 on the Peaceful Uses of Atomic Energy and is making a similar contribution this year in the preparation for a second such conference to be convened in Geneva next September 1st.

Perhaps I might at this point mention a question of procedure which may be of particular interest in this House of Parliament. In order to overcome in this Committee the difficulties which necessarily arise because of predominant political conflict, and to get unanimity or, at least, to reach agreement, I have, as Chairman ruled—and I have got it accepted from the beginning—that no vote is ever taken. Instead of a vote, the Chairman sums up his conclusions from the debate, and any member of the Committee is free to go on record with his objections to the summing up. Never in the course of these years has any such observation been put on record in the Committee.

It does serve one purpose—and that is that, if we can get over some of the procedural hurdles, the meeting of minds is closer at hand than one would sometimes believe from reading what is published about the very same questions.

Let me revert to the question of the second Atomic Conference. We already know enough about the scope and character of the papers which will be presented at the coming Conference to assess the remarkable extent to which barriers have been and are being broken down in this important field.

Another point: while it was the General Assembly which voted in public session for the creation of an International Atomic Energy Agency within the United Nations' family, agreement on the statute for this Agency was reached only after months of patient and private negotiation among the Member States named to prepare the way.

The United Nations Radiation Committee established by the General Assembly is another organ on which 'East' and 'West' are represented which also has met consistently in private in the preparation of its forthcoming report. There has been, in this committee of specialists, a consistent effort to arrive at conclusions which will represent the consensus of the best scientific thought of the whole world, regardless of political considerations, about a problem which deeply concerns all the peoples of the world.

My second example concerns the establishment and operations of the United Nations Emergency Force which has done so much to bring quiet to the Armistice Line between Egypt and Israel and to act as a stabilizing influence in the entire area. You will recall that the General Assembly decided to establish UNEF and gave the Force its terms of reference by an overwhelming vote within a couple of days. This was, of course, an emergency situation, but it was possible to achieve this result only because the informal procedures of private diplomacy had been very intensively exercised during the short time available. When the Assembly created UNEF, it also established a UNEF Advisory Committee to advise the Secretary-General on the many questions that arose concerning the operation and functioning of the Force. This Committee, meeting in private, has continued to play a most valuable role ever since. We have, in this case, an example of a three-stage operation which is natural in the United Nations and can be very helpful in getting constructive results: private diplomacy preceding public debate and then employed again to follow through.

Also, this second Advisory Committee, by the way, applies the somewhat extraordinary procedure to which I referred—and, so far, with the same happy result.

I might perhaps add here another word by way of a kind of footnote on this Emergency Force, as an illustration of how we work in the United Nations. The Force was created in an emergency situation, and for that reason we had to improvise. We had to improvise in the field of international law, in the field of military organization, in various fields where usually one does not really like to jump into cold water and start swimming without having learned how best to swim. That means that the Force, as established, cannot, in my view, serve as a good foundation on which to build anything permanent of the very same form. But it does serve as an extremely useful and valuable experiment. We have learned very much. And, in the Secretariat, I have started a study which will digest our experiences, work out some kind of blueprint, master texts of the kind needed for this kind of operation. That means that, if another operation of a similar type should arise, where the same need would be felt, we would not have the Force but we would have everything ready in such a way that we would not again improvise. We would not again make those unavoidable mistakes into which, so to speak, you rush when you just must get the thing going without having had the time to study it carefully before.

In a sense, what I have said here is a reply to the question of whether or not, at the present stage, we should work for a permanent Force. I think the counsel of wisdom is, in the first instance, to digest the experience, to work out what I call the blueprints, the master texts for agreements, for orders, and so on and so forth . . . to get that firmly in hand, and then work with that as the emergency arrangement.

Those who are interested in the financial question may, I think, take special pleasure in the fact that this does not cost anything— and the other operation is an extremely costly one, as our experience has shown.

To turn to a more regular field of United Nations activities, I believe that a greater use of private diplomacy in the work of the Security Council might also yield fruitful results. There is an unused paragraph in the United Nations Charter, Article 28, paragraph 2, which reads: 'The Security Council shall hold periodic meetings at which each of its members may, if it so desires, be represented by a member of the government or by some other specially designated representative.' In his commentary to Parliament at the time the Charter was being considered the then Secretary of State for Foreign Affairs of the United Kingdom said of this paragraph, 'It is by these meetings in particular that governments would be able to carry out the fourth Purpose of the Organization'. This fourth purpose is 'to be a center for harmonizing the actions of nations in the attainment of these common ends'.

I do not suggest any move at this time to give formal effect to this paragraph, but I do think that its application from time to time to the negotiation of appropriate questions might contribute not only to the processes of conciliation but also toward developing in a new direction the important role that the Security Council is intended by the Charter to play in the task of peace-making.

Another example relates to the special responsibilities borne by the United Nations for the Armistice Agreements between Israel and her Arab neighbors and in encouraging a course of development that we hope will lead in time to conditions more favorable to the peaceful settlement of the Palestine question than now exist. This

United Nations responsibility is, as you know, shared by the Security Council and the Office of the Secretary-General. Each has its part to play in upholding the Armistice Agreements and its obligation to seek, whenever opportunity presents itself, to move toward restoring these agreements to their full application and toward lowering the temperature—even if it be by only a few degrees—in an area where, as you well know, the temperature has fluctuated wildly.

It so happens that the Office of the Secretary-General has a place in many of the examples I have cited. But this need not be so. There are many opportunities open to the Member governments and to their representative organs in the United Nations which do not involve my office for the greater use of private diplomacy of a traditional kind, side-by-side with the public procedures of parliamentary diplomacy, either through the use of additional formal procedures or on a purely informal basis. . . .

Those who fought here in these precincts in past centuries for the rights of men belonged to the world and not only to England. Across the earth many lands can fairly boast of such champions of freedom through the centuries. In this sense, the United Nations is not a new idea. It is here because of centuries of past struggle. It is the logical and natural development from lines of thought and aspiration going far back into all corners of the earth since a few men first began to think about the decency and dignity of other men.

Now the lines between national and international policy have begun to blur. What is in the national interest, when truly seen, merges naturally into the international interest.

I am reminded of a memorandum written in 1907 by Mr. Eyre Crowe for the British Foreign Office. He advised then that Britain's best safeguard for the future would be a national policy that is 'so directed as to harmonize with the general desires and ideals common to all mankind, and more particularly that . . . is closely identified with the primary and vital interests of a majority, or as many as possible, of the other nations'.

This seems to me to be a policy—and a principle—which it would be both right and wise for all nations to seek to follow. It is, in effect, the policy and the principle of the United Nations Charter.

PRIVATE DIPLOMACY IN THE
SUEZ SETTLEMENT

From press conference transcript, 1 May 1958

QUESTION: On Tuesday, the very important Suez Compensation Agreement was signed in Rome, signalling the liquidation of the Suez crisis. We feel—at least in our fingers—that your initiative in this whole operation was quite important. I wonder if you would care to comment, now that this Agreement has been signed.

THE SECRETARY-GENERAL: I agree with you that one of the really good pieces of news that we have had in recent times has been the signature of the Agreement on principles. I think that if it has not resolved the problem, as you say, it has at least brought us a long distance in the direction of re-establishing a normal situation. The main credit for this solution rests, of course, with those who have been negotiating: the Government of Egypt and the representatives of the shareholders. We in the United Nations have been very happy to cooperate closely all the way through, from the beginning to the end, with the representatives of the International Bank, which in this case has, I think, ventured—I do not know whether it is for the first time—into fields that we are trying to explore: namely, the playing of a role where you are not a mediator but are, so to speak, a common denominator for the parties, making it much easier to achieve results. I really want to pay tribute to the Bank for the work it has done in pioneering in activities which I think give a lot of promise for the future.

If I am to write history at all, or write a part of history, concerning these negotiations, I may perhaps do it in these terms: This cooperation between the Bank and the United Nations in the early stages involved a division of responsibilities. We both had the same target: to help the parties. After all, it was a situation which was rather intricate and rather delicate, and for that reason, required the cooperation of several minds. This division of responsibility was simple and was indicated by the very terms of reference of the two organizations. It was for the Bank to work on the financial aspects of the problem; it was for us, and for me, to work on what I would call the political-legal aspects of the problem. You may remember that the very long delay which we suffered last year was explained, to a large extent, by the fact that it was not easy to find a formula under which one could establish two parties to this compensation negotiation. There was the Government of Egypt, obviously —but who was the party on the other side? Was it the governments? Was it the old company? Was it the new company? Was it the shareholders? That did present a problem, on which we spent quite some time—and it is for the parties to say whether the time we spent on it was usefully spent or was not usefully spent. The end result, however, as you know, was that we got negotiations going on the basis of a formula which has worked out—we got them going, I think, early in February—and in my private calendar I have put a star on the ceiling.

THE ARMS RACE AND DISARMAMENT

*The following comments in the Security Council and
at a press conference in 1958 reflect the Secretary-
General's deep concern over the continuing failure to
make any progress towards bringing the arms race
under control. They define his support for a step-by-
step approach as the most practical negotiating tactic
and, even more, constitute an appeal for efforts to
break out of the vicious circle of distrust with which
both sides have greeted each initiative by the other.
When he spoke in the Security Council the Council
was considering a USSR complaint against flights
over the Arctic regions by American military aircraft
and a USA counter-proposal to establish an Arctic
inspection zone against the dangers of surprise attack.
Nothing positive resulted. The majority voted
against the Soviet complaint and the USA proposal
was vetoed by the USSR.*

———————◆———————

I

*Statement before the Security Council,
29 April 1958*

It is most unusual for the Secretary-General to intervene in a debate
of the Security Council. Indeed, it would be out of order and
rightly criticized if such an intervention from his side would mean
a taking of sides in a conflict before the Security Council.

However, on a previous occasion I have stated as my opinion,
that the Secretary-General has not only the right but the duty to
intervene when he feels that he should do so in support of the
purposes of this Organization and the principles laid down in the
Charter. He cannot assume for himself the right to 'speak for man'
but he must subordinate himself to his duty to express the significance of the aspirations of man, as set out in the Charter, for problems before this Council or the General Assembly.

Some time ago in a press conference I found reason to welcome the decision of the Soviet Union to suspend unilaterally tests of the atomic bombs. I did so solely on the basis of an evaluation of the possible impact of that move on the stalemate reached in the disarmament debate.

In the same spirit and on the same basis I wish today to welcome the initiative taken by the United States in presenting a proposal which might break up the stalemate from the angle of a limited system of inspection. I note that this is in response to the expressions of the Soviet Union of their fear for the possible consequences, in a direction of immediate concern to them, of the present state of extreme preparedness in the field of armaments.

It would be against my rights and duties to comment on the background of the Soviet initiative or of the United States' response. I am concerned only with the consequences.

The stalemate in the field of disarmament has been permitted to last for far too long. Attempts to break it through negotiations have so far proved of no avail. I think there are reasons of different kinds behind this deeply worrying failure. One is that in a sense governments have been too ambitious, not being satisfied with just making a dent in this intricate and vital problem from which a rift could develop, opening up the possibilities of a true exchange of views. Another reason has been the tendency for each government to wait for others to take the first step. Still another reason and, of course, the basic one, is the crisis of trust from which all mankind is suffering at the present juncture and which is reflected in an unwillingness to take any moves in a positive direction at their face value and a tendency to hold back a positive response because of a fear of being misled.

Such initiatives as those to which I have referred, one of which is today being considered by the Security Council, are steps which could make a dent in the disarmament problem. They might have a major impact if treated in good faith—which is not the same as to let down one's guard. And they could, if followed through, provide a first frail basis for the development of some kind of trust.

Each government is in close contact with the opinion of the man in the street in its own country. For that reason, I am sure that all governments are in a position to confirm my statement that the peoples are eagerly and anxiously expecting leadership bringing them out of the present nightmare. The government taking a fruitful initiative will be hailed as a benefactor by the peoples. The governments responding in a positive spirit so as to give effect to such an attempt to turn the development, will share the merit with the one who took the first step.

I have felt it incumbent on me to state these few simple reactions. I have done so under my obligations to the peoples whose voice is reflected in the Charter under which I am acting. I trust that my intervention will not be misinterpreted as a taking of sides, but merely as an expression of profound feelings which are current all over the world and which have a right to be heard here also outside the framework of government policies.

I hope that each one of the governments, represented around this table, will wish to try out the line of trust as a way out of the disintegration and decline under which we now all suffer.

II

From press conference transcript, 1 May 1958

QUESTION: Sir, your intervention in the Security Council has created some concern among some UN delegates who felt it may affect the position of the Secretary-General in his relationship to one of the big Powers. It is being said particularly that there is a difference between your support of the ban on nuclear tests by the Soviet Union (in a press conference) and the support of the United States position with regard to the control of the Arctic. . . . Would you please comment on these viewpoints.

THE SECRETARY-GENERAL: That is a broad question. First of all, it is very kind of you and some of your colleagues to express concern. I think it is, however, not very necessary.

As to the first part of your question—my relation to this or that government, in this case in particular one of the big Powers—I am personally firmly convinced that that depends on the maintenance of their trust in, let me say, my independence, my sincerity, my impartiality, and my sense of responsibility. I do not for a second believe that the Secretary-General, with due reserve and due tact, going on record with his general views on one of the key United Nations problems, will shake such trust. . . .

As to the other question—press conference or Security Council—

I think that you make an unnecessary distinction, especially in this case as the very fact that I, so to say, read into the Security Council record my welcome to the Soviet decision, gave it exactly the same standing politically as my welcome to the United States initiative. I think, also, that it would be helpful if you read the text of what I said quite carefully. What I said was what I felt about the sense of urgency at the present state of disarmament efforts and talks to explore to the full the positive results which may be derived from this or that initiative. An appeal for that, irrespective of the substance of the specific initiative and, of course, irrespective of where it comes from, does not involve a taking of stands as to the substance. It involves in a very serious way an evaluation of the situation and an evaluation of what may come out of this or that initiative. Read it, and I think you are then on the safest basis. Read it as a general appeal to all governments, first of all, of course, the big Powers, to get all the positive value they possibly can out of any honest initiative taken by any government.

You know that I have expressed myself many times in press conferences on disarmament. It is, of course, an extremely complicated problem and it is bound to develop with slowness. But there is a point in the development of disarmament where every time an initiative is taken in good faith and its possible consequences, its possible values, are not fully explored, I have the feeling that we have missed the bus. And we should not be too sure that the road will remain open for buses in all the future. That sense of urgency, that sense of responsibility, in the face of every new opening, from wherever it comes and whatever its immediate limited substance, was what prompted me, what made me feel that it was one of those occasions where public statements by the Secretary-General are very much part of his duty and a very adequate supplement to private diplomacy.

This was a very long reply, but your question was, as I said, a rather broad one.

*   *   *

... QUESTION: In your Security Council intervention you indicated that you were motivated in your appeal by the feeling that the world must be gotten out of this nightmare—if I remember the sense of your remarks correctly—a nightmare of deterioration. And a few minutes ago you said that if we continue to miss the bus the road may not always be open for that bus. I wonder whether, in the context of those two definitions or, perhaps, warnings, you feel that there is a foreseeable time-limit ahead by which we must meet the challenge or face the consequences?

THE SECRETARY-GENERAL: No, there is no foreseeable time-limit because that is dependent on two rather irrational factors, human impatience and human failure as to the precision of operations which may be well intended but, all the same, may go wrong. What I meant with those words, which you rightly combine, is that it is all right to continue disarmament talks if it is just a high political game of some kind of refined chess, or something else, provided nothing develops in the meantime. But if, in the meantime, the armaments race continues up to a point where it does represent a risk of failure, of breakdown, of collisions which are unintentional, then, of course, an element of urgency is introduced which makes it impossible to look with equanimity at the diplomatic game.

I do not believe that any of the governments concerned have less of a sense of urgency than I have. But it may be that the way in which discussion has been pursued has tended to mislead public opinion so that they have felt: 'Well, this is in the hands of the governments, and they talk and write letters and discuss matters and meet, and we can go on in the shadow of that somewhat costly but not harmful operation. Time may work wonders.' I have this sense of urgency; I think the governments have it.

What I wanted to do in using those two phrases was to bring it out into the open. In particular, the use of the word 'nightmare' may shock you as it in a certain sense shocked me, because it is the kind of language I rarely use. However, it was completely adequate for me as a description of what I had in mind. The people who give thoughtful consideration to the news know that there is a margin of failure everywhere in everything and that there is a factor of impatience. They might rightly feel that it is not in keeping with their reasonable rights to life to have to live under the kind of threat which is created not by any specific policy of any country but which emerges from the total situation as it develops while the discussions are going on.

I believe that gives you the background thinking. This is certainly a statement which normally would have been given off the record, but I do not think there is any reason for me to ask you to place it off the record.

DANGERS OF A 'POLITICIZED' WORLD

*Extract from an address at the State Dinner of the
50th Annual Meeting of the Governors' Conference,
Miami, Florida, 19 May 1958. The Governors' Conference brings together once a year the governors of all
the states of the United States.*

. . . Politics in general, and international politics in particular, was
once an area in the main reserved for experts and of comparatively
limited significance to the common man. Our time, however, is one
of an expansion of politics into increasingly broad areas of common
life. This is as true of international politics as of national politics.
Anyone who today tries to disengage himself from the political
aspects of life cuts himself off from developments of the deepest
direct significance for his own destiny.

It is natural in these circumstances that political questions should
claim much of the time and space of all the media of mass communication. To the extent that this means that each and every one
of us is enabled to develop his own knowledge and judgment concerning the way that a society is growing and the way its leaders are
trying to frame its future, it is certainly welcome. But we cannot
disregard the fact that the expansion of the part played by political
concerns in the life of our society may create dangers of which
especially we, whose professional responsibilities are in the political
sphere, must remain aware.

A 'politicized' world is a world where individual reactions have
to be disciplined and subordinated to group interests, and where
for that reason conformism easily becomes an ideal. It is a world
where tactics often are given priority over substance and in which,
for this reason, we may lose sight of the real interests in our search
for propaganda points to be scored. To use a comparison, it is also
a world where the preacher may be tempted to give greater effort
to winning the approval of the converted than to converting the sin-
ners. If we succumb to such dangers, we lose the ability to communi-
cate our sincere reactions to others who are of a different view,
forgetting also how to listen to what they may have to say in explanation of their stands. To the extent that this is permitted to happen, a
politicized world becomes a de-humanized world.

These indications of risks implied in the life of today may be considered as exaggerated. I am afraid that they are not. Any student of politics and its impact on common life today could easily find examples showing to what extent the intrusion of politics into common life has had the consequences to which I have referred.

I have found it justified on this occasion to recall these dangers because I believe that it is impossible to reach a clear understanding of the present international situation without taking such factors into account. They explain in part the seeming paradox that certainly no single people wants anything but peace and no single government would take the responsibility for starting a war, but that, all the same, the world situation, politically, represents a picture of interlocking stalemates.

It is one of the surprising experiences of one in the position of the Secretary-General of the United Nations to find in talks with leaders of many nations, both political leaders and leaders in spiritual life, that the views expressed, the hopes nourished and the trust reflected, in the direction of reconciliation, go far beyond what is usually heard in public. What is it that makes it so difficult to bring this basic attitude more effectively to bear upon the determination of policies? The reasons are well known to us all. It might not be understood by the constituency, or it might be abused by competing groups, or it might be misinterpreted as a sign of weakness by the other party. And so the game goes on—towards an unforeseeable conclusion. . . .

THE WALLS OF DISTRUST

Address at Cambridge University, 5 June 1958

We meet in a time of peace which is no peace, in a time of technical achievement which threatens its own masters with destruction.

We meet in a time when the ideas evoked in our minds by the term 'humanity' have switched to a turbulent political reality from the hopeful dreams of our predecessors.

The widening of our political horizons to embrace in a new sense the whole of the world, should have meant an approach to the ideal sung in Schiller's 'Ode to Joy', but it has, paradoxically, led to new conflicts and to new difficulties to establish even simple human contact and communication.

Korea, China, Indonesia, Kashmir, Palestine, Hungary, North Africa. There are fires all around the horizon, and they are not fires announcing peace. More perturbing than all these smoldering or barely controlled conflicts are the main underlying tendencies, which we all know only too well and which preoccupy our minds and darken our hopes.

We may well rejoice in having taken the first steps towards the establishment of an international democracy of peoples, bringing all nations—irrespective of history, size or wealth—together on an equal basis as partners in the vast venture of creating a true world community. But we have taken only the first steps, and they have often proved painful. There is a maturity of mind required of those who give up rights. There is a maturity of mind required of those who acquire new rights. Let us hope that, to an increasing extent, the necessary spiritual qualities will be shown on all sides.

Today we are in the middle of this development, and, naturally, we tend to judge it from the viewpoint of our own past and our own immediate interests. This may explain why many now show reactions which seem to reflect a kind of despair of Western civilization. But, where is the reason for such defeatism? Is it not possible to establish and maintain a spiritual leadership, whatever the changes in other respects?

Our lives today are coloured, first of all, by the long and bitter strife between the Western world, with its traditional ideals, and a new power bloc, grown out of the great revolutions after the first World War and representing views of society and of man's place in society different from ours although partly inspired by thinkers of the West. However, this is not the place to comment on that strife and the harassing political problems to which it gives rise.

The conflict between different approaches to the liberty of man and mind or between different views of human dignity and the right of the individual is continuous. The dividing line goes within ourselves, within our own peoples and also within other nations. It does not coincide with any political or geographical boundaries. The ultimate fight is one between the human and the sub-human. We are on dangerous ground if we believe that any individual, any nation or any ideology has a monopoly on rightness, liberty and human dignity.

When we fully recognize this and translate our insight into words and action, we may also be able to re-establish full human contact and communications across geographical and political boundaries, and to get out of a public debate which often seems to be inspired more by a wish to impress than by a will to understand and to be understood.

This generation can boast of scientific achievements, the scope of which goes beyond the sum of what had come out of scientific research up to our days. In laboratories here in Cambridge and many of its sister institutions Rutherfords and Diracs—may the names of these two Cambridge men of different generations be permitted to represent them all—have laid the basis on which the potentialities hidden in matter have now been explored up to a point where the use of nuclear energy has become a practical reality.

Parallel with this development—and also in this case, ironically enough, partly as a by-product of war efforts—we see the beginning of a penetration into outer space, with all the possibilities for new progress and new difficulties which this entails.

May it be enough to recall here how, through these achievements, doors that were locked have been broken open to new prosperity or to new holocausts. Warning words about how the development of social organization, and how the growth of moral maturity in the emerging mass civilizations, has lagged behind the technical and scientific progress, have been repeated so often as to sound hackneyed—and to make us forget that they are true.

What, then, is wrong? Why is it that a situation with so many achievements both in the political and in the technical fields should lend itself to comments of this kind? The reasons, of course, are many and complicated. I guess that we, all of us, may have developed our own views on what has led up to the present situation.

It is easy to turn the responsibility over to others or, perhaps, to seek explanations in some kind of laws of history. It is less easy to look for the reasons within ourselves or in a field where we, all of us, carry a major responsibility. However, such a search is necessary, because finally it is only within ourselves and in such fields that we can hope, by our own actions, to make a valid contribution to a turn of the trend of events.

With your permission, I would in this context like to quote one of the influential thinkers of our time, whose personal history and national experience have given him a vantage point of significance.

In an address in Carnegie Hall in New York, in 1952, Martin Buber had the following to say:

'There have always been countless situations in which a man believes his life-interest demands that he suspect the other of making it his object to appear otherwise than he is. . . . In our time something basically different has been added. . . . One no longer merely fears that the other will voluntarily dissemble, but one takes it for granted that he cannot do otherwise. . . . The other communicates to me the perspective that he has acquired on a certain subject, but I do not really take cognizance of his communication as knowledge. I do not take it seriously as a contribution to the information about this subject, but rather I listen for what drives the other to say what he says, for an unconscious motive. . . . Since it is the idea of the other, it is for me an "ideology". My main task in my intercourse with my fellow-man becomes more and more . . . to see through and unmask him. . . . With this changed basic attitude . . . the mistrust between man and man has become existential. This is so indeed in a double sense: It is first of all, no longer the uprightness, the honesty of the other which is in question, but the inner integrity of his existence itself. . . . Nietzsche knew what he was doing when he praised the "art of mistrust", and yet he did not know. For this game naturally only becomes complete as it becomes reciprocal. . . . Hence one may foresee in the future a degree of reciprocity in existential mistrust where speech will turn into dumbness and sense into madness.'

I excuse myself for having quoted at such length from this speech. I have done so because out of the depth of his feelings

Martin Buber has found expressions which it would be vain for me to try to improve.

If I have wanted, on this occasion, to draw attention to the aspect of the troubles of our time to which the quoted words have given such an impelling expression, this is because it is in a basic way related to the tasks and the spirit of an institution like this University.

Scientists of genius, working here and in other research centers around the world, have made a unique contribution to progress, prosperity and peace. If their achievements have been turned to uses sometimes very far from their original intentions, it is not their fault. Nor is it the fault of their colleagues in the fields of theology, law, medicine, history and philosophy, or other branches of humane letters, if their contributions have not sufficed to create such psychological and political safeguards as would guarantee that the achievements of science be turned to man's benefit and not to his destruction.

But all of us, in whatever field of intellectual activity we work, influence to some degree the spiritual trend of our time. All of us may contribute to the breakdown of the walls of distrust and towards checking fatal tendencies in the direction of stale conformism and propaganda. How can this be done better or more effectively than by simple faithfulness to the independence of the spirit and to the right of the free man to free thinking and free expression of his thoughts? So, attitudes in line with the liberal traditions of this University emerge as a deeply significant element also in our efforts to master the political difficulties.

I have used strong words, but they reflect deep concern. For someone active primarily in the field of international politics it is today natural to appeal to the spirit for which Cambridge may be taken as a symbol. Deep-rooted conflicts which have run their course all through history, and seemed to reach a new culmination before and during the second World War, continue. And destructive forces which have always been with us make themselves felt in new forms. They represent, now as before, the greatest challenge man has to face.

PRESS CONFERENCE COMMENT
ARISING FROM ADDRESS AT CAMBRIDGE
From transcript, 12 June 1958

QUESTION: During your recent trip, you delivered a speech at

Cambridge in which you cited at length the philosopher Martin Buber. During the five years you have been here, I have never noted any tone of pessimism from you. In this particular speech, however, I was very much surprised to note your use of what you yourself called strong words reflecting deep concern for the fate of mankind. You referred to 'a kind of despair of Western civilization', and, in concluding your speech, you said that deep-rooted conflicts which have run their course all through history continue, and destructive forces which have always been with us make themselves felt in new forms.

My question is this: Are we to note here an outlook of pessimism so far as mankind and the future of the World Organization are concerned?

THE SECRETARY-GENERAL: If you read the speech that way, you go too far. First of all, the despair about which I talked was a despair I was criticizing. As you may have seen in the speech, I said that I found the despair of Western civilization unjustified.

But the other accent to which you have referred is one which I do not think should surprise you. I think you can see three expressions, as it were, of very much the same attitude: in the much-discussed intervention in the Security Council on Arctic inspection, in the press conference following that intervention,* and in the Cambridge speech. On those three occasions, I was in fact talking about exactly the same subject.

My fear is related to one single thing which I think has been brought out very well in the Buber statement—that is, the drift into what Buber has called existential reciprocal mistrust.

* See 'The Arms Race and Disarmament', pp. 177-181.

ARAB COOPERATION AND THE U.N.

Opening statement before Emergency Special Session of the General Assembly on the Lebanon-Jordan Crisis, 8 August 1958. This is the statement referred to in the Introduction (page 12). In response to a complaint by Lebanon of intervention by the United Arab Republic in its internal affairs, the Security Council had established the UN Observation Group in Lebanon in June under the Secretary-General's direction. Immediately after the revolution in Iraq on 14 July, Jordan submitted a similar complaint against the UAR and simultaneously the United States and United Kingdom, acting independently of the United Nations, sent troops to Lebanon and Jordan at the request of their governments. This armed Western intervention in the Middle East evoked a strong and threatening reaction from the USSR and an emergency special session of the General Assembly was called to deal with the matter. The Secretary-General opened the session with this statement pointing the path to a peaceful solution. In essence, it was, on the one hand, an appeal to the Arab States to put Arab solidarity within the United Nations above their quarrels and, on the other hand, an appeal to the rest of the world, especially the Great Powers, to give support and respect to such a development rather than resorting to outside intervention. Later the Secretary-General was to follow the same policy line with the African States in the Congo crisis. This statement, supported by active personal diplomacy by the Secretary-General, was an essential element in the final constructive outcome. The Arab States united in proposing a resolution giving effect to this approach. It won unanimous support in the General Assembly and paved the way for the American and British troop withdrawals in October and for a turn toward a better and more constructive atmosphere in the relationships among the Arab States.

The item on the agenda of this emergency session of the General
Assembly refers specifically to situations in the Middle East which
have arisen only recently. However, seen in their broader context,
these situations draw attention to basic problems facing the United
Nations in the Middle East. In these circumstances, it may be
found useful by the members of the General Assembly if, at this
early stage of the deliberations, I were to outline some of the basic
needs for action in the region, which, in view of the experience of
the Secretariat, require urgent attention. It would be premature
for me now to indicate along what lines solutions might be sought.
I hope that in this respect the debate in the General Assembly will
prove to be fruitful. An indication of the needs, as seen by the
Secretariat, may serve as a basis on which Members might wish to
develop positive and constructive suggestions.

The arrangements by which the United Nations, through the
United Nations Emergency Force, assists the Government of the
United Arab Republic in Gaza and along the international frontier
between Egypt and Israel, and serves to maintain quiet in that area,
have worked out in a way which, I believe, may be a source of
satisfaction to all Members of the United Nations. Similarly, the
United Nations Truce Supervision Organization continues to
function, under the terms of reference established by the Armistice
Agreements. Although the scope of its activities has been restricted,
and in spite of difficulties, this body also represents an essential
element in the efforts of the United Nations to stabilize conditions
in the area.

On the basis of the resolution of the Security Council of 11 June
1958, the United Nations has organized a third operation in the
Middle East, the United Nations Observation Group in Lebanon.
It has already rendered very useful service and its further development is, in the light of our experience, fully justified. However, the
present operation is related to conditions which may be temporary,
and the time may not be distant when a change of those conditions
would call for a change of approach. Recent experiences may be
taken as indicating that some form of UN representation in the
country might be a desirable expression of the continued concern
of the Organization for the independence and integrity of Lebanon.
If that proves to be the case, forms should be sought by which such
representation would adequately serve the purposes of the Organization in the region. However, the arrangements that should be

made, once the time has come to reconsider the UN representation in Lebanon in the light of developments in the country, will depend, ultimately, on the attitude of the Government of Lebanon itself.

Another part of the region, which presents specific problems, is the Hashemite Kingdom of Jordan, with its central location on the map of the area. In the period through which we are passing, it appears that the UN should give special attention to the essential role which this country has to play in the efforts of the Organization to assist in creating conditions for peaceful and constructive development. Under present circumstances, some strengthening of the Truce Supervision Organization, within the framework of the General Armistice Agreements, may have to be considered. Were it to be felt that special measures would be desirable, in addition to the activities of that Organization, the question would arise how such measures should be developed so that they are adequate in the specific situation prevailing in Jordan. Consideration should also be given to the question how the measures taken might best be co-ordinated with the other United Nations arrangements in the region.

However, activities like those of the UNEF, the UNTSO, the UNOGIL and such other organs as the General Assembly might wish to consider, are only safeguards created to assist the governments concerned. The developments in which the UN and all Member countries within or outside the region are interested, can be supported by such measures, but ultimately they must depend on, and will be effectively shaped by, actions of the Member nations in the region.

Arab nations already have cooperated within the Arab League, and they all have subscribed to the principles of mutual respect for each others' territories, integrity and sovereignty; of non-aggression; of non-interference in each others' internal affairs, and of equal and mutual benefit. Were the States concerned, in the present troubled situation, jointly to reaffirm their adherence to such principles, that step would be of considerable assistance to the general efforts in which the UN is engaged. Steps that might be taken in the direction of an agreement or a declaration to that effect, and of accommodations of policies to those principles, should, therefore, have the support of the Organization.

To the extent that the Arab nations would find it possible to translate the principles mentioned into joint practical action, the Organization should be prepared to render assistance of a technical nature and to give the necessary support. This is so especially in the field of economic cooperation, since one of the major aims of the United Nations is to make its contribution to the efforts of the governments and peoples to improve, in cooperation, their economic and social conditions. By studies made within the Secretariat, and with the assistance of the International Bank, we have, in the Secretariat, tried to prepare ourselves to afford such assistance as the countries concerned may request.

The need for arrangements for economic cooperation within the region has been strongly felt in the work of the UN, especially as regards the financial field, where the creation of the proper institutions would considerably facilitate the flow of funds needed in the region. However, arrangements for economic cooperation also in other fields would, in the light of our experience, be helpful. I have in mind especially arrangements giving a proper framework to the cooperation between oil-producing and oil-transiting countries, or made with a view to a joint utilization of water resources.

The need for a closer cooperation in the various fields to which I have just referred, could best be met through institutions created by the free initiative of the countries in the region. The Organization could make an essential contribution by extending its encouragement, support and technical assistance to the independent efforts of the nations in the region to fill that need.

Finally, it is clear, in the light of experience, that both the arrangements for direct UN representation in various parts of the area to which I have referred, and such arrangements for cooperation as might be made by agreement among the Arab countries, will require the recognition by the world community of the particular problems and possibilities of the region. Most countries in the area have only recently emerged with their present political character of independent sovereign States, with close mutual ties and with a strong sense of the rights and duties which flow from the particular heritage of the Arab peoples. We know that the problems and aspirations of these peoples meet with general respect and understanding. It would be helpful in promoting the purposes of the United Nations in the area if this respect and this understanding were to be given general expression, assuring the peoples there that they may shape their own destinies in the best interest of each nation within the region and of the region as a whole.

It is my belief that, if the General Assembly in its present deliberations could find a way toward furthering developments to meet the needs I have indicated, a basis would be provided on which we could hope to deal with the other serious problems of the area with which the Organization has been engaged for years. First among those problems stands the question of the refugees. It continues to be urgent, but its solution may have to await the creation of the more favorable general conditions which would follow, were the other needs to which I have referred to be successfully met.

SCIENCE AND HUMAN RELATIONS

Address at the Atoms for Peace Award Ceremony,
29 January 1959, The Rockefeller Institute,
New York.

Within the span of one man's life, science, technology and economic and political developments have brought a greater and more world-embracing change in the life of mankind than had previously taken place in centuries or, in some respects, even millennia.

The last half century has brought to fruition, with revolutionary consequences, ideas and initiatives of generations. The change is in no way complete; we are perhaps only at its beginning. The final results are still undetermined, but, to a large extent, will be decided by our way of reacting to the developing situation.

In very simple words, one of the leading nuclear physicists* has formulated our personal problem when he says that the ways that we learned in our childhood are now only very meagerly adequate for the issues that we must meet in maturity. His words stress how developing knowledge and technology, and a developing society, require of us a continuous development also of the individual.

In an often quoted statement, Arnold Toynbee has pointed to the awareness of the responsibility of the more highly developed societies for those who have lagged behind in the race as the most characteristic new fact of our generation. This new awareness, however, seems to me to be rather a symptom of change than an independent and decisive factor in the change. We can easily trace its roots in the past and its background in the present.

How much of this new awareness is spontaneous, and how much of it is a response to a demand for a share of the place in the sun by that vast majority of mankind which has been left behind? Back of the demand and back of the response we find ideas that, in national communities, broke through long ago in the French Revolution, in the American Revolution and—not to be forgotten—in the Soviet Revolution.

These ideologies of past and present generations would not have brought our world to the ferment in which we find it at present, had it not been for the development of communications over the last decades. I, myself, and certainly many of us, have had the

* J. Robert Oppenheimer.

194

privilege of meeting pioneers who penetrated into Gobi or to Lhasa by foot, or men who crossed the Arctic ice-cap with dogs. Today the same regions are easily reached by plane by anybody, while the voice of the political leaders now can penetrate to the innermost recesses of what was *terra incognita* only some decades ago. Members of a family who starve in the Indo-Chinese jungle nowadays are people we all may meet. It is no longer a feat to visit the clay-huts of the desert. And we have no excuse not to tackle with our modern equipment the diseases of children in the igloos of the Arctic region. Likewise, difficult though it may be to envisage what the standard of life and the political liberties in highly developed countries mean to such societies, the road has been opened to everyone in the most remote places of the globe to compare his position with that of more fortunate peoples. Thus, ideas and ideologies peculiar to the West have in our time, in their practical application, become factors in global development and of global significance.

The discoveries and inventions which have opened the doors for personal contacts all around the globe, and for the written and spoken word in every quarter, have, at the same time, put at our disposal means by which we have unprecedented possibilities to change conditions of life for the better, for all people. Our increased knowledge has given us new sources of power and new insight into the nature of disease. It may be that we are still far from mastering disease, and it may be that we are still far from mastering the new sources of energy sufficiently well to meet the demand of a quickly growing humanity for a life in dignity without fear. But, the newly developed perspectives are such that political economy need no longer be the 'dismal science' of the days of Malthus.

Thus, in this epoch of change we see science as a *primus motor* but likewise as a human activity from which we may expect many of the replies to our present-day problems as they are determined by our concepts of man and society in their new, world-wide application.

The half-century which I have characterized here as an epoch of change, has also seen two global wars of unprecedented violence and destruction, the last one having the additional—and doubtful— honor of having introduced the ultimate results of modern science into the destructive arsenal of men.

The more than thirteen years of peace which have followed the end of the second World War have been characterized by two major sets of conflicts, both of which have shown possibilities of leading to a situation where a new global conflagration might strike us—I mean both the Cold War, in all its ramifications, and the manifold tensions between the historical West and the peoples of the Asian and African continents.

Obviously, these conflicts are closely related to the developments I have just mentioned. They point to the relations of man to man, of man to his environment, and of groups to groups as an overriding problem of our time which must be solved not only in order to preserve the peace necessary for survival, but also to induce an atmosphere in which science and technology may find it possible to yield results which would enable us to meet the demands which science itself has in part created.

I have referred to some spectacular aspects of the problem of human relations at the present time. Considering them, and what they represent, we finally are led back to problems of the individual in the present phase of the development of the international community, of the nation and of the many units and groups of which the individual is a member.

Mass movements, means of mass communication, pressures of mass interests, the access to new enormous resources of strength and wealth, together with the rapidity of change, have taken the individual unaware and created situations which he still has to learn how to master. Indeed, 'the ways that we learn in childhood are only very meagrely adequate to the issues that we must meet in maturity.'

One risk facing equally the worker, the artist, the scientist and the politician, is the suppression of the inner freedom of the individual through demands for subordination and conformity. There is less tolerance for the personal, perhaps erratic, experiment in life than in times which could afford more tolerance. However, the need for such tolerance is as great as ever in the very interest of progress and in the interest of peace.

At this point, I would like to quote two leading nuclear scientists.* The first one is an American, who has said 'the open society, the unrestricted access to knowledge, the unplanned and uninhibited association of men for its furtherance—these are what may make a vast, complex, ever-growing, ever-changing, ever more specialized and expert technological world, nevertheless a world of human

* J. Robert Oppenheimer and Francis Perrin.

community'. The other one is a leading scientist from Europe who, speaking with the full authority of a wide personal experience, stated at the Second International Conference on the peaceful uses of atomic energy: 'Science actually requires a perfect sincerity with oneself as well as with others, an objective pursuit of truth which goes beyond its own field and penetrates the nexus of relationships between men. It demands a discipline of thought and expression that rejects the empty emotional bombast which is so particularly apt to put peoples against each other.'

We honor today one of the pioneers in the modern scientific revolution, and therefore also in the general revolution of our time. Professor de Hevesy, like last year's laureate, Professor Bohr, is one who, as an individual, has made a great creative contribution to those developments which have formed our present society with all its problems not only in scientific and technological terms but, likewise, in human terms.

The history of Professor de Hevesy's work illustrates well the growing unity of natural science. We see before us how a great advance, rooted in pre-reactor nuclear physics and developed in chemistry, reaches its final flowering in the study of life. It also shows how a major break-through in one great intellectual discipline —physics—may lead not only to a vast new technology but also, by paths not always anticipated, to great new vistas in other ancient disciplines of thought, such as the life sciences whose technological achievements, as in medicine and agriculture, are in some ways closer to the ordinary people of many lands than the mysteries of the atomic nucleus.

It is, indeed, the duty of society to honor such men in words, but it is also its duty to honor them in deeds, by treating the problems of modern man in a way worthy of the advance of knowledge to which they have made such decisive contributions.

Thus, it is for society to shoulder its responsibility in the fight against poverty, disease, inequality and lack of freedom, by the means put at its disposal by science and technology. It is, likewise, the duty of society to shoulder the responsibility for the development of ways in which men can live together in this shrunken world, turning the dynamics of change into the stability of peace.

It is here that the Organization I have the honor to serve comes into the picture as an—admittedly still crude—instrument for the construction of relationships among groups and nations which, taking into account the underlying economic and ideological problems, may make it possible to turn the achievements of science fully to the benefit of men, and to create a climate and environment in which the individual, successfully and in freedom, can pursue his exploration of the possibilities of the future. Using the Organization for such purposes, scientists and politicians can meet, and do meet, in a common effort, inspired by the same ideals and speaking the same language.

The United Nations is only a first approximation to the world order which we need and which one day must be brought about. It is in the field of international politics something like Niels Bohr's model of the atom in the field of nuclear physics; not the final reply, not even a tentative reply which, though incomplete, is correct in its details, but a reply which, if properly understood and developed, provides an approach leading us ahead, step by step, on the long road toward a satisfactory solution.

The United Nations is part of the great pattern of change of our time. It functions as a tool in the hands of governments and peoples, and of individuals, in their effort to give to that change a constructive direction. The Organization is based on the recognition of the fundamental unity of all mankind in its interest in peace and in progress based on justice and freedom. Its basic idea is not one of an enforced unity with a deadening subordination of the nation, the group or the individual under a global pattern. The concept which it reflects is what the American scientist I have already quoted once characterized in some words about the unity of science. He said that this unity is 'far more a unity of comparable dedication than a unity of common total understanding'. He continued: 'This heartening phrase, the unity of science, often tends to evoke a wholly false picture, a picture of a few basic truths, a few critical technical methods, and ideas, from which all discoveries and understanding of science derive; a sort of central exchange, access to which will illuminate the atoms and the galaxies, the genes and the sense organs. . . . The history of science is rich in examples of the fruitfulness of bringing two sets of techniques, two sets of ideas, developed in separate contexts for the pursuit of new truth, into touch with one another. The sciences fertilize each other; they grow by contact and by common enterprise. Once again this means that the scientists may profit from learning about any other science. . . . It means that the unity is a potential unity, a unity of the things that might be brought together and might throw light one on the other. It is not global or total or hierarchical.'

These words about the unity of science are, I believe, profoundly true about all those human activities which create society and determine human relations. Especially do I know that they apply to the interests and activities which are brought together within the sphere of the United Nations. If the United Nations is to succeed in giving to the development of the world all that this experiment in organized coexistence can yield, it will be on the basis of a recognition of our fundamental unity, in the sense described in this quotation, and through the devoted efforts of men, who, like today's prize-winner, dare to be pioneers in their field of activity and who dare to risk 'a fruitful mistake' in their effort to meet the challenges of an ever widening knowledge and of ever widening—but also ever more complex—human relationships.

Our world of change is one in which only those who show this intellectual and moral courage—and who are free to exercise it—will be able to face the challenge of the future.

DO WE NEED THE UNITED NATIONS?

Address before the Students Association, Copenhagen, Denmark, 2 May 1959. This address was given a few days before the 1959 meeting of Foreign Ministers of the Western Powers and the USSR. There had been much preliminary discussion and speculation about a possible role for the United Nations in relation to the future status of Berlin. The Secretary-General used the occasion of this address to put on record his views of both the limits and possibilities for such a role, in negotiation and in the performance of executive functions. Later, in a press conference at Geneva, he described the address as 'a little "handbook" concerning United Nations practices, United Nations history and United Nations law which is handy for anybody who wants to form his own view regarding the possible role of the United Nations.'

[TRANSLATION FROM SWEDISH]

We are in the midst of a period of intense international negotiations. Every day, the press brings news about conferences among leading statesmen, correspondence between governments and meetings of various political organs such as the NATO council of ministers. It may appear as though the significant developments we are witnessing were taking place entirely outside or independently of the United Nations. One may well ask where the Organization is in this puzzle. Since it is not visible, one may wonder what role it plays in world politics. Has it been side-tracked by other organs? Have difficulties and failures broken its ability to make contributions of value? In attempting to answer these questions, it may be natural to tie the answers in with the present international discussion and some of the problems it poses.

Let me begin by making some distinctions which may help clarify the problem. The United Nations is, on the one hand, *an organ for negotiation*, and, on the other hand, an *executive organ* with practical functions. These functions can be of various kinds: military functions, police functions, diplomatic-political or administrative functions. In appraising the need for the United Nations in the present situation, it is necessary to keep apart the tasks of the Organization in connection with negotiations, and its possible executive functions along the lines I have just mentioned.

It is true, as I have already said, that so far the United Nations has not entered the picture as a forum for those international negotiations concerning Germany and the European security problem which have dominated events during the past months. But this means neither that the Organization has been without importance in the current negotiations, nor that those forms of negotiation which it offers may not play a crucial part later on.

In the United Nations, representatives meet face to face, not only from countries with a direct interest in the German question and the European security problem, but also from the many States for whom the outcome of the international deliberations may indirectly have a vital importance. Of course, something similar takes place, although in varying degrees, wherever the majority of States have diplomatic representation. There is, however, a qualitative difference between New York and these capitals. Over the years, the diplomatic representatives accredited to the United Nations have developed a cooperation and built mutual contacts in dealing with problems they have in common, which in reality make them members of a kind of continuous diplomatic conference, in which they are informally following and able to discuss, on a personal basis, all political questions which are important for the work of the Organization. These continuous informal deliberations do not lend themselves to publicity, and they receive none. But it would be a grave mistake to conclude from this that they are unimportant. On the contrary, the flexible and confidential forms in which these discussions can be pursued have given them a particular value as a complement to other diplomatic contacts and to all the various conferences and public exchanges about which we are being informed through the press and which constitute the normal operating procedures in a more traditional diplomacy.

In these circumstances, it is natural that contacts concerning the security problem and European questions have developed of late at United Nations Headquarters, too. My own experience is that, in this informal way, the Organization has become the framework for important exchanges between Member States about the questions simultaneously dealt with at foreign ministers' meetings, in the NATO council, etc. It is all the more natural that such has been the case, since it is within the realm of the possible that the United Nations will be given certain functional tasks later on or will be used as a central negotiating organ concerning some special facet of the European problems.

While the negotiations on the official level have so far predominantly been conducted among the Powers on one side or the other in the international conflict, the unofficial contacts within the United Nations have naturally not been similarly restricted. Public debate in the United Nations is dominated by the same differences among the parties as international political life as a whole. But behind closed doors these differences are diluted. The human factor carries more weight there, and confidential exchanges are possible even across frontiers which otherwise appear impassable.

One illustration of the position of the Organization is that it serves as host to the foreign ministers' meeting in Geneva about a week from now. This, of course, does not mean that the meeting takes place under the auspices of the United Nations, or that the Organization is in any way a party to the deliberations. But it does mean that it has been found that the United Nations can offer a framework within which it is natural that such discussions between the two sides take place. This is more than a purely formal relationship. It reflects the fact that, should the parties find themselves in need of the kind of assistance the Organization can render in any other respects, they can ask for such assistance and will get it. To begin with, this means only various practical arrangements, but the assistance can go further without changing the basic situation, which is that the foreign ministers' conference as such is independent of the Organization, and that the United Nations at the present stage neither has nor can have any policy position as a party to the conference.

It is easy to minimize the importance of the manner in which the United Nations enters the negotiating picture in these respects. For my part, I do not want to exaggerate, but I know that the Organization facilitates or can facilitate impending diplomatic operations of such a degree of difficulty that even the relatively modest support they can gain from the United Nations as an external framework for negotiation or as a kind of unofficial sounding-board must be highly valued.

There is no reason for me to prophesy about the future, but in this context it is worth recalling that when a meeting at the level of heads of government was discussed last year, the intention was to have it take place on the basis of, within, or in intimate connection with the Security Council. Should present plans also develop in the same direction, it would mean that the functions of the Organization which I have already mentioned would reach their full development. The Organization, in that case, would become not only the framework of an unofficial exchange or the unofficial support for formal deliberations between the governments, but the forum of the ultimate negotiations which are the aim of all the extensive diplomatic preparation.

The reasons which last year led to preliminary agreement that the meeting of heads of government should take place within the framework of the Security Council, illustrate the possible role of the Organization in such negotiations. Not only would the Security Council have provided a firm procedural foundation for the planned discussions between the heads of government; more important, it would have provided them with a clearly defined legal frame and would have eliminated elements of uncertainty concerning purposes and principles which easily might complicate deliberations in other forms, unless far more extensive preparations had been made than are required for a meeting of the Security Council.

When a meeting is formally held within the framework of the Organization—even if this occurs in circumstances which lend it a relatively independent character—it means that the United Nations Charter as a whole emerges as the background of the deliberations. It means that the negotiating parties, without their having to be openly stated, accept as guiding them those basic rules of international coexistence of which the Charter is an expression. Before this body, I need hardly recall the most important of these principles: the obligation to find a peaceful solution of emerging conflicts, the respect for the integrity and independence of each Member State, the right of collective self-defense in case of armed aggression, etc.

In characterizing the three different respects in which the Organization enters into the present picture as an organ of negotiation— or, rather, the three degrees in which it is possible to visualize the utilization of the possibilities of the Organization as an organ of negotiation—I have left aside the role in possible negotiations which would devolve upon it rather automatically, in case the conclusion should be that the cooperation of the United Nations as an executive organ is needed in some respect or other. A decision providing such cooperation can only be made by the General Assembly or the Security Council. Should there be agreement about requesting the assistance of the Organization for certain practical tasks in the field, this question would thus have to be referred to those main organs for a decision. In this situation, the United Nations would obviously become a party to the negotiation.

Chapter VII of the United Nations Charter authorizes, in certain circumstances, the Security Council to use military force to maintain peace. It is important to realize what this means. This is not collective security of a kind which a defensive alliance can provide. The Charter expressly permits the formation of such alliances, but the United Nations itself is something else again. The possibilities of the Organization to use military force are limited to acts of coercion in the name of the world community against a nation which violates the peace. Such an action requires unanimity of the Great Powers. This unanimity has a two-fold significance. Without it a military police action lacks the foundation necessary to be fully effective. And without it the United Nations would also, in contrast to the fundamental idea on which it is built, be capable of transformation into an instrument of military force in a conflict between the Great Powers—with all that this might mean for the other Member States. The rule of unanimity in combination with the right to form defensive alliances defines the position of the Organization. It has never been meant as an organ of collective security of the alliance type, but it is aimed at a universal system for the maintenance of peace which may have, as a natural complement, defensive alliances.

The circumstances in which the Organization has functioned during its first thirteen years have made so far a dead letter of the provisions in Chapter VII about recourse to military force. Instead, the executive functions of the Organization for the peaceful solution of conflicts, under Chapter VI of the Charter, have developed along a much broader front. Under this chapter, the General Assembly has even created a quasi-military organ of the United Nations when it found this necessary for that very purpose—peaceful solution—in a situation where the unanimity rule had rendered the Security Council incapable of action. As you know, this measure was taken under the so-called 'Uniting for Peace' resolution which has established procedures for the exercise by the General Assembly of certain functions when the Security Council fails. The resolution has not changed the Charter. If the General Assembly decides to create a quasi-military organ of the United Nations, it has therefore been found that such an organ, irrespective of the form of the decision, can have only tasks which are in substance compatible with the provisions of the Charter on the peaceful solution of conflicts under which the General Assembly has acted. Experience has shown that such a military organ of the United Nations, even if, like UNEF, it has no military tasks in the conventional sense, can be a decisive factor in preventing hostilities and restoring calm in a troubled area.

For the General Assembly or the Security Council to create such an organ as UNEF to represent the United Nations in helping to maintain peace is an extreme case. It turned out to be necessary and useful in the case of Gaza, but it would have been too extreme a measure for Lebanon, and it would have been out of the question in Jordan—to name two other current instances of executive operations. In Lebanon, an observation group was formed, which at its peak numbered about 500. It was recruited from the officer corps in a score of countries, but no matter how useful their military training was, the group did not even have those military functions accorded to UNEF and, of its three leaders, two were civilians. In Jordan, where many expected the United Nations to form a military organization, it was decided to station a purely civilian organization of a very limited size, which has turned out to fill the need extremely well.

The instances I have recalled—I might of course have named others—are interesting because they show how the United Nations may fill vital needs in maintaining peace by executive measures. In these respects there is at present no substitute and no alternative for the Organization. The tasks of this kind which it has assumed could not have been fulfilled outside the United Nations framework by any single country or group of countries. These are security needs in the widest sense, which can be met only on the basis of universality and neutrality in the sense of freedom from partisan interests. Whatever role may be accorded to defensive alliances and similar arrangements, experience shows that there are essential tasks in the maintenance of peace which fall, and must fall, entirely outside the province of such groupings.

In various public statements and in what has been published

about deliberations on Germany and related problems, there have been hints that, without any commitments about what should be done, the possibility of using the United Nations for functional tasks has also received attention. What has emerged has naturally been quite vague, since more concrete proposals require a far clearer picture of the political solutions which may be reached than it has been possible to obtain until the principal parties have met in common deliberations. The ideas seem to have been exclusively focused on some form of what has come to be called, in international parlance, a 'United Nations presence', a common term used to designate all the various forms of functional representation which have been tried or may come up under Chapter VI. The possibilities existing under Chapter VII have, of course, had no place in the debate.

In this connection, let me say that in my view practical considerations alone prevent even the kind of quasi-military arrangements which are possible under Chapter VI and which fall within the competence of the General Assembly, from being used except to a very limited extent, if at all. Nor do I find it reasonable to envisage civilian tasks for the United Nations that would place an ultimate constitutional responsibility on any one of the main organs of the Organization exceeding what they are equipped or ready for. This excludes the imposition in this case of executive authority on the United Nations for administrative tasks which require political decisions. The possibilities I have thus written off still leave a wide area within which the United Nations could lend assistance, should such assistance be requested by the negotiating parties.

It is interesting to discuss the role and the capabilities of the United Nations in the relatively narrow perspective you get when applying them, as we have now done, to an actual international complex of problems. But there is good reason to consider the matter in broader terms too. It is one thing to try to form an opinion about the importance of the United Nations in bringing a critical situation under control. It is another to examine the preventive capabilities of the Organization, how it may be used to forestall the emergence of conflicts requiring specific actions.

Only to a limited extent does the United Nations have an existence and possibilities of action independent of the will of the Member governments and the policy of the Member States themselves. In comparing the General Assembly to, for instance, a parliament, it must be recalled that the authorized representatives of governments in the various United Nations organs do not have a position comparable to that of an individual legislator, and that only to a small extent can they contribute to the making of a policy which goes beyond the fundamental national reactions. It may be said of a parliament that the whole is more than the sum of its parts. Although the same can be said about the United Nations in certain respects, to which I shall come presently, it applies far less to the Organization than to a parliament or related national organs.

It is therefore hardly reasonable to reproach the Organization as such for not having been able to cope with, let us say, the so-called Cold War, or for not having taken action in the Hungarian question, confining itself to an expression of principle. In the first case, it is obvious that the Organization can advance no further than the intentions of the parties permit. In the latter case, it is worth remembering that, with the exception of one or two of the smaller countries, no government in the United Nations urged measures going further than those which were actually taken.

But no matter how realistic it may be to view the relations between the Organization and the Member States in the way I have done here, and to evaluate the capacity for action of the Organization as I have now done, something essential is missing from the picture. There are other elements which require attention and point ahead to a situation with other possibilities.

I have described the United Nations as an organ which offers the framework and the foundation for negotiations. But a negotiation as such may affect the parties and their representatives. Granted that States are far less inclined than individuals and groups to be affected by the fact that negotiations are taking place and by the way they are going; still, they are affected. Therefore, it means something essential that membership in the United Nations forces all States to subject themselves to such an influence. One may agree or fail to agree to a foreign ministers' meeting on a certain question, for instance. But only with difficulty is it possible to avoid entering a reply if the same question is brought before the United Nations in the prescribed form.

The importance of this is increased by the fact that not the parties alone, but practically all the States in the world, are represented at the negotiating table in the United Nations. The parties thus have to meet both the arguments coming from the other side, and the judgments and reactions expressed by States which, even if not directly engaged, are interested. It is dangerous, and in my view highly presumptuous, to describe this situation as one in which the parties are confronted with 'world opinion' and its 'moral judgment' at the negotiating table in the United Nations. But it is true that within the Organization they are being forced to confront their stand with that taken by States for whom the principles of the Charter may weigh more heavily than direct or indirect partisan interests. I spoke before of what I called a continuous diplomatic conference without publicity, for which the Organization is a framework, side by side with the public debates. This is the respect in which that continuous contact assumes its greatest importance. The independent opinion which gives the negotiations in the United Nations their special character is formed as much outside the conference halls as inside them.

It is possible, however, to go further and say that increasingly, although in a way difficult to define, something like an independent position for the Organization as such has found expression both in words and deeds. The roots of this development are, of course, the existence of an opinion independent of partisan interests and dominated by the objectives indicated in the United Nations Charter. This opinion may be more or less articulate and more or less clear-cut but the fact that it exists forms the basis for the evolution of a stand by the Organization itself, which is relatively independent of that of the parties.

Here the office I represent enters the picture. The Secretary-General is elected by the General Assembly, but on the recommendation of the Security Council, and this recommendation requires unanimity among the five permanent Council members. The purpose of this arrangement is to ensure that the Secretary-General shall, as far as possible, be placed outside or lifted above conflicts which may split the Assembly or the Council. From another point of view, the rules of election aim at ensuring that the Secretary-General, as one of the main organs of the United Nations, shall have the opportunity of functioning as the spokesman of the Organization in its capacity as an independent opinion factor. This desire is natural and not particularly difficult to satisfy concerning administrative questions, which of course should be insulated as far as possible from all political conflicts. The problem is pointed up when the political and diplomatic responsibilities of the Secretary-General come into play.

There are two possible lines of action for the Secretary-General in the political questions falling within the competence of the Organization, two lines which have both had their advocates in the debate about the office. The Secretary-General may interpret his constitutionally objective position in such a way as to refuse to indicate a stand in emerging conflicts in order thus to preserve the neutrality of the office. He may, however, also accord himself the right to take a stand in these conflicts to the extent that such stands can be firmly based on the Charter and its principles and thus express what may be called the independent judgment of the Organization.

It goes without saying that, to the extent that the Secretary-General follows this latter course, his office assumes an importance quite different from what happens if he chooses what one might call negative neutrality as his leading principle. If the Secretary-General represents an independent but positive evaluation, free of partisan influences and determined by the purposes of the Charter, this means not only that he reinforces the weight that independent opinion may come to carry in the negotiations. Step by step, he thereby also builds up a practice which may open the door to a more generally recognized independent influence for the Organization as such in the political evolution.

The difficulty of a policy along these latter lines is obvious. A positive influence, politically, for the Secretary-General can be imagined in practice only on two conditions. First, he must have the full confidence of the Member States, at least as to his independence and his freedom from personal motives. Second, he must accept the limitation of acting mainly on inner lines without publicity. In nine cases out of ten, a Secretary-General would destroy his chances of exerting an independent influence on developments by publicly appealing to opinion over the heads of the governments. Only in rare exceptions—in the tenth case, one might say—this is what the situation requires, and then he must of course be prepared to see his future value as a negotiator endangered or even lost. In the latter case, he ought, naturally, to resign from his post.

Sometimes, it has proved difficult to gain understanding of the fact that the independent influence of the Secretary-General largely is indirectly proportionate to his degree of discretion. Cases such as the Suez and Hungary crises, when on the basis of the Charter he took a direct political stand in public, have been considered instances of what he ought to do more often. Everybody is free to judge for himself. What I have just said reflects my own experience and the conclusions I have reached.

To the extent that events have led the governments to accord an independent position as spokesman of the United Nations to the Secretary-General even politically, this has also given him wider opportunities for independent diplomatic activity. One instance during this year may be mentioned. On the basis of an invitation from two Member States, the Secretary-General recently sent a personal representative on a good offices mission to these countries.* This was a measure of a kind that used to be taken exclusively by the Security Council. In this case it was taken without a decision by the Security Council, after the Secretary-General had informed the Council of his intentions in order to give its members an opportunity to raise objections if they so desired.

This action, which may lead to the development of a new pattern —other governments have made two or three proposals of a similar nature—is an example of what I should like to call active preventive diplomacy, which may be conducted by the United Nations, through the Secretary-General or in other forms, in many situations where no government or group of governments and no regional organiza- tion would be able to act in the same way. That such interventions are possible for the United Nations is explained by the fact that in the manner I have indicated, the Organization has begun to gain a certain independent position, and that this tendency has led to the acceptance of an independent political and diplomatic activity on the part of the Secretary-General as the 'neutral' representative of the Organization.

It may have struck some of you that the possibilities I have touched upon in connection with the present international debate, and the evolution I have just dealt with as well, have little explicit support in the United Nations Charter. This is true if you apply a restrictive literal interpretation to the Charter. But it is not true if the Charter is regarded as an international treaty, establishing certain common goals for international cooperation and creating organs which the Member States may use in their cooperation towards these goals, but without aiming at limiting the development

---

* Cambodia and Thailand had broken diplomatic relations. These were restored as the result of the good offices exercised by the Secretary General's personal representative, Ambassador Johan Beck-Friis of Sweden.

of its procedures. The statement of objectives in the Charter is binding, and so are the rules concerning the various organs and their competence, but it is not necessary to regard the procedures indicated in the Charter as limitative in purpose. They may be supplemented by others under the pressure of circumstances and in the light of experience. This freer interpretation permits an evolution departing from what has been explicitly stated, to the extent that new procedures, perhaps combined with a modified balance in the use of various organs, prove productive in practice for the efforts to attain the objectives of the Charter. Seen in this perspective, the developments I have dwelt on appear entirely compatible with the Charter and well fitted into its framework. What we are seeing is an evolution on the basis of a fundamental charter of sufficient flexibility to permit a continuous adaptation of constitutional life to the needs.

At the outset, I asked the question whether the United Nations is needed. The reasons for my affirmative answer are clear from what I have said, and yet I have not touched on the role of the Organization in the economic and social fields or in the transition of peoples from colonial status to independent nationhood.

We need the Organization in the present situation for the negotiating possibilities it opens up. We need it as an executive organ. We need it for the constructive additions it offers in international attempts to resolve conflicts of interest. And we need it as a foundation and a framework for arduous and time-consuming attempts to find forms in which an extra-national—or perhaps even supra-national—influence may be brought to bear in the prevention of future conflicts.

In none of these respects do any of the other forms of international organization which have been tested offer a viable alternative. Therefore, the work must go on. To write it off because of difficulties or failures would mean, among other things, to write off our hope of developing methods for international coexistence which offer a better chance than the traditional ones for truth, justice and good sense to prevail.

ASIA, AFRICA AND THE WEST

*Address before the Academic Association of the
University of Lund, Lund, Sweden, 4 May 1959.*

[TRANSLATION FROM SWEDISH]

In one of the capitals of the Orient—one of the smallest and least accessible ones—I had a conversation recently which happened to turn on questions of religion. This happens often in that part of the world. All about us, there was a row of pagodas from different centuries, and life was strongly colored by the position of the city as a Buddhist shrine. But the representative of the country with whom I was talking said that for many Buddhism was hardly more than a thin cloak over animism. He added: 'But what is there for you as a Scandinavian to say? Think of Knut Hamsun or Selma Lagerlöf!'

The story may serve as a starting point for some thoughts about the confrontation of East and West in present-day international life, and the problems posed by this confrontation. No matter how overwhelming other world problems may appear to us because of their proximity, it is possible that the future will attach greater importance to the rebirth of Asia and Africa in the historical evolution of the present epoch, than to the questions now uppermost in the news.

The little anecdote has many illuminating points, important to an understanding of the situation. It offers an instance of how much an educated Asian may know of Western culture—far more than the Westerner generally knows about that of Asia. At the same time, the reaction is typical of the matter-of-fact way in which references to religion may be made by leaders in a part of the world, where yet, without exception, religion is a dominant political factor. Another aspect worth noting is the one apparent in the semi-ironical equating of spiritual development in East and West. Finally—even though the anecdote shows this only indirectly—conversations like this one offer striking proof of how openly a discussion can be conducted between a Westerner and today's spokesmen of Asia or Africa. We have advanced far beyond the world once mirrored by Kipling or Sven Hedin.

To understand the present situation and to see the future in the right perspective, it is useful to go back in history a bit. In doing so, the limits set for a speech like the present one, of course, force me both to generalize and to simplify the argument.

In today's perspective, the Europe of the early nineteenth century appears as a tightly closed cultural world, highly developed but essentially regional in character. Goethe's 'universality' was combined with a firm conviction of the supremacy of the European man of culture, a supremacy which erected invisible walls around his spiritual life in relation to other parts of the world.

As time went on and the military and political influence of Europe was extended further and further in Asia and Africa, this conviction of supremacy found increasingly concrete—and increasingly simple —expressions. In many cases, it came to be represented by persons whose only superiority over those they had to deal with lay in the power they had back of them. Nobody should minimize the admirable achievements frequently attained by the colonizers of the nineteenth century. But nobody should forget that colonization reflected a basic approach which may have been well founded in certain limited respects, but which often mirrored false claims, particularly when it touched on spiritual development. Applied generally, it was untenable.

One consequence of the basic approach in the unfolding events of the nineteenth century was that contact with the Asian and African peoples did not break down the closed character of Western European culture. Other peoples were approached from points of departure which made it very difficult to assimilate what they, in turn, had to offer. The ethnologist, the geographer or the religious scholar could impart his findings, but largely these remained exotic information of interest to experts alone, not integrated into the mainstream of culture. Such integration is difficult in any case. In this setting, it was made almost impossible. To make it a reality required an intellectual humility and an open-minded set of values, which came about only when European man was shaken in his self-confidence and saw the walls around his closed world crumble before the pressure of new forces which Europe itself in large part had called into being.

To a Westerner of a later generation who is facing today's Asia and Africa, it is a useful exercise to go back to the works about these areas written by distinguished Europeans whose mental attitude was shaped in the main before the first World War. What strikes one in the first place, perhaps, is how much they did *not* see and did *not* hear, and how even their most positive attempts at entering into a world of different thoughts and emotions were colored by an unthinking, self-assured superiority.

The first World War brought the world across the Atlantic into the picture in earnest. The second World War opened the door for Asia and Africa. Between the wars, Europe passed through a period in which old forms and norms were dissolved. Nineteenth century Germany existed no more. In the fields of politics and culture, the other European great Powers underwent parallel changes. The whole closed European cultural circle was broken up in reappraisal of all values.

Many of us have had contact with the European world of the fading nineteenth century—the typical attitudes of which have, of course, reached far into our own—and then experienced the breakdown of the European circle of culture, spiritually, politically and geographically, finally seeing at least the beginning of a new synthesis on a universal basis. Depending on temperament and background, reactions to this evolution may vary. One may reach back for the imagined calm of the closed world. One may find one's spiritual home in the very disintegration and its drama. Or, one may reach ahead towards the glimpse of the synthesis, inspired by the dream of a new culture in which there is achieved, on a level encompassing the whole world, what once seemed to have become a regional reality in Europe.

He who chooses the latter course will be disappointed, if he believes the task to be easy or the goal close. But he can count on the richest satisfaction in meeting different spiritual traditions and their representatives, if he approaches them on an equal footing and with a common future goal in mind. He will also find rich satisfaction in the progress he will note in the direction of a human community which, while retaining the special character of individuals and groups, has made use of what the various branches of the family of man have attained along different paths over thousands of years.

I have tried to outline the evolution from a West European point of view. The form of my statements, however, has naturally been colored by such experiences as that illustrated by the opening anecdote. Let me return to that story for a moment.

The man I was talking to was deeply conscious of the unsatisfactory economic and social conditions in the country he represented.

He was also aware that its spiritual life might appear primitive, measured against the severe yardstick offered by Buddhism in its pure forms. But he did not apply such a yardstick. He saw and respected the view of life held by the people. He did not find it basically inferior to views of life which he had encountered in prominent representatives of European culture. And he certainly did not see it as any reason whatever for his own people to remain in the economic and social state which prevailed in the country even after many decades of Western colonial rule—with the progress these were said to have meant. What he asked for his people and his country was cooperation with others, based on solidarity and mutual respect, without any false distinctions between cultures or races, with gratitude for what Europe had done, but also with a critical eye towards all unfounded claims.

What I have now said about the meaning of the words I quoted is not based on any direct statements made at the time. Explanations were unnecessary. The interpretation of the answer is my own, but it has a firm basis in what I have learned through years of intimate contact with representatives of the Asian and African peoples.

I used the word solidarity. It is a key word in this connection and to me it is the answer to the irritable questions and reactions which are still sometimes forthcoming from those who have entrenched themselves in the past and view almost as a traitor any European who does not weep over the receding power of Europe.

The health and strength of a community depend on every citizen's feeling of solidarity with the other citizens, and on his willingness, in the name of this solidarity, to shoulder his part of the burdens and responsibilities of the community. The same is of course true of humanity as a whole. And just as it cannot be argued that within a community an economic upper class holds its favored position by virtue of greater ability, as a quality which is, as it were, vested in the group by nature, so it is, of course, impossible to maintain this in regard to nations in their mutual relationships.

I believe that no anthropologist nowadays would say that the various branches of the family of man represent fundamentally different potentialities for contributions and development in various fields of intellectual and material activity. If I may speak on the basis of my own experience, which in one way is of course limited, but in another very extensive, I would say that for my part I have not been able to discover any such differences.

We thus live in a world where, no more internationally than nationally, can any distinct group claim superiority in mental gifts and potentialities of development. What may in practice seem to point in another direction is explained by the vast differences which have prevailed in opportunity to bring the gifts to fruition and expression. Those democratic ideals which demand equal opportunities for all should be applied also to peoples and races.

In these circumstances, it appears evident that no nation or group of nations can base its future on a claim of supremacy. It is in its own interest that the other groups have opportunities equal to those it has had itself. To contribute to this is an act of solidarity which is not only good for the whole but, in the long run, redounds to the advantage even of those who take the action. It means that leadership is substituted for power—leadership both in giving other peoples their chance and in assisting them, without issuing commands, to find the best way to develop their spiritual and material resources.

On a modest level and to an all-too-small extent, the Organization I represent is working in the direction I have indicated. It is based on a philosophy of solidarity. It attempts to convey to the less favoured nations, in the first place, knowledge, but also material resources which will give them the chance for a development and position corresponding to their potentialities. It tries to find forms in which the ancient nations which are now gaining or have gained their freedom, may find their new place without frictions. It accords them all an equal voice in the councils, independent of race, history and physical or economic power. The latter respect is one in which, in particular, one encounters a skepticism similar in nature to that which once formed an obstacle to universal suffrage. One may be conscious of the hazards of such an experiment and yet be convinced that it is necessary and has to be carried out. In this case, the experiment must succeed. To achieve this, those who work for the new synthesis must not deny or question the principles on which it must be based.

To an increasing extent, experts from the West have gone out to the new nations in Asia and Africa to help the governments in different posts. In this, they have embarked on a career entirely in the spirit of the age, and one which belongs to the future. I hope that from Sweden, and indeed from this university, men and women will go out into the world in the various forms which are

available, not as some kind of missionaries either for the West or
for a world community, but in order to serve, by practical work, the
evolution towards the synthesis which is on the way.

They can do it, aware of the riches of the cultural heritage which
is theirs and of all that Europe stands for, but they should do it in
awareness, also, that the best and soundest way to perpetuate this
cultural heritage is to meet other peoples and other cultures in
humble respect for the unique gifts that they, in turn, have offered
and still offer to humanity.

They should realize that it is a sign of the highest culture to be
really capable of listening, learning and therefore also responding
in a way which helps the less favored ones; while it is a privilege
reserved for the half-educated who is unaware of his limitations to
be a poor listener in a feeling of his own false superiority. Leadership—the word I have used to designate what may come instead of
superior power—is a dangerous word if one does not keep in mind
that the most influential leaders in the European cultural evolution
were askers of questions like Socrates or the carpenter's son from
Nazareth.

Much has to be overcome by a Westerner choosing the road I
have here spoken of, not only within himself but also within those
he is serving. I believe what I have said to be enough concerning
those problems of his own he has to solve in facing the East in
international cooperation. A few words more may be in order
concerning the difficulties the Asian or African encounters in the
same confrontation.

On the simplest level he comes up against the difficulties unavoidable when poverty and relative opulence are confronted with each
other. A needy person who knows that assistance is given in a spirit
of solidarity, and knows that he can put it to such use that he will
one day be able to repay it even in kind, may still find difficulty in
avoiding a feeling of dependence and a distrust of the motives and
attitudes of the helper. The same man I quoted before also said: 'I
suppose you realize that it may be more difficult to receive assistance
than to give it?' This situation becomes doubly serious if those in
need of help take justifiable pride in what their own nation has
achieved but have a feeling, only too often well-founded, that its
value is not realized by the other party.

A related difficulty is created by the differences in the scales of
values. In the eyes of the East—and perhaps in actual reality—the

overwhelming technical progress which is the mark of the West has marked us more than we ourselves realize. The Asian admires the material achievements of the West, he knows what they may mean for the improvement of living conditions in his own world, and he is anxious to make use of their results. But he is not willing to pay for the improvement by changing his way of life in a manner which may seem to him an unavoidable concomitant of technical progress, but incompatible with the spirit and traditions of his own people.

Poverty is relative. When life has been made safe and elementary needs filled, people are hardly made happier by being exposed to influences creating needs which fundamentally are foreign to them and tend to grow more rapidly than new means of satisfying the needs can be created. This is no argument for the contentedness of the poor as it was worshipped in the Victorian fairy-tale world. Nor is it a question of the poverty which is borne with equanimity because it is shared by all. What we must remember in this connection is that strong and living spiritual traditions in the Afro-Asian world still make for an approach to life and its blessings which vouchsafes happiness on a level where we would speak of misery. The obligation of all of us, and of the international community, to give economic security and raise the living standards for those two-thirds of humanity who live close to the level of starvation or below it, is inescapable. But the representative, for instance, of the Buddhist world is more conscious than we are of how true it is, even in the most elemental context of everyday life, that man lives not by bread alone.

Finally, there are difficulties explained by the fact that we are still very close to the epoch when the West lived happily in its feeling of superiority, thus innocently creating a corresponding uncertainty in minds and hearts of representatives of other cultural regions. For an Asian or an African, it may be difficult to enjoy the spiritual heritage of the West without a sense of cleavage which may be pushed all the way to rootlessness, or without an uneasiness as though in the face of treason, while the Westerner, from his point of view, may widen his cultural range and absorb other traditions without corresponding tensions. Here we meet what may be the most serious of the obstacles to be surmounted. Can we solve the problem without, as it were, *growing* out of it, the way we do when the same kind of difficulties occur in our personal lives? Here, the greater responsibility rests on him who believes he is the stronger.

I once knew a man from Asia of the highest culture. Educated at European universities during and after the first World War, he was at the Great Divide in the evolution I have spoken of. He once told me how, in his early youth, he lived with and loved *The Rubáiyát of Omar Khayyám*. He thought he had made the original text entirely his own, until he came to Britain and became acquainted with Fitzgerald's translation. Then, this in turn became—in the academic surroundings that began to transform him—his 'real' *Rubáiyát*. He returned home, however, and again found Omar Khayyám's poems such as he had once made them his own. The pendulum kept swinging, and, he concluded, 'even today I do not know which *Rubáiyát* is mine, Omar's or Fitzgerald's.'

The story needs no comment. Figuratively, there are still millions upon millions who do not know which *Rubáiyát* is theirs, Omar's or Fitzgerald's. We must reach the day when they, and all of us, can enjoy in common the *Rubáiyát* and the fact that we have it both in Omar's and in Fitzgerald's version.

FROM THE INTRODUCTION
TO THE ANNUAL REPORT 1958-1959

22 August 1959

THE ROLE OF THE UNITED NATIONS

The past year has been characterized by intense diplomatic activities mainly outside the United Nations although in some cases within its precincts or in informal contact with the Organization.

The discussions among representatives of three nuclear Powers on a controlled cessation of tests, which were started at Geneva in the course of the summer of 1958, have continued through the year. Negotiations were also conducted in Geneva during the spring and summer of 1959 by four of the permanent members of the Security Council regarding the Berlin question and related wider problems. In both cases, the United Nations has served as a host for the conferences and provided them with extensive practical assistance.

Important discussions, of relevance from a United Nations point of view, have been conducted among members on a regional basis also, as for example, within the Organization of American States, the Arab League and groups of African and Asian States.

Finally, there has been in recent months an increasing number of exchanges of visits of leading statesmen for purposes of personal contact and discussion on current political issues. These will now be continued by visits of the Chairman of the Council of Ministers of the Union of Soviet Socialist Republics to the United States of America and of the President of the United States to the USSR.

This intense diplomatic and political activity has a dual significance. On the one hand, it indicates that various international problems have been brought to a point where they call for renewed and urgent efforts to find a solution. On the other hand, the broadening and deepening of personal contacts on different levels, to which this situation has given rise, has introduced a new constructive element which may strengthen the hope that ways to reconciliation and to a reduction of tensions may be found.

In both respects, these are the virtually unanimous evaluations voiced by governments, and they are naturally also those of the United Nations. However, from the point of view of the United

Nations, the development requires also special consideration for the light it may throw on its role and on the way in which the Organization should serve its purposes.

The Charter is quite clear about such diplomatic efforts. It states in Article 33 that 'the parties to any dispute, the continuance of which is likely to endanger the maintenance of international peace and security, shall, first of all, seek a solution by negotiation, enquiry, mediation, conciliation, arbitration, judicial settlement, resort to regional agencies or arrangements, or other peaceful means of their own choice'.

Further, it states in Article 36, regarding the Security Council, that the Council should take into consideration any procedures for the settlement of a dispute which have already been adopted by the parties. This rule has been understood to have reference especially to efforts on a regional basis or through regional organizations like the Organization of American States.

Thus, while the Charter establishes for its main organs the primary responsibility for the achievement of the purposes of the Organization, and gives access to its procedures to any State which appeals for its assistance for these purposes, the United Nations is not intended to be a substitute for normal procedures of reconciliation and mediation but rather an added instrument providing, within the limits of its competence, a further or ultimate support for the maintenance of peace and security. Viewed in this light, the various diplomatic and political activities in the course of the past year are in full harmony with the intentions expressed in the Charter. They may even be said to reflect obligations which Member nations have assumed in the Charter. Also, irrespective of this formal aspect of the matter, those who support the work of the Organization must welcome all such serious efforts to further the purposes for which it was set up, whatever the specific form such efforts may take.

Nevertheless, recent diplomatic developments call for attention insofar as they might reflect a situation which in other respects should be of concern to the governments which cooperate in the Organization and are interested in developing it to its full capacity. This would be the case if the extended use of diplomatic negotiations and political contacts outside the Organization reflected a neglect of the possibilities which the Organization offers, because of a lapse into bilateralism, disregarding legitimate third-party interests. Likewise, the situation would be a reason for concern if it reflected a view that the Organization is not able to meet the demands which Member nations are entitled to put on it.

There is no reason to give to the developments which have taken place an interpretation along either of the lines to which I have just referred. These developments are not only in keeping with the principles of the Charter but are also free, I believe, from implications which impair the position of the Organization in principle. They do, however, give a natural reason for a renewed consideration of the ways in which the United Nations functions and fulfils its purposes, if only because they remind us of the need continuously to test the Organization and its value in the light of current requirements so as to ensure that it is always in a position to meet situations as they arise, through the means for diplomatic action which it provides, as effectively as the political realities of the moment may permit. It is for each Member government, as well as for those who individually serve the Organization, always to keep this need in mind. This is so, not only for immediate practical reasons, but also—and perhaps even more so—with a view to the future. The work of today within and for the United Nations is a work through which the basis may be laid for increasingly satisfactory forms of international cooperation and for a future international system of law and order, for which the world is not yet ripe.

It has so often been said that the world of today is one which requires organized international cooperation on a basis of universality that one repeats it with hesitation. However, there are reasons to do so. It still seems sometimes to be forgotten that—whatever views may be held about the United Nations as an institution—the principle of organized international cooperation on a basis of universality which is at present reflected in this Organization is one which has emerged from bitter experiences and should be now considered as firmly established. No international policy for the future can be envisaged which does not recognize this principle and is not willing to give it adequate implementation in practice.

The United Nations is the means to an end, not an end in itself. While the principle of cooperation on a basis of universality is now a definite part of international politics aiming at peace and security, this does not necessarily apply to the Organization as the practical instrument for such a policy, and especially not to its specific working methods. Were it to be felt that the Organization with its present procedures failed to provide the best means by which this basic principle could now be implemented, we would be facing a situation where the choice would be one between revolution and evolution. We should have to choose between the creation of a new international organization, based on the principle of universality like the United Nations although different in other respects, and an evolution of procedures of the present Organization which would make it a more adequate instrument for implementation of the principle.

Certainly, nobody would feel that there are reasons for even a hypothetical consideration of the first alternative. In fact, were unforeseeable developments to threaten the Organization with disintegration, there would undoubtedly be a rallying of Members in its support which would carry it on fundamentally as at present conceived. Therefore, the only practical question is, whether an evolution of procedures should be envisaged in order to adapt the United Nations more adequately to the needs as experienced and, if so, what the development should be.

This leads, in turn, to two questions. What, in *constitutional* terms, is the degree of adaptability of the procedures of the Organization; and what, in *practical* terms, are their capacity for adaptation and the directions in which such adaptations might be indicated?

As regards the first question, it should be noted that the Charter as an international treaty establishes certain common goals for international cooperation and creates certain organs which the Member States may use in their cooperation towards these goals. The statement of objectives in the Charter is binding and so are the rules concerning the various organs and their competence, but it is not necessary to regard the working methods indicated in the Charter as limitative in purpose. Thus, they may be supplemented by others under the pressure of circumstances and in the light of experience if these additional procedures are not in conflict with what is prescribed. As is well known, such an evolution has in fact taken place, and it has thus been recognized that such new procedures may be developed when they prove productive in practice for efforts towards the objectives of the Charter. In this respect, the United Nations, as a living organism, has the necessary scope for a continuous adaptation of its constitutional life to the needs. How fully the opportunities thus offered have been utilized so far and how they might usefully be explored further are questions which need more study and evaluation before a complete reply can be given.

Such studies must, in the first place, be undertaken by the Member governments themselves in support of, and in the course of, deliberations in the various organs of the United Nations. The subject is very wide and it is possible here to make only a few observations.

A development of special significance is the establishment of permanent delegations at United Nations Headquarters with standing senior representation there for all Members of the Organization. While in one sense reducing the practical importance of the public sessions of the various organs, this development has, basically, tended to give these organs greater real weight in present-day diplomacy. The public debate, and the decisions reached, gain added significance when the attitudes presented in public result from practically uninterrupted informal contacts and negotiations. Thus, it does not belittle the importance of the formal proceedings in the General Assembly, the Councils and other United Nations organs if it is understood that, to an increasing extent, their role has come to provide for a public confrontation of views which have developed in negotiations under other forms, and for the registration of a resulting consensus, or, when this has not been achieved, of a difference of opinion, with the relative support apparent from the votes.

The importance this evolution has given to the experienced work of the permanent delegations is obvious. They are today to a decisive extent pioneers in the development of international cooperation within the United Nations, giving to the work of the major organs a perspective which is not less valuable for being less publicized. The permanent representation at Headquarters of all Member nations, and the growing diplomatic contribution of the permanent delegations outside the public meetings—often in close contact with the Secretariat—may well come to be regarded as the most important 'common law' development which has taken place so far within the constitutional framework of the Charter. It is to be hoped that it will continue and increase in strength.

The observations just made have a bearing on the evaluation of the work of the principal United Nations organs and on the way their work may be furthered.

In a previous annual report I made some comments on the significance of voting in the United Nations. There is no reason to repeat here what was said then beyond observing that later experiences have confirmed the view then expressed that, whatever legal standing the Charter may provide for the results of the votes, the significance of these results requires further analysis before a political evaluation is possible. This observation applies to the composition of majorities and minorities as well as to the substance of resolutions. These resolutions often reflect only part of what has, in fact, emerged from the deliberations and what, therefore, is likely to remain as an active element in future developments. In these circumstances, it is natural for those who are not close to the United Nations sometimes to underestimate the results of the work of the General Assembly and other organs, and equally to over-estimate the significance of a formal voting victory or a voting defeat.

Well known factors have in recent years tended to reduce the public role of the Security Council. However, what has been said above applies with equal force to the Council. Constant talks and negotiations among, and with, members of the Security Council have given the Council a continuing life and importance and enabled it to exert its influence during the intervals when it does not meet in public. It may be asked if the time is not now ripe to give formal expression to this fact by the organization of regular meetings of the Council in executive session. Such meetings would not as a rule be devoted to particular issues brought to its attention, but to any aspect of the international situation which may prove of concern to the Council because of its responsibilities under the Charter. Sufficient experience seems now to have been gained in the Council of the value of the kind of deliberation for which such meetings might give an opportunity to warrant that the suggestion be given serious consideration by Member nations.

For several practical reasons it is difficult at regular meetings of the Economic and Social Council, without special arrangements, to organize the work in such a way as to render possible a searching examination and discussion of key issues of decisive general importance at a policy-making level. At the summer session of the Economic and Social Council this year, I suggested that the Council consider a development of its procedures to meet this need. I believe that short special meetings at the ministerial level, within or under the aegis of the Economic and Social Council, might make an invaluable contribution to the formulation of international economic policies adequate to vital requirements for concerted action. Were the suggestion to meet with the sympathy of Member

15

governments and appeal to the Council, the Secretariat would, in consultation with Member governments, devote further study to the question and in due time present concrete proposals to the Council. It is my opinion that, in this or in such other ways as might be considered preferable, efforts should now be made to add to the usefulness of the Economic and Social Council and to give to the United Nations, through this Council, better possibilities of playing a role of the same significance in the economic field as the one which is entrusted to it in the political sphere.

In considering the evolution of procedures of the principal United Nations organs, attention may also be given to the developing functions of the Secretariat. There have been, in the first place, various decisions taken in recent years by the General Assembly or the Security Council under which the Secretary-General has been entrusted with special diplomatic and operational functions, which he is responsible for carrying out within the wide framework of general terms of reference laid down in the resolutions and, naturally, in the Charter itself. This, also, represents an evolution of the procedures of the United Nations for which no explicit basis is to be found in the Charter—although it may be said to fall within the scope of the intentions reflected in Article 99*—and to which neither the League of Nations, nor the United Nations during its earlier years, presented a significant counterpart. These decisions should not, of course, be considered as setting precedents changing the constitutional balance among the various organs of the United Nations. However, they have pointed to the possibility of developing new methods of approach of great practical significance, which, after the thorough testing needed, may become part of a common law of organized international cooperation.

It should also be noted that in some recent cases of international conflict or other difficulties involving Member States the Secretary-General has dispatched personal representatives with the task of assisting the governments in their efforts. This may be regarded as a further development of actions of a 'good offices' nature, with

---

* Under Article 99 'The Secretary-General may bring to the attention of the Security Council any matter which in his opinion may threaten the maintenance of international peace and security.' In his statements at the time of the 1956 Suez and Hungarian crises Dag Hammarsjköld informed the Security Council that he would have invoked Article 99 if the United States had not acted first to bring the issues before the Council (pages 123 et seq.). Article 99 was first formally invoked in the Congo crisis in 1960. For further discussion of this Article see especially his lecture at Oxford (pages 335 et seq.).

which the Secretary-General is now frequently charged. The steps to which I refer here have been taken with the consent or at the invitation of governments concerned, but without formal decisions of other organs of the United Nations. Such actions by the Secretary-General fall within the competence of his office and are, in my view, in other respects also in strict accordance with the Charter, when they serve its purpose. As a matter of course, the members of the appropriate organ of the United Nations have been informed about the action planned by the Secretary-General and were given an opportunity to express views on it. These cases also should not be considered as setting precedents, especially as it always remains open to the appropriate organs to request that such an action, before being taken by the Secretary-General, be submitted to them for formal decision. However, in these cases too, what has been tried may provide experiences on which, later, stable and agreed practices may usefully be developed.

The main significance of the evolution of the office of the Secretary-General in the manner referred to above lies in the fact that it has provided means for smooth and fast action, which might otherwise not have been open to the Organization. This is of special value in situations in which prior public debate on a proposed course of action might increase the difficulties that such an action would encounter, or in which a vacuum might be feared because Members may prove hesitant, without fuller knowledge of the facts or for other reasons, to give explicit prior support in detail to an action which, however, they approve in general terms or are willing should be tried without formal commitment.

It goes without saying that none of the developments to which I have referred has changed the basic character of the office of the Secretary-General, or its place in the Organization in relation to the General Assembly, the Security Council or other main organs. They represent, from a constitutional viewpoint, an intensification and a broadening of the interplay between these main organs and the Secretariat for purposes for which these organs maintain their primary responsibility. Thus, the wider functions which in specific cases have been exercised by the Secretary-General fully maintain the character of the United Nations as an organization whose activities are wholly dependent on decisions of the governments. On the other hand, the development reflects an incipient growth of possibilities for the Organization to operate in specific cases within a latitude of independence in practice given to it by its Member governments for such cases.

I cannot leave this general subject without, finally, again drawing the attention of the General Assembly to the position of the International Court of Justice, which offers opportunities for constructive progress that, in my view, have been seriously neglected. I have on previous occasions noted with regret the failure of many Member States to accept the compulsory jurisdiction of the International Court of Justice or to resort to the Court for the judicial determination of legal questions. This situation continues to be a cause for concern. The development and acceptance of international law impartially administered by judicial tribunals is essential to progress towards a more just and peaceful international order. It should also be recognized that there are many international disputes which involve legal questions along with the political elements and that submission of such questions to the Court for judicial determination would clear the ground for processes of peaceful negotiation in the political organs of the United Nations. Neglect of the legal elements in international conflicts, and of the means by which they may be clarified, thus stands in the way of progress in the political field and, in the long run, may tend to weaken the weight of law in international affairs. . . .

DIPLOMACY AND THE PRESS

From transcript of extemporaneous remarks at UN Correspondents Association Luncheon, 10 September 1959.

. . . . Diplomacy, basically, is something rather undramatic. Events are not produced daily. Major changes are not common occurences. Major achievements are often very difficult to display to the public. All these things present you with a problem, and us with a problem: you with the problem that people want to know and are entitled to know, but also with the problem that people want to get what they want to know in a form which strikes them and, if possible, produced in the sense of something which is interesting and easily understood. To translate diplomacy into that kind of language, into the language of the daily press and the headlines of the daily press, is not only a very difficult job, it is also a highly responsible job because, as we know, finally, public opinion is one of the decisive factors in the modern world—perhaps the most decisive factor in the creation of policies, international policies in particular.

For that reason, caught between the undramatic character of diplomacy and diplomatic developments and the need for, so to speak, daily drama from the point of view of news, I can easily see what kind of difficulties you must sometimes have. I would be overjoyed if I could give you, daily, good news for the headlines. I would not be overjoyed to be able to give you, daily, bad news. I may perhaps have a certain inclination, in view of the fact that bad news is likely to have greater interest than good news, to underplay the bad news at the expense of the good. I think subconsciously, we might have that tendency, all of us, when we approach developments in which, after all, we do not want to stir up feelings prematurely or unjustly and where we want, on the other hand, to create an atmosphere as profitable as possible for constructive work for those in responsible positions in the various nations.

However, I think that we all can recognize that the outcome, in some cases, of this effort to strike a delicate balance between news and undramatic diplomacy in the stories we have to tell, is sometimes one where, certainly without any intention at all, something comes about which comes close to what I, in a personal phrase of my own, have come to call 'diplomatic back-seat driving'; and I think that the phrase expresses my whole idea. We have all had the pleasure of having back-seat drivers, and we all know for that reason what the feelings may be of those who are at the wheel. That does not mean that those in the back seat may not be very wise, may not have the right to claim the fullest understanding of the one at the wheel; but one should realize that, in diplomacy and in politics, the one in the back seat sees less of the road than the one at the wheel. I mention this because it has, over the years, developed into a problem of my life.

I have underscored to you my strong understanding of the problem which you are facing and I must pay tribute to the exceedingly responsible way in which the members of this corps at the United Nations play their game and strike their balance. But after that I should like to mention my problem. My problem is that in this or that operation where there is this or that kind of chance to assist, after a big build-up in public—necessarily under the pressure of need and requests for guesses, anticipations, etc.—again and again one has to face situations which render the work a great deal more difficult—and sometimes impossible. Impossible in a very serious sense because the best effort in the direction of peace is frustrated, when you meet and have to face an atmosphere where people simply believe that the movement is in the opposite direction. . . .

ON AFRICA

INTERNATIONAL COOPERATION IN AFRICA

I

From transcript of extemporaneous remarks at inauguration of the Congress for International Cooperation in Africa at the University Institute of Somalia, Mogadiscio, 14 January 1960.

....This year saw, on the 1st of January, the creation of the new Republic of the Cameroons. It is the first Trust Territory to become independent. It will soon be followed by the Republic of Togo, and soon indeed, gentlemen, by the Republic of Somalia*. That is a date we are all looking forward to; together with the other events, it marks this year indeed, as it has been said, as a Year of Africa, and we know that, beyond these Trust Territories which will reach independence and membership in the United Nations in 1960, there will be other African nations coming to and joining the family of nations and its organizations. By the end of this year I think that the group of African nations will be one of the strongest continental groups in the United Nations and in the family of nations. Thus it is timely to give thought to the question of international cooperation in Africa.

I have had the privilege of visiting many, many countries and territories in Africa starting in the far west and reaching on this long Odyssey, at present, Mogadiscio and Somalia. I have had the privilege to meet the present generation of leaders, of, let me say so, *remarkable* leaders of this continent. I have had the privilege to visit the universities of Ghana, Lovanium and Makerere, three great institutions of learning which may serve as nucleus organizations in the vast work of education and studies which is going on and which is so vital for the future of this continent and indeed for all of us. Now, I come here.

Trying to look backwards over the experiences of the last few weeks, I would say that there are a couple of things which have

---

* Formerly Italian Somaliland, first a colony, then a Trust Territory and, upon reaching independence, joined with the former British colony of Somaliland.

struck me with special vigor. One is the vitality, the vitality of the present generation and the present leaders of the African world. It is a somewhat superficial and sometimes misused expression to talk about an African renaissance, but I think that the word can be taken in a much deeper sense and here, in a setting where thoughts naturally go to Italy or the Renaissance, I think it is right to recall things which this time and that time have in common.

It is not only the vitality, it is not only width of perspective, it is also the emerging strong sense of the dignity of man, of the dignity of the individual and of his rights. There are many features in the present situation in Africa and among its leaders, and among its young people, which unavoidably lead our thoughts to great men of that time in Italy and in Europe. That time was also the time of a new resurgence of learning; and, going around Africa and meeting these people, I would say that one of the things which have struck me most is the deep sense of responsibility for a widened and intensified education as a basis for the present phase in the development of Africa.

It is an enormous task which is facing our African friends. It is an enormous task by way of administration where fairly few hands have to do the job, and at the same time they have to foster and guide those who will help them and will succeed them and will build up that strong organization we wish to see all over the continent. In doing so—in devoting themselves to that great and sacred task of building these nations from within and making them strong through the constructive approach to education which we see as one of their main aims—in doing so they will face an interesting and two-fold problem which, alas, I am not sure that the European Renaissance solved in the right spirit. The ideas were there, but the solutions were not always the happiest. The two problems they will have to solve is to create an international world, a world of universality and unity, and on the other hand to save not only what I would like to call the personality of Africa, but the personality of each country, each group, in this wonderfully rich continent.

I think it is possible; I think it is possible because also, my African friends, you can learn from mistakes in other parts of the world, in other phases of history. I think that you will see that what is needed is unity with diversity, diversity respected within the framework of an even deeper respect for unity. You *can* create, and I know you *will* create, the African personality as part of the picture

of mankind today. But I know that, in doing so, you will preserve
all the richness you have inherited; each group, each people within
this continent. That means, however, that you will have to face the
great practical task of finding the proper forms of cooperation,
administratively, politically, economically and in the field of education. For that reason, anything that can be done in order to explore
how that should best be accomplished is now an essential contribution to the future of this continent. . . .

II

*Extract from statement at the second session of the
UN Economic Commission for Africa, Tangier,
Morocco, 26 January 1960.*

. . . . There is one aspect of independence in Africa to which I
referred last year and to which I feel compelled again to draw the
attention of this Commission. The process of emancipation does
not always permit the creation of states with a geographic con-
figuration most conducive to rational economic development. This
is not the first example of such a phenomenon in human history.
It should, however, be one of the determining factors in the definition of the role and orientation of this Commission. The sharing of
experiences, the discussion of common problems on the basis of
comparative studies and the initiation of technical cooperation—all
those are within easy reach of the Commission and will, no doubt,
occupy a great deal of its time and energy. They follow established
patterns and can rapidly be organized without creating difficulties
for governments. But they will not solve the problems to which I
have referred. It seems to me that this economic commission will
not fully realize the hopes placed upon it a year ago if it does not
boldly enter the field of direct economic cooperation through the
harmonization of policies, through the expansion of regional trade,
through concerted action in transports and basic investments. I do
not say that many opportunities for such types of action are immediately at hand, but rather that work should be initiated early with
this type of action in mind, and that such opportunities as already
exist and can be readily identified should be fully exploited. This
may for some countries represent something of a sacrifice, or at

least an additional effort; for others, it may mean the forming of a new habit; but it is clear that advancement will be much more difficult if each country must proceed on its own and only with whatever direct help it can get from outside this continent.

We must recognize the fact, inevitable under historic circumstances, that very often political borders will cut across natural economic regions in a manner which will make useful development schemes impossible without concerted action among contiguous areas. Coming from a cross-continental tour, it is perhaps not unnatural that I should mention the overriding importance of a national network of inland transport and communications and of international rivers without which the economic potentialities of Africa cannot be realized. Perhaps also, in this context, may I be permitted to single out, as a pointer in the right direction, the agreement recently signed between the United Arab Republic and the Sudan for the further development of the Nile, beneficial to both countries.

Contemporary experiences in other parts of the world clearly demonstrate that economic cooperation, and even association of an intimate type, is possible without political integration or federation, and need not be predicated upon the possibilities of such developments.

It would be wrong to postpone action until conditions are quite appropriate, until the time can be considered quite ripe, before Africa begins to establish the close links, the tight weaving of economic and other relationships among its own countries which is one of the conditions to its future development, probably no less important than is the inflow of help from outside the continent. . . .

AFRICAN IMPRESSIONS

From press conference transcript, 4 February 1960

THE SECRETARY-GENERAL: Ladies and gentlemen, it has been quite a time now that we have not met and the reason, as you know, is a rather long journey in Africa. I guess that you would expect me first of all, to say a few words about that trip. . . .

Africa today is in one sense a unity. There are some well-known and very deep currents which sweep across the whole continent through all its countries. It is reflected in very different ways indeed in various parts of the continent, but you can never understand the way in which it is reflected at one point without knowing how it is reflected at other points, and you can never evaluate the totality of this remarkable movement without having, so to say, seen it in its various and different facets.

For that reason the period during which I have been away has been one of very intense work with very little glamour and very rich experiences which I am sure I can put to the benefit of the operation of the United Nations and, in particular, to the benefit of those old Members or new Members which we have on the continent. . . . The general trend on the African continent is something which most recently was summed up by Mr. Macmillan when he characterized as his main impression the strength of the awakening of national consciousness on the continent.

. . . That is not news, but, just as for Mr. Macmillan it was for me a rather extraordinary experience to see how this awakening, how this new national consciousness was reflected in individuals and by political leaders in their thinking, in their reactions, in their perspective of the future and, not least, in their philosophy regarding the United Nations.

I emphasize again, and for good reasons, the element of personal contact, of personal experience. You can talk endlessly in general terms about Africa, Africans or African leaders, and you do not say a thing which is not, so to say, just banalities, but you can experience the same things in their concrete incarnation, so to say, in this or that man, in this or that people, and it takes on another dimension and presents you both with problems, perhaps with some feeling of concern and also, I must add, with an enormous sense of encouragement.

I said when I arrived at Idlewild that I was less prone than ever to generalize because another predominant impression was the infinite variety of problems in Africa. The first impression, as I said, referring to Mr. Macmillan, is, of course, the one of the common urge, the common awakening. The second one is how varied the forms this psychological and political reaction takes in various parts. This is natural because historically, economically, ethnically and sociologically, indeed in all usual respects of significance for the evaluation of the situation in a country, the various parts of Africa have had very, very different fates in the past, and for that reason they approach the present phase on very different assumptions. There are also, in the very differences and the varying problems, common elements which should be emphasized here. There is the problem of personnel. There is the problem of money. There is the problem of education and there is the problem of, let us say, moral support in the reshaping or the shaping of a nation.

I said there is the question of people. There are extremely able people all around the continent in all the various countries, but they are few. The period of growth, of education and of political formation in Africa has been a very short one—we need not go into the reasons why—and in such a short period, and with efforts on a fairly limited scale in most cases, it is quite natural that there has not emerged the kind of social grouping, the kind of social classes, from which you can recruit a broad administration and a broad political leadership. The countries will have to live with few people, and quality will have to make up for numbers and quantity. But there is a limit to what any man can do, and for that reason, if we are not to overburden these people, if we are not to put them before an impossible task, they must get assistance in human terms, they must get people, experts, technicians and—why not?—officials to the extent that they want, temporarily and transitionally, to employ foreigners.

We have as you know, in technical assistance and the so-called OPEX* scheme, certain possibilities to do so, but, alas, how modest—I would even say how ridiculously modest—in relation to the needs.

I further said that there is a question of money. In most of these countries some striking investments have been made, and some good development schemes are under way, but it is quite common to note that we lack what I would call the economic infrastructure for a national life as a political unit.

To such an infrastructure belongs a network of communications, the necessary school buildings, some few basic industries—I need not prolong the list. You know it well from various experiences and perhaps most recently from the picture we have given you of the situation of Laos, which is a typical case where the first efforts must be to create what I call here the economic infrastructure of the political life of a nation.

---

* Operational and Executive Personnel Program. See 'An International Administrative Service', page 114.

I also mentioned education, and education naturally is a key point in the whole situation. It is, if you please, part of the infrastructure but a part of such significance that it has to be mentioned specifically. Education is not only broad education at the bottom; it is not school teaching and book learning. It is civic education. It is the method by which you bring people not only to national awareness but to the point where they form as free individuals their judgment on political issues. Education is also the method through which you get the doctors, the engineers, the administrators and, to some extent, of course, also the political leaders, although I do not believe that there, any more than other places, the universities will be the main breeding ground for political leaders; political leaders, after all, are mostly made in the field, in practical life. Anyway, the problem is there on all the levels—primary, secondary, college, specialist training and so on, and the nuclei are there in several parts of Africa, but insufficient. For that reason, one of the major efforts must be to get this part of the infrastructure developed as quickly and as wisely as possible: wisely because it is a question of how, within the framework of limited means, to get the most possible out of those means; wisely also because there must be an adjustment to the specific social traditions, economic life and ideological approaches of each region.

I had the privilege of visiting some few of the great universities in Africa, and I must say that I admire their work. It is, as I said about the chief political leaders and administrators, a question of very high standards indeed, but again quality has to make up for the lack in quantity.

Finally—and I mention it last not because I regard it as the least significant—I refer to the necessity of moral support. In fact, I guess that it is the most significant, because people and money and education do not mean a thing unless they are given and provided in the right spirit. By the right spirit, by the moral support, I mean such attitudes from the outside, and from those who work with the governments, which reflect an understanding of the problems facing those countries, a sympathetic understanding, neither a feeling of false superiority, nor a feeling of sterile pessimism, nor a feeling of facile optimism. What is needed is realism and understanding, joined into something which really helps those leaders and those peoples. And why shouldn't it be provided? Why shouldn't it be provided by all the Member States of the United Nations and by

the Organization itself, which has pledged itself to self-government
and to independence as part of the human rights spelled out in the
Charter?

How this has to be translated into action is another matter. You
have examples of it already in United Nations practices over the
past few years. Those examples may not perhaps be repeated in
exactly the same form, but similar patterns are possible. It is something very striking that from the far west coast and to the south-east
coast as a belt all across Africa south of the Sahara, there is one
standing demand, one standing hope. It is less for money or for
experts, because those countries know very well that we haven't
got much money and we are not likely to get much money in this
Organization. It is much more for what I have called here the moral
support which is expressed even in the most modest action through
the right people.

I will not in this context repeat what is common knowledge. For
those countries, it is infinitely easier to receive financial assistance
and technical assistance by experts and so on through an international body than on a bilateral basis, and it is infinitely easier for
them to receive it through an international body of which they are
themselves members than through any other international body of
which they are not members. That is to say, internationalization of
aid is not achieved by switching from the system of one country
giving another country aid to a system where one group of countries
gives a country aid. The bilateral character is then maintained. It is
not until and unless the receiving country feels that this is an act of
solidarity within an organization where they have equal rights with
the donors that you really reach the optimum point not only
psychologically but politically and economically.

Under such circumstances, you are not surprised to hear that,
every place, there was one wish reiterated—that as much as possible
of international assistance should be channelled through the United
Nations. But, as I said, they looked at it realistically. They knew
that the time perhaps was not ripe. I must, on the other hand,
endorse their feelings. I understand their motives and I share their
conclusions. . . .

* * *

. . . QUESTION: My question is in regard to your trip to Africa.
You spoke a while ago about the ideology in Africa and I wonder

whether you could assess for us what the ideological trends are today in Africa, whether they stem from the inner realities facing African life today or whether they reflect the often repeated clichés of foreign ideology.

THE SECRETARY-GENERAL: I do not think that the rights of man is a foreign ideology to any people and that, I think, is the key to the whole ideological structure in Africa at present. It may be that the most eloquent and the most revolutionary expressions of the rights of man are to be found in Western philosophers and Western thinking, but that certainly does not make the idea a Western idea imposed on anybody. . . .

BILATERAL AND
UN PROGRAMS OF AID IN AFRICA

From press conference transcript, 4 February 1960

. . . QUESTION: You endorse strongly the principle of channelling aid through the United Nations, but I suppose you are probably aware that just as much, or at least as much, as the role of the United Nations is being undermined in the political field it is more actively even being undermined in the field of giving economic aid. One of the two world Powers—a latecomer in economic aid—the Soviet Union, is more than ever devoted to bilateral aid. The United States, which has more experience, is switching to multilateral aid, but outside the United Nations. My question is this. Are you aware of this—for the United Nations—very dangerous trend and would you consider an appeal to the Heads of State meeting in May in Paris for a joint enterprise in this very important field which, at the same time, could be a very important if not the only topic on which they might agree?

THE SECRETARY-GENERAL: I am very well aware of the trend you mentioned. I think less in terms of that trend as a danger to the United Nations—the United Nations, as I have often said, is not an end in itself—but I think of it as something which really reduces the usefulness of the aid from the point of view of the receiving countries. That is to say, the billions put up would be better billions in terms of peace and world progress if they were put up in a form which was more adjusted to the real political needs of the receiving countries. However, I take the situation less dramatically than you do because, if I look at it from the angle of the United Nations, the United Nations has possibilities and, I would not call them arguments, but tools which put it in a position where it can never really lose its ground if we live up to our responsibilities.

I guess that aid through the United Nations to countries will always be only a fraction of aid received from big Powers or from power blocs, but that does not mean that it cannot be decisive. It depends entirely on where we put it in and under what kind of leadership. Eight hundred thousand dollars does not mean the same as 80 million dollars from the point of view of investment, but from the point of view of what I call moral support it may be used in such a way as to carry greater weight.

That leads me to one aspect which I should perhaps mention, because it is essential for an evaluation of technical assistance through the United Nations at the present juncture. I have already referred to the interest taken by the African leaders and the African regions and States in the United Nations. Why this interest, as we are, from their point of view, poor as concerns finance and not very rich when it comes to the question of the number of officials and technical experts? The reason is quite obvious. The United Nations is now, or will be, their Organization. The United Nations can give them a framework for their young national life which gives a deeper sense and a greater weight to independence. The United Nations has not had a past in any of these regions in the sense that any one country necessarily has had. The United Nations, for these reasons, without pushing, without, so to say, becoming a party in their development, can through proper means, even on the basis of fairly small amounts of money, come into the picture in such a way as to help considerably in the framing of their political life after independence and in the building up of the national state.

That is a role which cannot be taken over by anybody else, and I see our technical assistance, even with modest means, as part of the pattern which naturally follows from this role and from the philosophy of African leaders when they look at the United Nations in this light. This applies, of course, especially to areas which have been Trust Territories, because there we have had a continuous experience, but I would not like to exaggerate the difference between Trust Territories and other territories.

We have responsibilities which I think we can carry out, and if we carry them out it is not decisive that tens or hundreds of times more money will come through other channels; although frankly I would, as I have said before, prefer to see it go through United Nations channels because it does make the money more effective, it does help the receiving country by more than the money. It helps it also in its effort to find its place on the world map.

KNOW YOURSELF—
KNOW YOUR WORLD

*Address at the 75th Anniversary Meeting of the
Swedish Tourist Association in the Concert Hall,
Stockholm, 27 February 1960. Mr. Hammarskjöld
was serving as Vice-President of the Swedish Tourist
Association and had been a member of its Executive
Board since 1940. He delivered this address in his
capacity as an officer of the Association rather than
as United Nations Secretary-General. It is included
in this volume for reasons similar to those applying
to his two addresses to the Swedish Academy.*

[TRANSLATION FROM SWEDISH]

After long years of wandering, far from the forest of Tiveden and
Lake Vättern, Heidenstam in a couple of poems in *Thoughts in
Solitude* found pregnant words to express the deep roots he felt he
had in his native soil and the openness towards the world beyond
the borders of his own country which, in apparent contrast, had
grown out of his rich experiences from other parts of the world.
  One poem ends with the well-known words:

' . . . I yearn for the ground,
  I yearn for the stones where as a child I played.'

The other poem, likewise in the confessional first-person form,
begins:

'Around half the world I have searched
For a point I might call the most beautiful.
So beautiful were they, all of them,
That none excelled the others.'

On the one hand the pilgrimage of emotion to a country so dear
to the poet as to make the very stones seem to speak to him. On
the other, the wanderer experiencing a world of such abundant
beauty that this country had no prior claim to it. His feeling of

deep roots in Sweden, which might have degenerated into compla-
cent provincialism, was balanced by his alert awareness of all that
the world had to offer, in a way which in turn, without its counter-
poise in his lively feeling for the homeland, might have transformed
him into a rootless cosmopolitan.

When the founders of the Swedish Tourist Association rallied
around the maxim 'Know your country', this was surely no mere
popular propaganda catch-phrase for them. What they had in mind
was not just superficial publicity for more travel, no matter what
ideas in such a direction the name of the new organization might
evoke, at least with the connotation the word tourist has gained in
everyday parlance. We have a right to assume that the founders of
the Association looked farther and wanted more. They belonged to
the same generation as Heidenstam, those vital people of the late
1850's and the 1860's who were to pour new life into Swedish art
and letters, as they did into Swedish politics and economics. The
new national feeling of which these generations were the bearers
grew out of a reaction both against the patriotism of hollow phrases
and banquet toasts and against a weakness for spiritual imports
caused by uncertainty about one's own abilities and values. Without
violating psychological truth, this background permits us to interpret the sentence the founders chose as the motto of the Swedish
Tourist Association in the light of the twofold sentiment and insight
reflected by the Heidenstam poems.

'Know your country'—the formula was directly linked to the
famous classical maxim. It demonstrates that the knowledge sought
was seen as a way to increased knowledge of oneself. As always,
and in all contexts, such a knowledge of oneself can widen the
understanding of the worlds of others. In the situation confronting
the founders of the Association the road they chose appeared as a
road ahead. But it was also a road that led inwards. Therefore, it
could in the end become a road outwards. 'Know your country'
meant both 'Know yourself' and 'Know your world.' Thus interpreted, the slogan excluded just as emphatically both an empty
internationalism and a narrow isolation within the limited confines
of the homeland.

The present generation, with its increased opportunities of seeing
for itself the world around it, can fully appreciate the importance,
in a wider sense, of the experiences to which the Tourist Association
extended an invitation. Just like Heidenstam during his years of

wandering, Swedes of today, during easily organized tours to more colorful countries with a different heritage and different problems, may learn to see their own country in a free perspective which must sharpen their eye for its limitations and weaknesses, but at the same time strengthen their feeling for its individuality and their awareness of what it, and it alone, has to offer.

Faced with the worlds of others, one learns that he who has fully absorbed what his own world has to offer is best equipped to profit by what exists beyond its frontiers. Nothing is more natural. Is it not our profound childhood familiarity with the fields and forests round the corner from our own house which enables us to move with assurance on the soil of others? Is it not on the basis of a deeper feeling for and insight into our mother tongue that we learn to speak other languages most easily?

We go to other countries and other continents. We may experience the overpowering greatness of the mountain ridges of Asia, the other-worldly calm of the deserts of Africa, the rain forests of South America or the wide water expanses of Polynesia. We meet people of other races and other creeds. But the more we see and the more we widen our contacts with our fellow beings in other parts of the world, the more it is also revealed to us that the essential beauties and the ultimate human values are equally present among 'the stones where as children we played' as in these other, far larger worlds. The road inwards can become a road outwards. For the traveller with open eyes and alert senses, on the other hand, the outward road can in a deeper sense become a road home. For Heidenstam, the wandering ended in pilgrimage. As happened to him, our experience of the wealth of the world may form the basis for a new love of the homeland. 'The world nomad' returns, and he it is who explains to us *The Grasses of Thule*.*

Recently I made a long journey through Africa. It may seem surprising, but my contact with the young representatives of the population in the various countries and territories I visited often evoked that period in Swedish and Scandinavian history which counts the Swedish Tourist Association among its offspring.

There is much talk today about a new nationalism. In the first place, this refers to the deep and strong currents on which the

* Title of a collection of poems by Harry Martinson, Swedish poet and writer, born 1904, who in *Cape Farewell* (English translation by Naomi Walford, London 1934) referred to himself as a 'world nomad.'

freedom movements of the Asian and African peoples are forging ahead. When these things are discussed, it is often done in a tone of critical superiority which does not limit itself to the primitive, or at least immature, expressions these currents sometimes find, but which actually regards the basic attitude itself as naive and obsolete.

To counter this new nationalism, there is created the image of a new internationalism, characterized by awareness of all that unites people and nations, regardless of race, history, ideology or economic conditions. The attempts to argue that there is such a contrast are superficial and unfair. They are as unfair as are tendencies to deride the spirit which carried our own national renaissance forward during the final decades of the nineteenth century.

I recall a small occurrence which in its own way sheds light on how the question of a new internationalism and a new nationalism appears to young intellectuals in Africa today. When I talked to a student at Makerere University in Uganda about the present phase in African history and about how exciting it must be, at this moment, to be trained for a professional task in Africa, he replied: 'Sir, I regard myself first of all as a citizen of the whole world. But, that being said, I am rather proud to be an African.' Is it too bold a parallel to trace in such a reaction the spirit which once inspired the founders of the Tourist Association and those who followed up their initiative?

A nationalism seeking self-glorification at the expense of others, or geared to an aggrandizement of power or territory, undoubtedly appears as the expression of a social concept we have to overcome. Such a nationalism—no matter what historical, legal or moral guise it assumes—is quite different from the kind of national feeling I am thinking of. This was not the sort of nationalism which found one of its expressions in the creation of the Tourist Association. Nor is this the kind of nationalism one encounters in the young Africans who represent a new-born national consciousness at such universities as those of Ghana, Nigeria, the Congo, Uganda or the Sudan. In neither case is there a question of overrating what one has to offer oneself or of underrating the world outside one's national borders and the necessity of full integration in this world of ours. But there has been an awakening to a living sense of heritage and resources, and to a healthy pride in the awareness of one's individuality, regarded not as a limitation but as an asset. That which is one's very own is experienced not as something provincial on the outskirts of the world, but as an essential part of the resources humanity as a whole has to manage.

Such a national feeling can be harmoniously merged with a feeling of international responsibility. Within the borders of the homeland it seeks to lay the groundwork for international influence and international respect. Regardless of the differences in almost all those respects which are primarily relevant in comparing peoples and countries, they can share, in common, an attitude such as the one I have now described. It can appear in the 1960's south of the Sahara as well as in the 1880's and 1890's in Scandinavia. A young nation which is a mature nation knows itself without overbearing or self-infatuation, but it also feels its strength in being faithful to its heritage and its individuality.

These thoughts may seem to have led us far outside the framework of today's celebration. But I think they are justified. The 75th anniversary of the foundation of the Swedish Tourist Association and the problems of the period we are commemorating give ample cause for reflection on our view of the homeland and of the world, and on the orientation of our national feeling. The Tourist Association is too modest an organization to serve as a point of departure in judging these delicate and far-reaching problems. But it is fully justified to place the Tourist Association, with the tasks it has taken upon itself and the place it has gained in Swedish everyday life, in the wider perspective which these questions create.

The Tourist Association has only a very limited role in the large problems of how we are to fit into the world of today, but in its field it has such a role. And this role assumes increased meaning and increased value if it is viewed in clear awareness of the larger problems and the greater demands now placed on us all.

The Tourist Association might have contented itself with the task of being an organization for leisure, with obvious and practical services to offer travellers. Its leaders have given it a wider task and have tried to mould it into what I venture to call an instrument for self-education. Such self-education is going on in many forms, here as well as in other parts of the world. It is a task which has to cover a wide field, and ultimately may help us attain a coexistence of nations in harmony with themselves and with respect for others. How has the Tourist Association transformed its program into action and how has it sought to carry out its self-assumed responsibility?

'Know your country!' If we go back to the earliest yearbooks it is evident that regardless of possible larger purposes the first concern was to use the limited means at hand to help the Swedes get to know *the country*. The attempts were somewhat groping and at times strike us as a little pathetic in their lack of perspective and their amusing tendency to a kind of exoticism. Top priority was given to the mountains of the north, and this led to important initiatives both in the creation of huts, stations and hiking trails and in the publication of elementary hiking manuals. Sometimes, the difficulties may have been overrated, and the experiences to be expected may have been overdramatized. But it would be misleading to apply the perspective of today, not least because mountain tourism has become so much easier and simpler nowadays largely thanks to the pioneer contributions of those we may feel tempted to criticize. And, anyway, did not the pioneers have the most august examples? We probably all remember the self-admiration and urge to dramatize evinced by Linnaeus in his *Lapland Journey*.

Apart from the mountains, what may be called the romantic provinces were given prominence: Dalecarlia, Värmland, the Uppland of the runic stones, Scania, Bohuslän. The interests of the Tourist Association naturally ran parallel to literary and artistic currents. The view of scenery and history of the '90's, the color scheme of the '90's, put their stamp on the work of the Association to open up the country and spread knowledge about it.

But the viewpoint of the '90's faded. And, as it did, the program of the Tourist Association underwent changes also. Fröding's* Värmland and Karlfeldt's† mining region of Bergslagen were followed by Bo Bergman's and Sten Selander's‡ Stockholm or Fridegård's and Moberg's§ share-croppers' country. From the romantic mountain world with overtones of Nietzsche there was a descent to the marshlands and river valleys of Eyvind Johnson and Stina Aronson.‖ The sweeping nocturnal vistas of Eugène Jannson were succeeded by the Hagalund streets of Olle Olsson, the bright-colored Lapland slopes of Leander Engström, by the bushy foothills of Folke Ricklund.¶ The names are chosen at random, but they

* Gustaf Fröding, Swedish poet, 1860–1911.
† E. A. Karlfeldt, see footnote, page 30.
‡ Bo Bergman, 1869–, Sten Selander, 1891–1957, Swedish poets.
§ Jan Fridegård, 1897–, Vilhelm Moberg, 1898–, Swedish novelists.
‖ Eyvind Johnson, 1900–, Stina Aronson, 1892–, Swedish novelists.
¶ Eugène Jansson, 1852–1915, Olle Olsson, 1904–, Leander Engström, 1886–1927, Folke Ricklund, 1900–, Swedish landscape painters.

represent a turn we all know that developments have taken during the past half-century.

While in earlier years the Tourist Association was principally concerned with living up to its motto of teaching the people to know their country, the changes I have recalled have led to a greater interest in *the people*. 'Know your country' came to mean 'Know your people.'

The tinge of exoticism vanished. Romanticism was subdued, although the strong Swedish feeling for nature always retained it in the picture to some extent. Instead, attention was focused more and more on Swedish workaday life. Industrial Sweden entered the arena. Castles and manors were succeeded by crofters' cottages and the homesteads of poor small-farmers. The new city landscape and the beauty of its life gained a place side by side with natural scenery.

During the period of the life of the Association I now have in mind, there were of course other changes in Swedish life than those reflected in poetry and art, and they have also affected the work of the organization. The democratic break-through, followed by a democratization also of the economy, with the large popular and civic organizations as dominant factors in the social make-up, caused a certain change of course in the activities of the Association and created new tasks for it. The Tourist Association organized and conducted the hikers' hostel project. In this and other ways it tried to find forms of travel which offered a penniless schoolboy or an adult with limited resources wider opportunities of familiarizing himself personally with his far-flung country in all its facets. In these efforts the Association had the natural, welcome and efficient competition—and help—of, *inter alia*, the travel organizations of the civic movements. Close cooperation was organized with the trade union movement and with other mass organizations.

This evolution, conditioned by the times, has run parallel with a channelling of the interests of the Association in a new direction in one other respect. 'Know your country' and 'Know your people' have increasingly taken on the meaning also of 'Know its *history*', know it as it is reflected by the country and its people of today.

Interest in history has always existed, but as in other fields the tone and the perspective have changed. In this respect it is also appropriate to talk of a move away from romanticism towards matter-of-factness, from the large colorful vista to a living understanding of the telling detail and what it has to say to us. It may not always have been popular, but I believe that it has been right and essential for the Tourist Association, in its continuous description of the country and in its efforts to open it up to the people, to have striven increasingly for scientific accuracy and concrete enlightenment. This has lent a perspective in depth to the picture of country and people and helped to prevent the banalization which may easily result if one forgets the past or permits it to be simplified into a myth.

Among the numerous publications of the Tourist Association the yearbooks naturally take pride of place. This is where we can best follow the evolution which the interpretation by the Association of its own task has undergone. This is also where we can best see how its activities have been widened and received a new content. But aside from the yearbooks there is also a small volume, published in 1943, whose existence I want to recall here in particular because it may be seen as a comprehensive symbol of the aspirations of the Tourist Association such as they are expressed in its motto.

The book I have in mind is called *Swedish Nature*. How this title is to be understood emerges from the introductory words, which explain that the plan to publish this selection of nature descriptions from Swedish poetry and prose literature had come to fruition at a time when Sweden, threatened by war and isolation, had emerged for us all with renewed force as our country. The Association, it was said, wanted to place within reach of all, a book in which the cycle of seasons and the varieties of scenery from Sandhammaren in the far south to the Lapland mountains in the north wove together fragments of our literature into a picture of this country as it had been experienced by Swedes, separated in time, separated also by origin, philosophy and ambition, but joined in their ties to the soil out of which they had grown.

The words I have quoted indicate, in one limited field, what has been the aim of the Tourist Association over the years. What it has tried to do is to present the country and the people in the light of their history as it is mirrored in the living landscape—*our* country, directly experienced or as it has been seen and described in words and pictures by representatives of the people. In this, the Association has sought and found support from writers, scholars and artists as well as from Swedes of various social stations who have shared the desire of the Association to transform the words of its motto into action. Its gratitude goes out to them all today.

Let me conclude these remarks by quoting from the first few pages of the book I just mentioned. Here is Torsten Fogelqvist* speaking in a fragment from 'Odyssey in the Provinces':

'I see the first snowclouds flocking around the rhythmically towering Kebnekajse massif, I see the steep banks of Indal river decorated in the golden glory of autumn, I see the Järvsö peak blue as light ink. I see Sveg reeking in white cold, fifty degrees below freezing, and strong men in bearskin coats with icicles in their beards. I hear the spring ice crackling under the sleigh runners on the thawing lakes of Dalecarlia and see the long lumber hauls splashing ahead in the slush gilded by evening. I see the birches mirroring themselves in the early summer glitter of the Fryken lakes. I hear the Sunday chimes from the dark little medieval churches of Roslagen. I see the plains of Östergötland in a burning sun with trickling ditches and jubilant larks falling like drops in space. I walk ahead silently under the stars and firs in the somber forests of the Småland highlands. I see the meager ridges of Halland fade like silent melodies against an autumnal, troubled sea. And I see the farmer in Scania standing beside his willow hedge and his village pond, brown against the brown sod.'

Thus, in the perspective of memory, does a great Swedish traveller sum up his picture of this rich and varied land which it is our duty and our good fortune to know and to learn to know better.

* Swedish author and critic, 1880-1941.

THE DEVELOPMENT OF A
CONSTITUTIONAL FRAMEWORK
FOR INTERNATIONAL COOPERATION

Address at the special Convocation and dedicatory
Celebration marking the completion and occupancy of
the new Law Buildings of the University of Chicago
Law School, Chicago, 1 May 1960.

International law, in spite of the vast literature covering the subject, has on the whole been less favored by serious students than national law. And within the field of international law what might be called international constitutional law and its specific problems has attracted less interest than other parts with their far longer history in the Western World. In fact, international constitutional law is still in an embryonic stage; we are still in the transition between institutional systems of international coexistence and constitutional systems of international cooperation. It is natural that, at such a stage of transition, theory is still vague, mixed with elements of a political nature and dependent on what basically may be considered sociological theory.

Men organize themselves into families. The families join together in villages or tribes. The tribes and the villages fuse into peoples, and one day, out of the self-consciousness of a people, there develops a feeling of difference and separateness, the positive expression of which is a feeling of nationhood. The nation organizes its life within a set of constitutional rules, evolving in practice or crystallized as law. Under the constitution the people develop national organs with different functions and a division of responsibilities representing a balance of power. Through those organs laws are given, setting the pattern for the lives and activities of the individuals and the groups which constitute the nation.

Is that the end of the road of the development of human society? Of course not. Nation borders on nation, peoples get in touch with each other, and whatever differences there may exist and whatever conflicts of interest the people may see, they are forced to live together, fighting or in peace, as neighbors with limits put by nature to their possible self-sufficiency and for that reason with a need to develop forms for international intercourse, permitting more or less highly developed degrees of cooperation. So an institutional system of coexistence is developed with its rules and practices. Still there is no international society. Still the nation remains the highest fully organized form for the life of peoples.

However primitive a basic institutional pattern may be, it carries within it seeds for the growth of higher social organisms, covering wider areas and groups of peoples. To use my terminology of a moment ago, such an institutional system for coexistence, stage by stage, may be developed and enriched until, on single points or on a broad front, it passes over into a constitutional system of cooperation. When that happens, we get in a first, necessarily rudimentary form, a form of society which, while preserving and protecting the lives of the nations, points towards an international constitutional system surmounting the nations, utilizing them to the extent that smaller units are more efficient instruments for evolution, but creating rules which limit the influence of the nations in fields where bigger units present greater possibilities for development and survival.

I believe it is useful, in the discussion of the development of human society, be it national or international, to keep in mind this sociological perspective taken over from theories of biological evolution. It is a perspective which helps us to a more realistic appraisal of what it is we have achieved and what it is we are trying to do, as well as of the scope and significance of our failures and our successes. It also gives us a broader and more organic sense of the role of law —again I use the word in its broadest sense, including not only written law but the whole social pattern of established rules of action and behaviour—making us see the differences as well as the similarities between the national and international field, and warning us against false analogies.

In the light of this approach, the value of speculation about what should be the ultimate constitutional form for international co-operation is obviously limited. Those who advocate world government, and this or that special form of world federalism, often present challenging theories and ideas, but we, like our ancestors, can only press against the receding wall which hides the future. It is by such efforts, pursued to the best of our ability, more than by the construction of ideal patterns to be imposed upon society, that we lay the basis and pave the way for the society of the future.

Our century has established a rich pattern of approaches to the development of an institutional framework for coexistence, as well as for a constitutional framework for international cooperation. In this respect our time is as much in the front line of evolution as it is in the field of natural sciences. It would take me much too far if, on this occasion, I were to try to make an analysis of these various efforts. I must limit my brief comments to developments around which interest and activities have recently tended to center, such as the European efforts to tie the countries of the Continent together in new patterns, providing for intensified cooperation, and, especially, the United Nations family of international organizations.

In a galaxy of nations like the European one, there are, of course, strongly ingrained patterns and inherited sets of rules which integrate the area. The life of those nations develops within a system explained by a number of shared interests and basic concepts, which set a framework for trade, for travel and exchange of people, for movement of capital and for exchange of ideas. Within the system created by those rules we have, in a sense, a kind of 'common market', which, however, does not infringe on the sovereignty of any of the nations forming part of the market and which, therefore, still lacks completely what might be called a constitutional element. It thus remains a purely institutional pattern. With the recent creation of the European Common Market of six nations, the Coal and Steel Community, and similar bodies, a decisive step has been taken in the further development of this institutional framework. In fact, by these actions the system has been pushed beyond the border of institutional arrangements and has come to include some initial constitutional elements.

The institutional evolution in Europe has brought us a step in the direction of a true constitutional framework for cooperation which, through experimental stages of a confederal nature, may finally lead to some kind of federal system or even stronger forms of association. However, just as in the case of world federalism, I think it is wise to avoid talking of this or that kind of ultimate political target and to realize that the development is still in an early stage of institutional evolution, although a few vanguard penetrations into the constitutional area have taken place. What seems imperative is to push forward institutionally and, eventually, constitutionally all along the line, guided by current needs and experiences, without preconceived ideas of the ultimate form.

It may be worth mentioning that, according to statements made by the President of France, the present approach to the idea of a French-African community has essential elements in common with the attitude just described. If I understand the policy correctly, it works in the direction of a far-reaching development of institutional patterns without any definite stand now being taken on the constitutional element, which thus is permitted to grow out of the evolving institutional pattern, whatever the direction which the interplay of forces may later establish. When, for example, in the case of the Federation of Mali, it is said that the new federation will have full independence while, on the other hand, it will be in a close cooperation with France, provided for by a set of agreements, this seems to reflect a state of affairs characterized by a highly elaborate institutional framework which, however, does not reach into the sphere of constitutional arrangements.

It is known that Sir Winston Churchill, in his time, advocated an approach to the building of a world community through the creation of regional organizations as stepping-stones to more highly developed forms of international coexistence or cooperation. We see instead the advance being made in part only through regional arrangements, but in part—and mainly—independently of such arrangements and directly on the basis of universality. If Sir Winston's line had been followed, it would, with my terminology, have meant that regional organizations step by step would have developed a basic institutional pattern for universal coexistence by which, later on, a push forward, on the universal level, could have been tried in the direction of a constitutional pattern.

If we accept the interpretation given here to the European community and the French-African community, the United Nations could, in a similar sense, be called a 'community', although of a universal character. It represents in itself, with the methods of operation and the rules established, an elaboration of an institutional pattern of coexistence. It even has, in theory, points where it reaches into the constitutional sphere; I have, of course, in mind especially the authority given to the Security Council to act with mandatory power, provided the action is supported unanimously by the permanent members. However, as is natural with a more complex system, built up of a greater number of components, among which—to use the language of natural science—in many fields forces of repulsion tend to balance or outbalance forces of attraction, the cohesion is more unstable and the field covered by the institutional pattern less extended or more marginal than in the case of regional groupings.

Viewed in this light, the United Nations is an experimental operation on one of the lines along which men at present push forward in the direction of higher forms of an international society. It is obvious that we cannot regard the line of approach represented by the United Nations as intrinsically more valuable or more promising than other lines, in spite of the fact that, through its universality, it lies closer to or points more directly towards the ideal of a true constitutional framework for world-wide international cooperation, and notwithstanding the obvious weaknesses of regional approaches to such cooperation. However, if one cannot *a priori* give it higher value, it is, on the other hand, equally impermissible to regard it as less promising than experiments at present pursued on other lines. The effort carried on within and through the United Nations is an effort just as necessary as other experiments, and nothing short of the pursuit of this specific experiment with all our ability, all our energy and all our dedication can be defended. In fact, the effort seems already to have been carried so far that we have conquered essential new ground for our work for the future. This would remain true in all circumstances and even if political complications were one day to force us to a wholly new start.

When the United Nations was created, the founders had the experience of the League of Nations and also the experience of such a highly evolved constitutional pattern as that established on the American continent. A strong influence from both these experiences can be seen in the Charter of the United Nations.

We have an Assembly of State representatives with an equal voice in the deliberations and decisions, irrespective of the size of the nation for whom they speak. But the 'legislative' powers of the Assembly have been limited to recommendations which, legally, at present is likely to be the maximum attainable. We have one collective 'executive' organ, formed on the pattern of the Council of the League of Nations, but with voting rules adjusted to the political realities of the world, and, therefore, recognizing that mandatory authority cannot be vested in such an organ unless supported by the main Powers in the world arena. We have, on the other hand, also what may be called a one-man 'executive', with explicit authority in the administrative field, supplementary to, but not overlapping the authority of either the Council or the Assembly.

Further, we have two organs with elements of both 'legislative' and 'executive' power, of which one carries the special responsibilities of a political nature which belong to the United Nations under the Trusteeship System, and the other one has broad authority in the field of economic and social development regarding questions of coordination of action towards the targets established under the Charter.

Finally, we have the International Court of Justice as a counterpart to a national judiciary. It would have possibilities to develop into a more important element in the settlement of international conflicts than it now is, were the unfortunate and self-defeating reservations against its jurisdiction made by some Member countries to be withdrawn. It should be stressed that all these organs function within the framework of the Charter, a document that by its very nature and by the way in which it establishes solemn commitments to certain joint principles and purposes has a clear constitutional aspect, in the sense in which I am using this term here.

The system we find in the United Nations has its strength and its weakness. In the light of the experiences of fifteen years, undoubtedly some changes of the pattern would be made if the Charter were to be revised. These changes, however, would probably not refer to the various organs as such, but rather to their relative authority—that is to say to the division of responsibilities—and to their methods of operation.

The experiment carried on through and within the United Nations has found in the Charter a framework of sufficient flexibility to permit growth beyond what seems to have been anticipated in San Francisco. Even without formal revisions, the institutional system embodied in the Organization has undergone innovations explained by organic adaptation to needs and experiences.

On this point a word of warning may be in order. The fact that important sections of the Charter—I think especially of Chapter VII, which lays down the rules for interventions of the United Nations with military force—so far have not been implemented and still seem far from application, does not mean that on these points we are facing a dead letter, and that to the same extent the power of the Security Council, as the executive organ entrusted with authority under Chapter VII, has withered away. It is not so because, with some changes in the world situation, the clauses of the Charter to which I have referred may come to be seen as providing the basis for an adequate response to the anticipated needs. If and when it should so happen, the activities of the Security Council would automatically show a corresponding expansion.

What I have said is not hypothetical, as may be seen from the current discussion on disarmament. Were developments now to lead the main Powers to an agreement on even limited disarmament, the need for an institutional evolution in the direction foreseen in Chapter VII would at once present itself with considerable strength.

So far I have referred only to the United Nations itself. At its side stand the Specialized Agencies with somewhat similar organizational systems. They are autonomous, though coordinated with the United Nations within the terms of the Charter. There are provisions for cooperation among the various organizations within the United Nations family. However, this cooperation is established mainly on the Secretariat level and the group of organizations as a whole has no organ which, through a majority decision, can lay down a common line of action. A committee of the administrative heads of the various organizations, established for cooperation, functions on a basis of unanimity which is made necessary by the autonomy of the organizations.

Experience shows that neither the central role of the General Assembly of the United Nations nor the fact that, generally speaking, the same nations are members of all the organizations, provides for an effective integration among them. Thus we see at the present stage the paradox that the organizations created for the development of an institutional framework for international coexistence are themselves bound together within such a pattern only in a very loose form, which is not reinforced to any considerable extent by an integration of policies within various member countries.

This fact, which is strongly indicative of the experimental and, one might even say, embryonic character of the present efforts, is of special significance when we face a need to expand the field to be covered by international cooperation. Historically we have to register a tendency to create new organs for each new major field of activity. Thus international cooperation in the field of the peaceful uses of atomic energy led to the establishment of the International Atomic Energy Agency, which for all practical purposes functions as a specialized agency. Similarly, in the case of control of the implementation of an agreement on nuclear tests, the creation of a new autonomous organ is anticipated. Finally, even in the field of

17

disarmament, which under the Charter is a central task of the United Nations, suggestions have been made to the effect that activities of decisive significance should be entrusted to a new organ which might be not only administratively but also politically independent of the United Nations.

In view of the tentative stage so far reached as regards coordination of activities among the various organizations working on the basis of universality, it may be questioned whether the tendency to which I have just referred will not prove to be a deviation leading us away from the most fruitful direction for an evolution of a framework for international cooperation. At least it seems to me that, if this tendency is accepted and continued, it should be counterbalanced by an effort to evolve new forms for integration of the work of the various international agencies. I am not in a position to say in what direction such forms may be found, but unless they are developed we may come to face a situation where the very growth of the framework for international cooperation tends to lead to an ultimate weakening. If I am permitted to fall back again on a parallel with biological developments, it is as if we were to permit the growth of a tree to be weakened by the development of too many branches, finally sapping its strength so that it breaks down under its own weight.

Having spoken about the risk of disintegration of the international framework through a proliferation of organs, I should mention also the opposite risk, that by combining too many tasks too closely within one and the same organ, you break it up, as of course no organization can carry an unlimited burden because of the simple fact that no leaders of such an organization can have the capacity to give satisfactory leadership over ever-expanding areas.

The two risks indicated call for careful thought before we push much further forward. We must seek the optimum balance between a system with a large number of autonomous bodies and a system with strong concentration of tasks within a lesser number of organizations. The way will have to be found by trial and error, but planning is necessary because of the difficulty to take a step backward or to change fundamentally what once has been established. Probably, new forms will have to be devised, not only, as already indicated, for an integration of activities among autonomous organizations, but also for the delegation of powers within this or that organization without a breaking up of its inner unity.

What is true of the United Nations family of organizations as a whole is true also of the United Nations. The developing activities over ever-wider fields, in response to the needs which we face, may serve to alert us to possible risks of a lack of integration even within the organization itself. The correctives exist. There is the unifying influence of the General Assembly itself and of other main organs. There are the coordinating activities within and through the Secretariat. But, again, the human factor comes into play, and I would in this context, in concluding, like to quote one example of interest as a comparison of constitutional problems facing an international organization with those we know from national administrations. You will excuse me if I refer to my own office.

The Secretary-General of the United Nations is the Chief Administrative Officer of the Organization and, as such, the only elected member of the Secretariat. The founders of the United Nations may in this context have looked to the American Constitution. The chief of any government, or the Chief Executive in the United States, has the assistance of a group of close collaborators who represent the same basic approach, and to whom he therefore can delegate a considerable part of his responsibilities. On the basis of universality, especially in a divided world but generally speaking as long as nations have opposing interests, no similar arrangement is possible within the United Nations. This may have been understood in San Francisco, but I guess that it was felt that it did not matter too much as the Secretary-General had mainly administrative responsibilities. However, the position of the Office of the Secretary-General within the United Nations, explained in part by the fact that he is the only elected officer in principle representing all members, has led to increasingly widespread diplomatic and political activities. This is in response to developing needs. If negotiations are necessary, or if arrangements with a certain intended political impact are to be made, but Member nations are not in a position to lay down exact terms of reference, a natural response of the Organization is to use the services of the Secretary-General for what they may be worth.

The tasks thus entrusted to the Secretary-General are mostly of such a character that, with the composition of an international Secretariat and of the group of his closest collaborators, with its naturally wide geographical distribution, he must carry out the work on a fairly personal basis. Obviously, there is no parallel to this in the field of national politics or diplomacy, and the case I have described, therefore, highlights one of those essential complications which characterize in the constitutional field the effort to work in the direction of organized international cooperation. At an experimental stage, such difficulties may be faced on a day-to-day basis, but in the long run they are likely to require imaginative and constructive constitutional innovations.

Perhaps a future generation, which knows the outcome of our present efforts, will look at them with some irony. They will see where we fumbled and they will find it difficult to understand why we did not see the direction more clearly and work more consistently towards the target it indicates. So it will always be, but let us hope that they will not find any reason to criticize us because of a lack of that combination of steadfastness of purpose and flexibility of approach which alone can guarantee that the possibilities which we are exploring will have been tested to the full. Working at the edge of the development of human society is to work on the brink of the unknown. Much of what is done will one day prove to have been of little avail. That is no excuse for the failure to act in accordance with our best understanding, in recognition of its limits but with faith in the ultimate result of the creative evolution in which it is our privilege to cooperate.

PRESS CONFERENCE COMMENTS

Extracts from verbatim transcripts, 1959–1960

———◆———

THE COLD WAR AND THE EFFECTIVENESS
OF THE UNITED NATIONS

Extracts from transcript, 5 February 1959

QUESTION: Mr. Secretary-General, there is so much emphasis on Cold War these days. Do you feel there is sufficient understanding as to what the United Nations does to try to prevent possible conflicts?

THE SECRETARY-GENERAL: No, I think that the prevalent picture is not quite just and does not give the right impression. People think, as you say rightly, so much in Cold War terms that they forget that there is a very wide political life indeed going on outside the orbit of the Cold War and that, irrespective of the influence of the Cold War on United Nations operations, the United Nations is very active and I hope, on the whole, also efficient in what it does in all the other spheres. I can refer to the recent activities in the Far East where, as you know, a representative of the Secretary-General has had a kind of good-office function, about which I have the very best hopes.* And I can refer to various aspects of the much-discussed Middle Eastern problems; I can refer to the extremely important constructive work which the United Nations is undertaking in Africa, not only in the economic field but in the field primarily of the Trusteeship Council, guiding and helping towards the establishment of the new national States.

All these things, I think, are very important political contributions, which of course in public debate have become a little bit overshadowed by the Cold War, and for that reason I would agree with you.

*   *   *

... QUESTION: Mr. Secretary-General, since there are few signs of a thaw in the Cold War, it would seem that the basic deadlocks hampering the United Nations must continue indefinitely. In view of the situation, is it likely that the time may be near when, let us say, alternatives to the United Nations will have to be considered?

* See pages 210, 264.

THE SECRETARY-GENERAL: I would like to ask the question, what would you mean by alternative? I find it very difficult to give a reply myself. Is there any alternative to a world organization including as many countries as can be included, based on universality, for the purposes which only world organization can serve? There are and there may be shortcomings in the life of the United Nations. Then we can develop the United Nations further; we can improve on it; we can try and find new means to meet the needs, but basically I think it must be on the same basis. I do not see for that reason really how the word 'alternative' should be interpreted. In my mind, what might come after the United Nations will be on the same foundation, perhaps with this or that kind of adjustment in the light of experience. But I would not call that an alternative.

*   *   *

... QUESTION: Sir, there has been considerable talk about a thaw in the Cold War. What role might the United Nations play in developing such a thaw and particularly with respect to what the role of the United Nations might be in regard to Germany and Berlin?

THE SECRETARY-GENERAL: I would not like to comment on the last part of your question because I do not yet see the role clearly. There is so much debate going on, on Cabinet level, and our contact is insufficient for me to form any clear conclusions. However, I do believe that the United Nations in fact is serving the purpose of thawing the Cold War the whole time, and I do believe that to the extent that such a thaw may come about, the United Nations will increasingly be a focal point for that development.

It is quite natural, as you know, in this very room and in the lobbies here, there are, after all, contacts which in themselves are a denial of the state of absolute frozenness, because they do represent human contacts, they do represent, at the least, an attempt at a meeting of minds, and they are, I think, very often imbued by and inspired by a spirit of personal confidence, even if the general temperature may be very low in the sense that it is characterized by, so to say, official lack of confidence.

*   *   *

... QUESTION: Mr. Secretary-General, may I come back to what you have just said about the Cold War and United Nations problems. Would it be fair to describe your endeavours or the policy of the United Nations as trying to insulate the world problems, or as many world problems as are being faced by the United Nations, from the Cold War and to show by experience that these problems would exist without the Cold War and basically are not being affected by the Cold War.

THE SECRETARY-GENERAL: Yes, you are on a line which corresponds very much with my thinking. I might perhaps express it this way: that I consider it a very natural function for the Secretary-General to keep problems as much as possible outside the Cold War orbit and on the other hand, of course, to lift problems out of the Cold War orbit to all the extent he can. That is for many reasons. One of them is that it is one way in which we can get over the difficulties created for the United Nations and United Nations operations by the Cold War. It is one way, so to say, if not to thaw the Cold War, at least to limit its impact on international life.

*   *   *

...QUESTION: You have expressed your confidence in the soundness of the basic United Nations structure. Do you, however, think that experience shows that within this structure there should be any, shall we say, operational changes—in particular, voting changes?

THE SECRETARY-GENERAL: When I expressed my confidence in the soundness of the basic United Nations structure, it was for the specific purposes of the international organization. You can see that in that sense the alternative would be an organization which, in principle, was not universal. That is an entirely different animal, and one could not ride it in the same way at all. I say that in clarification of what I said before.

As to internal developments, I can very well see this or that kind of change. I must, however, say that I am somewhat wary of efforts to spell them out in theoretical terms, to sit at a desk and say what should be done. After all, if one looks back over the last, let us say, three years, one sees that there has been a very considerable internal adjustment of the type of operation chosen in order to meet a situation. In my view, there have been some constructive gains: simpler and smoother methods have been initiated to arrive at solutions—partly through by-passing regular procedures and creating new, *de facto* procedures. In other cases, the efforts have shown that we have entered a dead-end street, which, of course, we should get out of as soon as possible.

But this kind of pragmatic development in the light of experience, and with a constant—I would not say spirit of adventure or experiment—flexibility as to the best way in which to meet the needs is, I think, the best method for finding, in practice, a reply to your question.

I may refer to the most recent experiment, which I have mentioned before in a somewhat different context. This is the good offices operation in South-East Asia between Thailand and Cambodia. Normally, a conflict of the type we had there would probably have gone to the Security Council, and we would have had a decision which, perhaps, in substance would have meant the same as the decision now taken. However, the parties agreed not to raise the issue in the Security Council but, anticipating a possible outcome, to direct parallel invitations, as it were, to the Secretary-General to send someone to assist them in getting over the difficulty. Without in any way making this a precedent, I responded to the invitations and a representative was sent there, with the acquiescence of members of the Security Council. You can see how much more effective and smooth-working such a technique is than the regular one, which involves all the meetings and debates, and so on. That is a good case in point to demonstrate how, pragmatically, we can find better ways to do the job, without at all departing from the Charter but, so to speak, adjusting the procedures so as to meet a concrete situation as conveniently and efficiently as possible.

Those examples could be multiplied. I believe that in the future we shall have further cases that we perhaps cannot think of now. All this builds up a sum total of experience which one day, I feel, may usefully be codified.

QUESTION: Would you include as an example the method used in preparing for the atomic energy Conferences? You have mentioned that before.

THE SECRETARY-GENERAL: Very much so. I think that we can regard this as already codified. As you may remember, the Advisory Committee had its mandate renewed for the second atomic energy Conference and, in the light of the experiences of that second Conference, the General Assembly again renewed the Advisory Committee's mandate, with some modifications in the direction of widening its functions. When the General Assembly for a second time endorses this arrangement, I believe that I can regard it more or less as a firm element in United Nations thinking and United Nations philosophy that such organs can usefully be established in cases where the work is not that of resolving a conflict, but that of studying and negotiating in the elaboration of a practical approach to major problems.

QUESTION: Am I correct in interpreting one of your recent speeches to mean that the United Nations constitutes the one hope and road to future world government?

THE SECRETARY-GENERAL: I have never used the words 'the one hope for the world'—

QUESTION: I believe that you used the words 'world order.'

THE SECRETARY-GENERAL: I have already twice indicated in this press conference why I believe that the United Nations is a 'must' in view of the problem before us. We need a universal organization, and for that reason the organization in which we work has to be universal. In that sense, you may say that it is the one—I would not call it hope—method by which we can approach the world peace problem from this angle.

Of course, the one hope is that people will show a solid will to compromise, to find ways out of the problems. The United Nations is only an instrument; it is not the creator of politics.

ON MORAL JUDGMENTS

From transcript, 5 February 1959. The following exchange reflects Dag Hammarskjöld's deep dislike for the habit of arrogating unto oneself the right to be a moral arbiter, especially in international politics, where considerations of national interest mainly determine the stands taken.

QUESTION: Mr. Secretary-General, do you feel that the United Nations would have greater influence and impact on the world if there were stronger emphasis in the UN organs on moral condemnation of wrong-doers?

THE SECRETARY-GENERAL: I am perhaps not a moralist.

*   *   *

... QUESTION: Sir, a moment ago you made a very intriguing statement when you said you were not a moralist. May I follow that up—I assume a moralist in a certain context—and ask, if UN decisions do not register moral judgments, what should be the purpose of UN decisions?

THE SECRETARY-GENERAL: They register judgments, and I hope they are moral.

ON RESPONDING TO NEW DEMANDS

From transcript, 2 April 1959

QUESTION: Since your trip* amounted to an integration of experience in two continents, could you say that, as far as you could experience, Asia is involved in the problems of Europe? In the light of your experience, would you feel encouraged or discouraged about taking on new responsibilities in Europe, in view of the needs of Asia which you have stressed?

THE SECRETARY-GENERAL: It is difficult, as you know, to generalize, but my own impression is that Asia really has its hands so full with its own problems that it does not feel very much involved in what is, so to say, primarily a European problem. On the other hand, realistically, they fully realize that the way in which these problems are handled is vital to their own success when it comes to the solution of their own problems. I think I am right in interpreting their attitude as one of keen interest in how the European problem is handled, while at the same time they say to themselves: 'We are one step or two steps removed; we feel the repercussions, but we are not in the front range of those who should either express views or make a contribution.'

It is natural, with such a background, that also in such a respect these countries regard the United Nations, if not as a natural agent in problems of the European type, at least as a natural bridge when it comes to questions of knowing about what is going on and in expressing views on what is going on. That is to say, I do not think there is any clamour for an active UN part, but, as they feel they should be in a sense indirectly a party to what happens, a contact for them with any relevant political aspect should be safeguarded through the United Nations.

The other part of your question related to being encouraged or

---

* The Secretary-General had just returned from a trip to Member countries in Asia and the Soviet Union.

discouraged. It is very difficult to answer in terms which make sense to myself. You see, it looks to me to be the other way around. To be discouraged or encouraged is an emotional thing. The basic thing is the policy line, and the policy line, as I see it, is that the United Nations simply must respond to those demands which may be put to it. If we feel that those demands go beyond the present capacity, from my point of view that in itself is not a reason why I, for my part, would say no, because I do not know the exact capacity of this machine. It did take the very steep hill of Suez; it may take other and even steeper hills. I would not object beforehand unless I could say, and had to say in all sincerity, that I know it cannot be done. Then I would say it. So far, I do not know of any question that has been put to which I would have to give that very discouraging reply. For that reason, my policy attitude remains the one which I tried to explain, namely that the United Nations should respond and have confidence in its strength.

BERLIN AND THE UN

From transcript, 30 April 1959

QUESTION: I have a couple of questions on Berlin. In France and Germany fears have been expressed that if the United Nations is given too large a role in any agreement with regard to West Berlin, in the event of disagreement subsequently the issue would be referred to the General Assembly, and then these French and German diplomats take the view that the smaller nations would take the problem away, the control of the issue away, from the Great Powers. I wonder whether you would have any comment on that?

While I have the floor, may I ask a second question and that is: How can the Foreign Ministers of the Big Four discuss some form of UN presence in Berlin without having someone there to tell them whether the suit they are cutting will fit the UN?

THE SECRETARY-GENERAL: On the first question, may we, so to say, cut it loose from the reported statements to which you refer and regard it as a general and abstract question in order to avoid any possible implication of debate from my side with those gentlemen, or criticism of their stand. On that understanding I would say that it seems to me that, if developments in Europe around Germany were to develop to the point where they represented a problem from the point of view of the United Nations, a threat to peace in some sense, the Charter rules would apply; that is to say, anybody can then bring it to the Security Council and, as you know, from the Security Council it may or may not go to the General Assembly if there is no agreement in the Council.

I mention this possibility only to point out that it seems to me that it is a bit unrealistic as a judgment of the situation to look at it as if it were possible to keep the matter out of the United Nations in the case that this matter properly under the Charter belonged to the United Nations. Whether or not it comes to the UN will depend on the many who have a right to bring it to the UN.

Another matter on which I have commented several times is the role of the small nations. I do not believe that the small nations have less of an understanding of central political problems of concern to the whole world than those who are more closely related to them and who traditionally wield greater power in the international councils. For that reason, I cannot—and this is not only the official stand taken by the Secretary-General; it is a matter of personal conviction—share the view of those who regard the possible influence of smaller Powers as a danger—I would add, in any context.

As to the other question, how it is possible to have discussions in any form without knowing whether the suit will fit—in the sense of UN cooperation or UN functions—I think that the gentlemen will know both the extent of their knowledge of UN operations and their possible need of further information, and if they were to conclude that they were not quite sure of the measurements of the body to which the suit should fit, they would be very likely to find ways of taking those measurements. If they should need any kind of assistance in that context, I don't think it would be difficult for them to get it. They certainly know how to get it.*

ON BLOC VOTING IN THE UN

From transcript at Dar-Es-Salaam, Tanganyika, 10 January 1960

QUESTION: We hear a good deal about the Afro-Asian bloc as a sort of voting body, sticking together on particular issues. Now that

* In fact the Secretary-General used his speech at Copenhagen two days later as one means of providing this assistance. See page 200 et seq.

the membership of that bloc is getting larger and larger, do you think it is becoming more and more powerful as a voting body or do you think that it is getting to be less cohesive?

THE SECRETARY-GENERAL: I would say generally that our experience has been that the widening of the membership of the United Nations has moved the General Assembly, in a certain sense, in a more democratic direction. There is less and less cohesion, which is quite natural with the widening of the groups. The Afro-Asian group, I think, was explained by the fact that, with a strong Asian group and a fairly limited number of African countries, the Africans associated themselves, so to speak, with the Asians. I do not think that there was a common denominator, either a positive or a negative one. For that reason, I would guess that, with the widening of the African group, there will certainly still be joint meetings of the Africans and the Asians but it is quite likely that, from a practical point of view, they will function more separately than before. Within each group, as I have said, the cohesion becomes less pronounced as the group becomes larger. That is the experience we have had.

ANTHONY EDEN AND SUEZ

From transcript, 4 February 1960

QUESTION: While you were in Africa Sir Anthony Eden was publishing his memoirs, more or less recollections, in more or less tranquility. One of the points he made was that he felt that after 6 November (1956), the cease-fire, it should have been possible to shape a lasting settlement of the Arab-Israeli conflict and get some secure guarantees about freedom of passage through the Suez Canal; that he never would have anticipated that the cards that were in the hands of the UN and the United States would have been thrown away as they were in that situation.

My question is whether you feel, in the light of the difficulties you have had in the past year with respect to the Canal—and I am sure you have worked very hard on it—whether the cards were not perhaps thrown away at that time; and what you think about the general merits of Sir Anthony's observations.

THE SECRETARY-GENERAL: Well, I would like to turn the question back to you. What were the cards that the United Nations had? The presence of French and British and Israeli troops in or close to the Canal Zone regarded as enemies by the country through which the Canal runs—regarded as enemies by the whole Arab world. Is that a card which is a useful one for a negotiation about peace if it is not an imposed peace, and do you believe that any peace imposed on the Middle East would be a lasting one?

ON THE RESPONSIBILITY OF
GOVERNMENTS FOR UN ACTION

From transcript, 18 February 1960

QUESTION: In the last few days, particularly yesterday, three high governmental representatives have again kicked the Israel-Arab ball right into your field—into the field of the United Nations; I do not mean you personally, Sir. Mrs. Meir of Israel repeated in Israel a few days ago that the solution of the grievances which Israel has in regard to freedom of passage through the Suez Canal is up to the United Nations.

President Eisenhower, at his news conference yesterday, reiterated the statement which he made in 1957 to the effect that any violation of the principle of freedom of passage should be handled by the United Nations and said that he still relied on the United Nations for that solution.

Mr. Lloyd, in Commons yesterday, said that the Middle East had drifted into what he called a dangerous situation and, again, said that it was up to the United Nations to handle the affair.

I wonder whether you would care to comment on these various official statements?

THE SECRETARY-GENERAL: I think the reactions are natural as regards the role of the United Nations, and I firmly hope that this expression of views—that is to say, that the United Nations carries a responsibility—will be followed, on the part of those who have made the statements, by appropriate reactions and actions in the United Nations and in support of the United Nations. . . .

You know as well as I do the various facts at the moment. It is definitely a situation with symptoms which indicate a deterioration. As to United Nations action, you know that such action can take different forms. It can be action in the Security Council or in the

General Assembly or through the Secretary-General. There is an area, so to say, reserved for each of these various types of action. I can do some things—which I have tried—that are easier for the Secretary-General to do in the ways available to him than for the other organs. There are things which the other organs can do and the Secretary-General cannot do. It is a question for everybody who has responsibility in this case to judge when we pass from a situation which should be handled by the means available to the Secretary-General to a situation which requires action by one of the other organs.

My own feeling is that there is a certain tendency at present in some quarters to forget this difference of responsibilities and to expect from the Secretary-General action which rightly belongs to the Security Council. I have done and will continue to do what is possible for me to keep this situation on the rails with the means at my disposal and with the support, or lack of support, which I have to register.

THE NEW COUNTRIES AND ASSEMBLY VOTING

From transcript, 2 June 1960

QUESTION: I hope I can ask a question as a sort of *advocatus diaboli*. There is widespread thought and whispers in the United Nations . . . that the more the African countries are admitted to the United Nations the more reluctant the big Powers, or at least some big Powers, may be to bring decisive questions before the United Nations just because they do not want African countries and underdeveloped countries deciding upon these questions. You are certainly aware of this widespread rumour which goes up to the French summit. Will you comment on this and discuss with us the question of whether the usefulness of the UN is being increased or diminished by the admission of new countries? As I said, I am just speaking as an *advocatus diaboli*.

THE SECRETARY-GENERAL: I appreciate that, because I do not believe that you hold the view to which you have referred.

I am aware of the rumors you have mentioned, and I find it quite natural that this or that individual may give expression to that kind of pessimism. To me, it seems to be a typical lagging reaction and not at all based on facts or serious analysis of the situation.

That already implies my reply to your question. I do, for my part, believe that the usefulness of the United Nations will be increased by the addition of African States to the General Assembly. I do believe very much in the ability of those various states to make valuable contributions as soon as they have found their way in the maze of the United Nations. And I have already said at a previous press conference that their admission will move the General Assembly more in the direction of a true democratic parliament than we have had so far. I believe that in that way they will add life to the debates and to the consideration of questions.

There is something very shocking in the idea that new States must take so-called irresponsible stands. I myself do not believe it for a moment. On the contrary, I believe that new States are likely to approach problems with very great seriousness and with a very great sense of responsibility. But, as I said before, it is quite natural that they, like all of us, will have to find their way through a political system and a framework of procedures which so far have been unknown to them.

*   *   *

. . . . QUESTION: Would you comment on Dr. Spaak's suggestion of a weighted vote? His idea was that all the countries represented in the United Nations should not have the same voice in deciding questions, but that their votes should be weighted according to population, resources and various other factors.

THE SECRETARY-GENERAL: I do not believe in the possibility of having weighted voting in the United Nations. I think that would go against some very fundamental notions in the Charter. Equal voting may in some cases cause some practical difficulties, but I think that the advantages far outweigh the disadvantages. That is quite apart from the fact that an approach to weighted voting—if a formula could be found with which everybody would agree—would, in my view, go against a very basic idea in the Charter, which is the equality of sovereign States.

THE UNITED NATIONS AND
FAILURE AT THE SUMMIT

*Statement to the Press, 19 May 1960, following the
collapse of the Paris Summit meeting of Presidents
Eisenhower and de Gaulle, Chairman Krushchev and
Prime Minister Macmillan.*

Earlier this week, regrettably, the efforts to negotiate certain outstanding international issues at the level of the Chiefs of State failed.
The reasons why that happened will undoubtedly be studied and
discussed for a long time. There is a need to do so in order to be
able to draw the proper conclusions from what has happened as
guidance for the future. Men may be criticized, their actions may
be criticized, their words may be criticized, the methods used may
be criticized and abuses of those same methods may be attacked.
That is not the essential thing, and that does not lead us forward.
The problems which would have been taken up in Paris remain with
us and require as much of our honest efforts as ever. They deserve
our earnest attention. And they require renewed initiatives toward a
solution—initiatives that should be wiser for what has gone before,
but not envenomed by the feelings to which recent events may have
given rise.

The responsibilities of the UN and for all those who work within
the UN were never reduced by the efforts to reach solutions made
by other means, but rather they may be said to have been increased
by the discouraging experiences accumulated in the use of those
means. The Organization provides the framework for public diplomacy and for conference diplomacy on any level which governments
may desire. But it does so as part of a regular procedure, without
the building up of both expectations and problems in the way which
it is difficult to avoid in such other approaches as tend to make
of the negotiations pioneering initiatives of a unique character.
However, the Organization provides also the framework for continued non-publicized negotiations in which it is possible to play on
the whole range of approaches which have grown out of the experience of traditional diplomacy. There is in such non-publicized
diplomacy within the UN an additional element of value: the
mediating influence of the participation of all those who are vitally

interested in peace, while free from an immediate involvement in the issues at stake in terms of prestige or national interest.

A major problem which would have been considered in Paris is one for which the UN carries a special responsibility. I refer, of course, to disarmament. I hope and expect that the discussions of the Conference of Ten in Geneva will be taken up again and pursued with all energy, unhampered by the failure at the Summit. I express the same hope for the discussions regarding nuclear tests. And, in general terms, I hope that all Member nations, big Powers and others alike, will use the potentialities offered by the UN and its organs to the full in order to overcome a setback which otherwise might threaten to tie us down for a long time ahead. From us, who work directly for the Organization, a ready response will come to all demands for assistance. We will also act on our own initiative to the extent that such action may be helpful.

INTERNATIONAL COOPERATION
FOR SUSTAINED ECONOMIC
GROWTH

The following statement, dated 6 June 1960, was circulated to members of the Economic and Social Council in advance of its annual debate on the world economic situation at the 30th session beginning in Geneva the following month. It is perhaps the most comprehensive of the statements made by Dag Hammarskjöld as Secretary-General on the problems, functions and purposes of international economic cooperation.

Fifteen years have now passed since the second World War ended and ten years since the physical effects of the war were overcome. During all this time the world has been preoccupied with the tension dividing east and west. Nevertheless, despite changing political fortunes, international cooperation has registered an unprecedented advance in the economic sphere. This is due mainly to the movement of world-wide solidarity demonstrated first in the reconstruction of the war-devastated areas, and later directed to the infinitely vaster and more enduring task of bridging the gulf between countries at different stages of development. It is also true that while political or conceptual difficulties have hampered the progress of economic relationships between east and west, the area of cooperation, based on a recognized coincidence of interests, has, in recent years, tended to widen. It is therefore fitting that in this year 1960 which marks the beginning of a new decade, the Council should have decided to meet at the ministerial level, and should now undertake a broad examination of the direction to be taken if the challenge of national as well as of collective responsibility is to be met.

Economic interdependence has been increasing rapidly. In part, this has been the inevitable outcome of advances in science and technology, in transport and communications, which tend not only to shrink physical distances but also to diffuse cultural patterns throughout the world community. The tendency has been reinforced by the powerful drive for national independence, beginning immediately after the war in Asia, and now reaching a rapid climax in Africa. Though in another context such a movement might have generated powerful centrifugal forces splitting peoples apart, in the context of responsible national and international statesmanship towards which the United Nations has undoubtedly made its contribution, the emergence of new nations has, in fact, been accompanied by a growing sense of sharing a common membership in a world community. Of no less importance have been the powerful economic forces making for a growing integration of the world community. As the major trading countries of the world, in response to persistent pressures for economic efficiency, have dismantled their controls over trade and payments and have returned essentially to a system of international convertibility of currency, the degree of their mutual interdependence has inevitably increased. Having discarded economic instruments which had been earlier fashioned to shield them from foreign economic crises, their economies have naturally become more sensitive to influence from abroad.

Growing economic interdependence has been recently reflected in major efforts to strengthen inter-governmental organizations outside the United Nations. This is currently exemplified in the measure now being contemplated to remodel the Organization for European Economic Cooperation. Such broadening of institutional arrangements for international cooperation and action is of great historic importance. It also creates for the United Nations new problems and challenges. Regional arrangements among neighbouring or like-minded countries are bound to play a major role in the formulation of international economic policies. Nevertheless, it would be far from realistic to assume that regional arrangements can alone suffice to cope with the urgent problems confronting the community of nations. The United Nations organization remains the only universal agency in which countries with widely differing political institutions and at different stages of economic development may exchange views, share their problems and experiences, probe each other's reactions to policies of mutual interest, and initiate collective action; it is inspired and bound by the solemn pledge of the Charter to take 'joint' as well as 'separate' action. Unless steps are now taken to increase the effectiveness of action within the United Nations, the danger will exist that the strengthening of regional economic organs outside the Organization may divide as much as it unites.

It is to be hoped that the present ministerial session can help in reappraising the scope and direction of the United Nations' work in the economic and social field under prevailing political circumstances and in the light of prospective institutional changes in the framework of international cooperation.

BALANCED GROWTH

Balanced growth is gradually emerging as a central concept permeating public policy thinking in almost all countries, regardless of the stage of their economic development or of the nature of their basic political institutions. This is a healthy sign. For more than a generation, the world has been preoccupied with major catastrophes and minor crises—with a world depression of great magnitude and with the second World War, with acute post-war shortages, inflation and international disequilibria, with the effects of the Korean hostilities and the resulting raw material price boom and collapse, with recurrent minor recessions and recovery. Little wonder that in such a context, the immediate problems have tended to obscure long-term needs. Governments may now take courage from the degree of success that has been achieved in overcoming the various crises and in containing the forces of instability which have for so long plagued the world economy, and it is natural that they should increasingly turn their attention to the even more fundamental goals of growth.

This tendency is to be witnessed everywhere, although under a great variety of circumstances.

It is of course in the under-developed areas, emerging, as they are, from centuries of stagnation, that maximum awareness of the problem of growth is to be found. Despite the progress of the last decade, populations of these countries still endure levels of living which do not reflect the extraordinary expansion in the world's productive capacity and which are so much at variance with the revolutionary rise in peoples' expectations since the end of the war. How to convert a social and cultural environment rooted in a stationary economy into one that is growth-oriented; how to spare adequate resources from current consumption to finance an increase in the productive capacity of each country's economy without intolerable inflationary pressure; how to acquire the imports of capital goods and other essentials without deficit in the balance of payments; how to decide on the optimum allocation of resources between alternative uses for economic and social development; how to provide for adequate economic incentives for the necessary managerial, entrepreneurial and administrative leadership and for a labour force with the proper training and skills required by modern technology; how to develop adequate markets for the goods the economy is capable of producing—these are among the questions relating to the various aspects of growth which governments of under-developed countries cannot afford to leave without an answer. In most of these countries, preoccupation with growth is reflected in some form of planning, or, at least, in 'the creation of a general perspective giving broad guide-lines and orders of magnitude and objectives,' to quote the Consolidated Report of the Council Committee on Programme Appraisals.

In the advanced industrial countries with a free enterprise system, governments are also becoming aware that satisfactory rates of growth cannot be taken for granted. It is true that the post-war years have carried their levels of living to new highs. But, if the average rates of growth compare favourably with those of the pre-war period, it should not be overlooked that the earlier rates include the effects of major depressions and wars. They do not, therefore, necessarily provide an adequate guide for optimum growth in the future. Moreover, in recent years, the rate of expansion of the

industrial countries has been a declining one, partly perhaps because
private demand for investment may have grown less buoyant as the
arrears from the war and the pre-war depression have been more
than made good, but partly also because government policies have
not always proved entirely adequate to cope with the problem of
combining optimum rates of growth with price stability and balance
in the international payments accounts. Increasingly, the question
is asked whether adequate provision has been made, on the one
hand, for the appropriate improvement of the economic and social
overhead capital, and on the other, for protecting the levels of living
of the economically handicapped—the aged, the infirm and the
lower income groups generally. With the vast potential for expansion
in productive capacity and with the growing realization of the ever-
mounting waste of resources in armaments, it is felt that the time
has perhaps come to focus attention upon neglected opportunities
for raising standards in such areas as education and medical care,
or for wiping out the blight which, despite a decade of building
boom, continues to attack our cities. It is most significant that some
of the most advanced industrial countries now find it useful to
establish long-term plans for economic growth as guide-lines for
economic policy, and others, recently including Canada and the
United States, have established national commissions on economic
and social goals and policies.

Finally, in countries with centrally planned economies the
problem appears in somewhat different terms. Sustained high rates
of growth have been narrowing the gap between these countries and
the advanced industrial economies based on private enterprise, and
the question asked is whether capital accumulation has not been
proceeding at too fast a rhythm to permit for balanced growth, or
whether the allocation of resources between various uses has always
been satisfactory. Economic growth in these countries as in the
rest of the world has not been altogether free from inflationary
pressures. Agriculture has continuously been lagging in relation to
industry, and consumption in relation to investment and total output. The need is more and more recognized to give greater attention
to strengthening economic incentives of labourers or peasants, by
providing more consumer goods and a shorter work week.

A generation ago, it might have been assumed that responsibility
for policies of economic growth should be exclusively national.
Today, such a premise is hardly tenable. This is already recognized

in the United Nations Charter which reflects a major transformation of the concept of international cooperation and clearly establishes a measure of collective responsibility in such matters. Post-war experience has amply justified the Charter in this respect. It has been repeatedly shown that even a moderate slowdown in the rate of economic activity in one or two leading countries may affect prices and income, production and employment, and even prospects for development, in many parts of the world. Similarly, advances in industrial technology, or new trade arrangements between groups of countries, may have major repercussions in the national income and production of distant nations, at times far exceeding in importance their economic significance in places where they originate. It is, therefore, quite natural that in the United Nations the stable and balanced growth of the world economy is also gradually emerging as a dominant theme and preoccupation. In fact the importance now attached to this question is mirrored in a number of recent debates and resolutions. To list only those in the past year, in resolution 741 the Economic and Social Council requested a comprehensive evaluation of the techniques of long-term economic projections as a means of aiding economic development; the General Assembly in its resolution 1428 laid the ground for intensified work in the study of long-term perspectives. During the debate leading to the creation of a Committee for Industrial Development the importance of a periodic review of plans and prospects for industrialization of under-developed countries was repeatedly emphasized, and in the Commission on International Commodity Trade the study of medium-term trends has become one of the major topics. It should also be recalled that almost all the operational activities of the United Nations under its Technical Assistance and Special Fund programmes are directed towards the objective of balanced growth.

If the concern with balanced growth is already underlying so many of the United Nations activities, it is probable that an intensified and more systematic action is needed. It is worthwhile considering how the Organization could make its most effective contribution in this field and what steps should be taken to make this contribution possible. In this respect, the function of 'consultation' inherent in the Council, but never as yet fully developed, should be highlighted. Through a rationally organized process of consultations, the Organization might, more than any other agency, play an important role in both the harmonization of national policies and the formulation of international objectives.

The importance of consultations relating to *national policies* and objectives is underscored in the Council Committee's Programme Appraisal in the following terms:

'In an increasingly interdependent world, there is still far too little known regarding the extent to which the economic and social policies and objectives of the different nations are mutually consistent. Under constant pressure of immediate needs, governments are continually forced to take decisions of great significance for the future development of their countries without anything like adequate information on the corresponding policies and objectives of other governments, and on the world-wide framework into which these objectives are expected to fit. The harmonization of policies is an important function of the United Nations, according to the Charter. Nevertheless, as pointed out earlier in this report, it is an area where relatively little progress has been achieved. This is an obstacle to the development of national policies and programmes within the context of broad international policies.'

The reply of the Government of France to the questionnaire on long-term projections appropriately stresses that in a national economy consistency of objectives need not be a major preoccupation as long as a modest rate of growth is aimed at, for under such circumstances, the margin of adjustment in the various sectors is relatively large; but when rapid expansion is desired, a minimum of coherence of objectives and means becomes indispensable, if dangerous tensions are to be avoided. The same may be said to be true in the international community. It is recognized that some preliminary expert work will have to be done before meaningful consultations on long-term economic policies may be organized. Action undertaken under existing resolutions on long-term economic projections is but a modest beginning of what should become a continuing function of the Organization. It will be necessary to clarify further concepts and hypotheses and to establish their comparability. The Organization is well equipped to serve as a clearing house for the work undertaken by national or regional agencies entrusted with the formulation of perspectives and goals. It would require that a closer relationship be established between the

Secretariat and these agencies than has existed heretofore. Such a process might lead to considerable progress in the formulation of operationally meaningful goals for economic growth and in the definition of priorities for the proper phasing of policies of countries at various stages of development and under different social systems.

When work at the expert level is sufficiently advanced, regular and periodic consultations at the policy-making level can be organized, aiming at the harmonization of national economic goals and policies. Consultations of this nature might significantly help in reducing the inflationary or deflationary bias which often creeps into national policies when they are based on inadequate knowledge of trends and plans in the rest of the world. It would, moreover, minimize the risk for every country, particularly for those at an early stage of development, that their national policies for investment, especially for exports and imports, might be frustrated by conflicting policies in other countries.

Such cooperative efforts for analysis and consultations are at present taking place, although still in a very timid way, within regional groupings in Europe. This makes it more indispensable, and at the same time should make it easier, to promote a similar undertaking within the universal framework of the United Nations. Periodic meetings of ministers could constitute the propitious framework where a measure of guidance and leadership for some important inter-governmental decisions relating to economic goals and policies for growth might be found. The time factor involved in the full development of a process of this nature is not to be overlooked. However, even in its early stages, the degree of co-operation implicit in it, both at the technical and at the policy levels, would, in itself, be highly beneficial.

One word of caution is necessary, for concern is sometimes expressed about dangers of economic planning. The concern is related to a variety of factors including the difficulties of forecasting, the risk that plans might introduce undue rigidity in the economic structure, that they might be over-ambitious and unrealistic or that they might be inconsistent with the maintenance of a vigorous private enterprise system. These matters are discussed both in the *Programme Appraisal 1959–1964* and in the *World Economic Survey*, and it emerges clearly from these documents that the formulation of long-term economic goals and policies, far from introducing economic rigidity, may in fact impart a high degree of flexibility and adaptability to the economic structure, provided that the task is approached in a pragmatic fashion and that objectives and policies are kept under constant review: nor does this approach entail in itself any change in the basic political or institutional concepts of any country; in particular, it is not inconsistent with the expansion of private enterprise, as the recent experiences in a number of industrial countries such as Japan, Italy and France clearly show. Finally, consultations on long-term objectives and policies should not be mistaken for world economic planning. It is implicit in the Charter that each country shall give its own meaning to the objectives of full employment, economic growth and price stability, in accordance with its own economic resources, its social and political institutions and its cultural traditions. Consultations are only a means of arriving at a more effective and realistic formulation of these objectives and of the policies necessary for their attainment.

*　　*　　*

As the concepts of 'balanced growth' and 'economic goals' increasingly enter in the fabric of national policies within individual governments, they cannot fail to influence United Nations' attitudes in regard to the pattern of the world economy and the formulation of international policies pertaining to trade and aid.

INTERNATIONAL TRADE

The concept of international division of labour, which at times fell into disrepute because of its association with colonial policies, is now gaining new favour, as under-developed countries realize that it is not necessarily contrary to their industrialization or the diversification of their economies, nor to their desire for economic independence, and as nations with centrally planned economies give increasing attention to considerations of comparative costs. International division of labour is nowadays understood not only in terms of static gains derived from the allocation of resources in accordance with comparative advantages, but even more in terms of the dynamic gains resulting from improvement in productive efficiency.

This is quite clearly one of the major motivations behind the drive for regional integration, whether in western Europe, in eastern Europe or in Latin America. It is notable, however, that this drive is regional rather than universal and that it is spearheaded by countries with an advanced or with a rapidly developing industrial base. Although a number of under-developed countries find advantages in one or the other of the existing or prospective preferential systems, others find themselves much less comfortable in regard to these arrangements.

Among the most notable of the recent efforts at regional integration is the establishment of the Latin American Free Trade Association that took place earlier this year when seven Latin American countries signed the Treaty of Montevideo. While obligations under the Treaty are limited to the liberalization of current trade, the signatory States express, in the Preamble to the Treaty, their determination 'to persevere in their efforts to establish gradually and progressively a Latin American Common Market.' Since the north of the Latin American region is represented among the participating countries as well as the south, the Treaty is more than a sub-regional grouping of the Latin American countries: it will, moreover, be open to accession by the other Latin American States. This event represents a most important new departure in efforts to promote economic development in the area, based on the conviction among the signatory countries that, to quote again from the Preamble, 'the expansion of present national markets, through the gradual elimination of barriers to intra-regional trade, is a prerequisite if the Latin American countries are to accelerate their economic development process in such a way as to ensure a higher level of living for their peoples.' Similar considerations are inspiring the attempts of the Central American countries to reach agreement on an integrated approach to their development problems.

It is a matter of satisfaction that these efforts have largely taken place under the aegis of the United Nations through the medium of its Economic Commission for Latin America. This is a precedent which should not be lost sight of, as trends toward closer intra-regional relationships assert themselves in other parts of the world, notably in Africa.

Apart from regional integration, activity in the field of international trade centers around the GATT* and the International Monetary Fund which are especially concerned with reducing the barriers to international trade and payments. The GATT already has much to its credit in the achievement of a multilateral reduction

* General Agreement on Tariffs and Trade.

of tariffs, and the International Monetary Fund has similarly contributed towards freeing most of world trade from arbitrary exchange restrictions and discriminations. The statistics of post-war world trade give evidence of the excellent achievements of these and other institutions in helping to clear away innumerable barriers to the expansion of international exchanges. Yet the record is far from even. Trade between the centrally planned economies and those based on private enterprise remains small, partly for economic reasons, but partly also on political grounds. In this respect, a separate document submitted to the Council examines the conceptual difficulties involved in the possible equivalence of principles between the GATT rules and the Eastern European system of trade. Important work has been undertaken over the years within the Economic Commission for Europe, work which is of interest to the world as a whole. It is believed that this question should be further explored by experts until the time appears appropriate for a confrontation at the governmental level.

Even more striking, since the factors are exclusively economic, is the lag in trade between the advanced and the under-developed countries, especially exporters of agricultural products. In this lies perhaps the major obstacle to a well integrated world economy and it is from this point of view that governmental policies and attitudes towards international trade should be examined. Their orientation appears to have been shaped more largely by the static concepts of the pre-war world than by the post-war objectives of economic development. In this area, at least, international activity continues to focus more upon questions of equity and general reciprocity—upon the elimination of arbitrary trade restrictions, discrimination and dumping—than upon the more fundamental needs for expansion of world trade in the interest of economic development. Granted that the GATT contains a number of important provisions recognizing the special needs of the under-developed countries, it still remains true that even these provisions relate primarily to the establishment of appropriate standards for the institution of controls upon trade—whether they relate to national restriction of imports in support of economic development programmes or to the formulation of international agreements for the stabilization of commodity prices. Yet, important as such measures may be for the under-developed countries, it may be asked whether they are sufficient to take into account what is perhaps the most vital consideration relating to trade and economic development. Expansion of trade is essential to under-developed countries, not merely because of the benefits to be derived from international specialization—until they have succeeded in diversifying their economy, their lopsided specialization in only one or two export commodities holds risks which may at times be incommensurate with any such gains. For these countries an expansion of trade is essential because it provides the key for the acceleration of economic growth without inflation and without balance of payment difficulties. The significance of such trade is that it furnishes the most generalized form of purchasing power, thereby permitting under-developed countries to overcome through appropriate imports the limitation on growth stemming from the rigidities of their structure of production. Viewed in this context, much the most important problem in world trade would appear to lie in the lag of world demand for most primary commodities in relation to the rate of growth in the advanced industrial countries. Because this lag—examined at length in the *World Economic Survey, 1958*—remains a central feature of world trade, the rate of economic development of under-developed countries continues to be adversely affected. Because of this lag, it is inevitable for import restriction to occupy a prominent place in the development programs of under-developed countries, not because of any predilection towards autarchy but only because of the need to avoid insolvency.

Many of the factors affecting world import demand for primary products lie outside the sphere of international public policy. Such factors include the relative shift in output as between countries, or the shift in the structure of production in favor of services and of durable goods with a relatively low input of primary materials. Other elements, such as economies in the use of raw materials, stemming from technological advance, it would not be in the long-run interests of the world economy to retard; the world as a whole can only gain from savings in input per unit of output, whether the savings are in manpower, equipment or raw materials. One range of factors, however, has rightly been singled out by a panel of experts appointed by the GATT as an appropriate area for international policy formulation. This relates to the effect upon import demand of industrial countries stemming from their policies affecting foreign trade, whether for revenue or for protective purposes. To the extent to which it might prove feasible to relax such policies of the industrial countries in the interests of promoting exports of under-developed countries, whether it be primary products or the output of newly established manufacturing industries, it would be possible to make a significant contribution to their economic development and to the economic integration of the world community.

In the national sphere, countries have learned that a dynamic economy is capable of solving problems of equitable distribution of income that in a static framework might only give rise to a fruitless struggle. At the regional level, likewise, many countries are acting to secure the benefits that may come from lowering of trade barriers and increasing the degree of economic integration. The time has perhaps come when the United Nations should consider whether concerted action for the expansion of international markets for exports of under-developed countries might not bear similar fruit. If so, the question of defining meaningful goals for such expansion might well be included in the formulation of international objectives for the development of the world economy.

Related to the problem of the long-term lag in trade of primary products is that of the violent short-term fluctuations in both volume and prices. The causes of the instability, its effect upon the internal stability and development of the under-developed countries, and the national and international policies for dealing with instability have been examined at length in the *World Economic Survey, 1958*. The subject is a major item on the work program of the Commission on International Commodity Trade (CICT), whose report is before the Council, and it has been repeatedly examined both in the Council and the Assembly. The replies to a questionnaire circulated to governments during the past year show that for the most part governments continue to believe that the most appropriate method for dealing with the problem of stabilization is on a commodity-by-commodity basis. Renewed interest has developed, however, in some proposals for general stabilization measures, and even more in measures for offsetting the effects of fluctuations in trade in primary products by more systematic action for compensatory financing. This problem which is also being examined in the CICT, will be the subject of an intensive investigation by a Committee of Experts to be appointed by the Secretary-General under General Assembly resolution 1423 (XIV). It is, of course, possible that the Council will not wish, at this stage, pending completion of the work of the experts, to give overall policy guidance on this point. On the other hand, statements of governmental positions and attitudes may assist in ensuring that the experts deliberate in the full knowledge of political realities. In any case, in view of the marked weakness in commodity trade in 1957-58 and the failure to achieve a strong recovery in prices in the course of the general upsurge of economic activity in 1959, it is clear that the problem of commodity instability will call for continued patient and sympathetic consideration in the United Nations.

INTERNATIONAL ASSISTANCE

It is in the field of public international aid that post-war policies have proved most dynamic. Though one may still question the magnitude and modalities of present programmes, assistance from governmental or intergovernmental sources has come to be accepted as a durable element of great importance in the world economy. It is a major channel for the dissemination of technology, the transfer of savings and the propagation of growth; in almost all the under-developed countries it provides, quantitatively and qualitatively, a significant component of development plans. At the same time, it has brought with it new problems: for some of the major industrial nations it represents commitments which, at times, decisively affect their balance of payments position. The readiness with which this new element has been incorporated in international policies testifies to a remarkable resiliency in attitudes. Moreover, as will be shown in the report on international economic assistance to the under-developed countries, policies relating to international aid seem to be under constant examination with a view to making them more effective and better adapted to the varying and changing requirements of the developing countries.

Studies and debates in the United Nations have significantly contributed to the elucidation in theory, and the initiation in practice, of programmes of international aid, and many governments remain desirous to see the Organization further develop its action in this field. This is to be undertaken in a universal agency of equal nations, where the distinction between donors and receivers tends to dissolve itself. Over the years, debates have shown that, because of this particular feature, a great number of governments felt that the resources entrusted to the United Nations agencies for aid purposes were far from adequate. While schemes long discussed for the creation of a capital fund within the United Nations remain a matter of controversy, a consensus of opinions might be reached on a certain broadening of the present United Nations role. In this respect, proposals are being made to this session of the Council motivated by the need to keep pace with the emergence of a number of new countries into independence, and their expectation of the kind of services which are to be found within the Organization. But, quite apart from these special historic circumstances, certain consequences must logically follow from the growing recognition of the importance of United Nations action particularly in the *pre-investment* field. As long as doubts remain about the capacity of developing nations to absorb capital, there should be no hesitation in fostering, to the maximum extent, those activities which now take place under the Technical Assistance and Special Fund pro-grammes and which aim at transforming latent opportunities for in-vestment into actual opportunities. The figure of 100 million dollars had been mentioned more than two years ago in resolutions of the Assembly and the Council as a reasonable target for such activities under prevailing conditions and this figure may very well be con-sidered too modest under present circumstances. It may be a matter of legitimate concern that pledges worked out individually have not proved adequate to build up the total which represents the collective judgment. Such are, of course, the hazards of voluntary programmes, but it is hoped that the intensification of inter-governmental con-sultations now advocated in organs where the major donor countries meet, will be more fully used to adjust individual efforts to global requirements.

Over the years a remarkable phenomenon has taken place without perhaps attracting sufficient attention: born as an instrument for multilateral diplomacy, the United Nations has grown into an operational agency of significant dimensions. Theoretical knowledge and practical experience have accumulated, technical services have developed to a point where the machinery is now capable of a greater and more diversified performance than that which is currently entrusted to it. In particular there is no inherent obstacle or weakness which would prevent the Organization from playing its part in the field of capital investment. This would appear possible even without new institutional developments such as SUNFED,*

---

* Special United Nations Fund for Economic Development, a long discussed capital fund not to be confused with the existing Special Fund which is concerned with pre-investment activities and is not a credit institution.

provided the present potentialities of the United Nations as an executive agency are fully recognized. Whether governments, for general reasons, desire to associate the United Nations with their assistance efforts, or find it convenient to use the network of regional and functional organs and agents for the initiation of specific projects, or regard the Organization as a focal point for joint enterprises involving several nations, there is now no real reason why the services at the disposal of the United Nations should not be used more readily, even beyond the pre-investment field. If the Organization were to act as an agent or intermediary for specific projects, this would only be a logical development of present activities, one without which these activities would not always achieve their full meaning. There is of course nothing in the present rules and regulations which would constitutionally prevent such developments from taking place and experience already gained under the schemes for the development of the Lower Mekong basin illustrates the type of arrangement which can be devised.* But official encouragement on the part of inter-governmental bodies might greatly assist in the development of this new function.

It is also probable that the need will be increasingly felt for more systematic information on aid activities if the waste or misdirection which may result from many unrelated initiatives are to be avoided and if opportunities for investment are to be at all times known to potential aid-giving governments. It should be noted that facilities of a clearing-house type exist, in a limited way, for South-East Asia, under the Colombo plan and that they appear to have worked to the satisfaction of all concerned. Possibilities for this kind of action are inherent in the structure of the United Nations. They would be just a further development in the function of consultation, as applied to the problem of aid. They might be particularly useful for the continent of Africa, under the aegis of the Economic Commission for that region, as relationships of African countries with the rest of the world become diversified, and as new sources of assistance become available. This seems to have been what the governments assembled in Tangier for the second session of the Economic Commission for Africa had in mind when they adopted a resolution expressing the view 'that the Economic Commission for Africa

---

* A project for flood control and multiple water resources development in which various UN agencies and individual Member governments are cooperating with the four riparian States—Cambodia, Laos, Thailand and Vietnam.

19

should play an important role in the consideration of any new proposals that may be made for multilateral economic and financial assistance to Africa.'

THE FLOW OF PRIVATE CAPITAL

With the recognition of public aid as a major instrument in international cooperation for the building of the economic and social infrastructure of the under-developed countries, controversies which have at times centered around the role of private capital, its scope and its limitations, have tended to recede. In fact the success of the programmes of public foreign investment has not restricted, but rather contributed to expand the opportunities for an increasing flow of private capital.

The most recent studies undertaken by the Secretariat show encouraging signs of greater flexibility as regards the forms and objectives of foreign investment. In the less-developed countries, many types of foreign-financed manufacturing industries are springing up alongside the traditional investments in natural resources and public utilities. This tendency also responds to definite policies whereby governments of under-developed countries seek to direct a scarce supply of foreign private capital into those particular fields of activity in which they are likely to provide the strongest impetus to the development of the national economy. In addition to special concessions and assistance offered to investors in such priority industries and locations, governments are increasingly turning to programmes of investment promotion which range from the provision of information on local investment conditions to the identification and preparation of specific investment projects likely to meet both the requirements of foreign investors and those of national development policy. Foreign private capital is frequently supported by public financing from domestic or international sources.

The variety in the forms of foreign private investment is highlighted by the increasing resort to joint ventures and consortia for the pooling of foreign and domestic capital, management and techniques. Access to scientific information and its adaptation to the needs and conditions of under-developed countries are essential prerequisites for rapid development in decisive areas of industry, especially for growth firms, in the chemical, electronics, pharmaceutical and plastics fields. Major firms in advanced countries, which specialize in product development, now find it advantageous to expand their markets by 'investing' their scientific know-how as partners or licensors in industrial enterprises of under-developed countries. Training facilities for engineers and research technicians are also being made available in foreign enterprises and the United Nations technical assistance programme is active in developing the use of such facilities.

The question very naturally arises whether the readiness of foreign enterprises to invest abroad could not be enhanced by measures limiting the non-business risks involved. The elimination of the so-called political risks, whether these are real or apprehended, is currently the subject of extensive deliberations in many parts of the world. A number of governments have already taken action in this respect, especially through the introduction of guaranty schemes for the insurance of their investors against loss of foreign assets, in particular through nationalization or foreign exchange restrictions. Numerous other national and international schemes for the protection of foreign investments on terms which would be acceptable to the capital-importing countries are currently under consideration. Interest in particular is shown for measures designed to assure the investor of an independent recourse in disputes with the government of the country in which he has invested. Such recourse would chiefly take the form of an international arbitration.

There is considerable precedent for the arbitration of disputes arising in connection with foreign private investments. Provisions to that effect are increasingly found in bilateral agreements to which some of the major capital-supplying countries are parties, as well as in investment promotion laws of developing countries and in individual concession agreements concluded between governments and foreign companies. While arbitration under treaties requires action by the investor's home government, in the other cases the procedure can be initiated and carried forward by the investor himself.

Recent debates in the Council show that while there was some hesitation on the part of certain States, further exploration of the matter was considered worthwhile. In this respect, it should be noted that in the question of commercial arbitration, the United Nations has been able to initiate useful action as exemplified by the Convention on the Recognition and Enforcement of Foreign Arbitral Awards, and one should not exclude the possibility that some facilities, if only of a modest nature, for international arbitration in matters of foreign investment might develop under the aegis of the Organization, or linked with the Organization.

*   *   *

Policies of growth, international trade and aid, the flow of private capital, although they are far from exhausting the list of responsibilities of the United Nations and the specialized agencies in the economic and social field, are all important topics on which a greater measure of understanding appears at once desirable and, in varying degree, possible. They are important in their own right, in terms of human welfare. They are also related to the other, and major, objective and criterion of United Nations action, the preservation of peace. Obligations assumed by Members of the United Nations under Article 55 of the Charter are expressly aimed at 'the creation of conditions of stability and well-being which are necessary for peaceful and friendly relations among nations . . .'. An essential link is thereby established, and with a background of persisting world tensions, Member governments might well find in it an additional and powerful incentive for strengthening the Organization in those fields where the road to progress appears open, and, indeed, promising.

INTRODUCTION TO THE
ANNUAL REPORT 1959-1960

31 August 1960

———◆———

I. AFRICA AND THE UNITED NATIONS

On 1 January 1960 the former Trust Territory of the Cameroons under French administration became independent. For the first time a territory previously under United Nations trusteeship became an independent State by itself, thus giving full effect to the objective stated in Article 76(b) of the Charter that the United Nations shall 'promote the political, economic, social and educational advancement of the inhabitants of the Trust Territories, and their progressive development towards self-government or independence. . . .'

The event which thus marked the first day of 1960 has been followed by the accession to independence by many more African States, among them two additional Trust Territories, the Togolese Republic and the Republic of Somalia. By the time the General Assembly meets, fourteen African States will have been recommended by the Security Council for admission as new Members of the United Nations. It can confidently be expected that the Federation of Nigeria will apply for membership soon after the opening of the General Assembly; the admission of all these new States would bring the number of African States Members of the United Nations from ten at the end of 1959 to twenty-five at the fifteenth session of the General Assembly.

Another new Member has also been recommended for admission: I have in mind Cyprus, the independence of which has brought to an end a long-standing conflict considered at several sessions of the General Assembly.

It is not only the development into independence and into membership in the United Nations of a great number of African States which, for the Organization, characterizes the year 1960, so symbolically inaugurated by the independence of an African Trust Territory. The developments in the Republic of the Congo have engaged the United Nations in the greatest single task which it has had to handle by its own means and on its own conditions.

In these circumstances it may be appropriate for this Introduction to the Annual Report of the Secretary-General to the General Assembly to give attention, in the first place, to the problem of Africa and its importance for the international community.

Historically, Africa is not a unit. While North Africa and parts of East and West Africa have significant traditional links to the Mediterranean, to Islam or even to southern Asia, West, East and Central Africa south of the Sahara have received a significant impact from different European colonial administrations, varying in length and intensity, linking them, however tenuously, to institutions of a few European countries. The southern part of the continent has a development of its own, which finds but few parallels in the rest of Africa.

Not only have these diverse influences in Africa's past relations with the outside world led to divisions on the continent, but the manner and form in which colonial rule has been exercised have tended to accentuate these divisions. There are great differences between the evolution in areas formerly under British control and those formerly under French control, and there are even greater differences between these areas and the territories which were administered by Belgium. This applies to language, to certain traditions established, to legal ideas transmitted, and particularly to the ways in which political development for these territories was conceived and advanced.

The differences thus superimposed by recent history are reinforced by underlying diversities of race and national history. In these respects, Africa is much less homogeneous than South or South-East Asia, not to speak of Europe or Latin America. There are not only basic differences between the Arabs and Berbers living in the northern part of the continent and Africans south of the Sahara, but among the latter the impact of the environment, and of the great distances and difficulties of communication, has tended to create populations with very distinct differences in attitude and approach which are deeper and wider than tribal differences existing in other parts of the continent.

Finally, in Africa the first beginnings can now be seen of those conflicts between ideologies and interests which split the world. Africa is still, in comparison with other areas, a virgin territory which many have found reason to believe can or should be won for their aims and interests.

It is in the face of all this that the United Nations has, in the great task which it is facing in the Congo, appealed to 'African solidarity within the framework of the United Nations.' As the developments have shown, this is not a mere phrase; it applies to something which has become a reality. It is my firm conviction that the African States cannot render themselves and their peoples a greater service than to foster this solidarity. Likewise, I am convinced that the United Nations cannot render its new African Member States and the whole community of nations in Africa a greater service than to assist them, within the framework of their own efforts, to mould their new national and regional life, now that they enter the community of nations, in ways that will give Africa its rightful place on the international scene.

It is for the African States themselves to define the elements which establish the basis for African solidarity. It is also for them to find and define the aims which this regional community should pursue. But, also, for one not belonging to the region, it is possible, in the light of experiences, especially as they have evolved during the Congo crisis, to give some general indications.

There are negative elements in the picture, only too natural in the light of history. I have in mind the strong anti-colonialism which has created a marked resistance against any suspected attempt to interfere or to impose from outside a will foreign to the will of the peoples. There are, of course, also elements of racism, just as understandable in the light of experience, which, however, are strongly rejected by forward-looking, responsible leaders. It is a mistake to see in any of these reactions a hostility in principle against peoples of other races or regions. Expressed in positive terms, as it should be, the attitude is one of willingness to cooperate with the rest of the world and one of eagerness to integrate into the rest of the world, combined, however, with a firm rejection of any attempts by others to turn the efforts of the African States to achieve this cooperation and integration into subjection, be it political, economic or ideological.

Reactions from the outside have been mixed. There are those who try to maintain what history has already judged. There are those who try to put in place of the past new and more subtle forms of predominance and influence. There are, on the other hand, also those for whom independence is an end in itself, irrespective of whether or not, in the form in which it can be offered, it serves the best interest of the people. There are, finally, those who, using these various reactions and counter-reactions, try to manipulate them for their own ends.

The attitude of the United Nations in this situation seems to me to be clear; it follows from the aims of the Charter. The Organization must further and support policies aiming at independence, not only in the constitutional sense but in every sense of the word, protecting the possibilities of the African peoples to choose their own way without undue influences being exercised and without attempts to abuse the situation. This must be true in all fields—the political, the economic, as well as the ideological—if independence is to have a real meaning. Working for these purposes, the United Nations can build on the confidence of the best and most responsible elements of all the countries of the continent. As a universal organization neutral in the big Power struggles over ideology and influence in the world, subordinated to the common will of the Member governments and free from any aspirations of its own to power and influence over any group or nation, the United Nations can render service which can be received without suspicion and which can be absorbed without influencing the free choice of the peoples.

These possibilities of the United Nations create a corresponding responsibility. If the Organization is willing and able to face its duties, it will have given the new nations of Africa the framework of which they are in need during the first and sensitive years of independence. It will also be helping the African world, in solidarity, to determine its own political personality in the setting of universality as represented by the United Nations. If it faces these tasks and succeeds in them, it will make a vitally necessary contribution to international peace and to a more stable world.

In spite of all the divisions mentioned, African solidarity is a fact. Its growth is something that rightly should be hailed by other regions and by all nations, whatever the legacy of past relationships and whatever immediate political aims may seem to be countered by the growth of such solidarity.

The African States have realized that to grow into independence means to grow into interdependence. But to grow into interdependence means also to assume international responsibility and such international responsibility must be based on national responsibility. The contribution made from independent Member States in Africa to the Congo operation has shown that African solidarity within the framework of the United Nations can build on a strong sense of national responsibility, radiating into the international sphere and creating the interdependence in which independence can yield its most rewarding results.

II. PARLIAMENTARY AND EXECUTIVE DEVELOPMENTS

The African developments are putting the United Nations to a test both as regards the functions of its parliamentary institutions and as regards the efficiency and strength of its executive capacity.

The considerable increase in the membership of the United Nations stemming from a region with short independent experience in international politics has led to doubts regarding the possibility of the General Assembly and its committees to work expeditiously and in a way which truly reflects considered world opinion. In this context the question of the voting system has again been raised.

In previous reports to the General Assembly I have touched on this problem, indicating as my conviction that there is no practical alternative in keeping with the basic tenets of the Charter to the present system of equal votes for all sovereign Member States. Naturally it may be said that the irrationality of such a system is demonstrated when a new voting balance can be achieved through a sudden expansion of the number of Members by some 20 per cent. However, this fails to take into account realities to which reference has likewise been made in previous reports.

The General Assembly is a body which reflects in its decisions on major questions the results of long and careful negotiations and consideration. During this process, common lines are elaborated and compromises reached which give to the decisions the character of a confirmation of a negotiated approach rather than of a solution achieved through the mechanics of voting. Furthermore, the background of the decisions of the General Assembly, which, of course, anyway have the character of recommendations, should be analyzed in order to arrive at a true evaluation of their significance. A voting victory or a voting defeat may be of short-lived significance. What is regarded as responsible world opinion as reflected in the voting and in the debates is in many respects more important than any formally registered result.

There is in the views expressed in favor of weighted voting an implied lack of confidence in the seriousness and responsibility with which newly independent States are likely to take their stands. Such a lack of confidence is not warranted by the history of the United Nations and must be rejected as contrary to facts. Neither size, nor wealth, nor age is historically to be regarded as a guarantee for the quality of the international policy pursued by any nation.

It is my conviction that the addition of a great number of new Member States will widen the perspectives, enrich the debate and bring the United Nations closer to present-day realities. I also believe that this development will exercise a sound influence in the direction of a democratization of proceedings by lessening the influence of firm groupings with firm engagements.

However, the widened membership does create certain practical problems. It may tend to lengthen debates, and it may make the General Assembly proceedings seem too cumbersome in cases where speed and efficiency are of the essence. For that reason, the development directs attention again to the possibilities for improving the methods applied in the parliamentary institutions of the Organization. Thus, I feel that Member nations may wish to consider a greater role for the General Committee,* so that it can assume a wider responsibility for the conduct of the work of the General Assembly and eventually ease the burden of the Assembly and its substantive committees.

If and when the question of Charter revision comes up for consideration, the evolution of the General Assembly also is likely to add weight to the question of the role, composition and procedures of the Security Council.

During the Suez and Hungary crises, a development took place through which increased responsibilities were temporarily transferred from the Security Council to the General Assembly. Since it is difficult for the General Assembly to act expeditiously if it is required to engage in detailed consideration of complicated legal and technical problems, the Assembly found that the most adequate way to meet the challenges which it had to face was to entrust the

* The General Committee is the Assembly's steering committee.

Secretary-General with wide executive tasks on the basis of mandates of a general nature.

Especially in the Suez crisis, when all the executive work was entrusted to the Secretary-General, this put the Secretariat to a severe test. However, it proved possible, in close interplay between the General Assembly and the Secretary-General, assisted by the Advisory Committee appointed by the General Assembly, to work smoothly and swiftly towards a speedy achievement of the established aims. The value and possibilities of the Secretariat as an executive organ were thus proved, a fact which has in significant ways influenced later developments.

Without going into detail, I wish to recall that in the Lebanon crisis the General Assembly came into the picture only at a very late stage, while executive action in the earlier phases of the crisis was guided by the Security Council, which for the purpose availed itself of the services of the Secretary-General. Likewise, the first part of the Laos crisis was entirely in the hands of the Security Council.

This year has seen a further return of the Security Council to its central role as the organ of the United Nations which carries primary responsibility for peace and security. Thus, the question of South Africa and especially the question of the Congo have been major tasks with which the Council has been exclusively seized. The reason for this return to the Security Council from the General Assembly is, naturally, that both these questions have been of a nature which has to a degree placed them outside the conflicts of today between the main power blocs.* The shift of the emphasis back from the General Assembly to the Security Council has, however, not led to a change of working methods, as the Council, following the recent procedures of the Assembly, has used the services of the Secretariat and the Secretary-General as its main executive agent.

The Congo crisis has put the Secretariat under the heaviest strain which it has ever had to face. The organization of a sizeable military force under very difficult geographical and physical conditions, the creation of the necessary administrative framework for the military operation, and the development of a far-reaching civilian program to meet the most urgent needs of the country's economy have proved

* At the time this was written the USSR had not yet switched to a policy of attack upon the conduct of UN operations in the Congo, although it had become increasingly critical in the latter part of August. The break came a few days later, after President Kasavubu's dismissal of Patrice Lumumba and the ensuing constitutional crisis.

possible only thanks to the unstinting willingness of all Secretariat members to assume added burdens and the availability of a great number of people of a sufficiently general background to take up new assignments, sometimes far beyond and far different from their normal professional work. I wish on this point to pay a tribute to all those members of the Secretariat who have made the Congo operation possible.

The activities entrusted to the Secretariat by the Security Council in the case of the Congo have been widespread and have required an unusual combination of elements which normally would have required a much bigger and more specialized machinery than the one of which the United Nations disposes. The interplay between parliamentary operations in the United Nations, political action, diplomatic negotiation, military operations and administrative measures has been subtle and exacting. To the extent that it may be said to have worked and to have led to the desired results, it bears witness of a flexibility in the organization of the work of the United Nations which is encouraging for the future.

Naturally, however, the experiences have demonstrated also weaknesses in the organization of the Secretariat. It does not dispose of a sufficient number of highly qualified senior officials for all the tasks that now have to be met—in spite of the feeling sometimes voiced that the Organization is 'top-heavy'. There is, generally speaking, within the Secretariat not enough of a diplomatic tradition or staff with training in political and diplomatic field activities to meet the needs which have developed over the years. And it is, finally, a considerable weakness that the Secretariat has not in its ranks a highly qualified military expertise which is able, on a current basis, to maintain a state of preparedness for the kind of situation which the Organization has suddenly had to face. It is, of course, not my intention that in these various respects the Secretariat should be normally organized so as to be able to meet without difficulty or added strain a crisis of the Congo type. What I have in mind is only that it is desirable to have within the Secretariat a nucleus which can be switched over to the present type of task with full knowledge of the requirements and proper preparation, while leaving the normal work of the Organization intact because of the availability of sufficient second-line reserves.

I have mentioned the need for some strengthening of the Secretariat on the military side. This, in the light of recent experience, would be my reply, as regards actions by the United Nations, to those who have found in the Congo developments new reasons for the organization of a standing United Nations force. As I have already clarified my views on this problem in earlier reports to the General Assembly, I have no reason to go into the matter in any detail here. It should, however, be stressed that the Congo experience has strengthened my conviction that the organization of a standing United Nations force would represent an unnecessary and impractical measure, especially in view of the fact that every new situation and crisis which the Organization will have to face is likely to present new problems as to the best adjustment of the composition of a force, its equipment, its training and its organization.

It is an entirely different matter if governments, in a position and willing to do so, would maintain a state of preparedness so as to be able to meet possible demands from the United Nations. And it is also an entirely different matter, for the Organization itself, to have a state of preparedness with considerable flexibility and in the hands of a qualified staff which quickly and smoothly can adjust their plans to new situations and assist the Secretary-General in the crucially important first stages of the execution of a decision by the main organs to set up a United Nations force, whatever its type or task.

The value of such preparedness can be seen from the fact that the organization of the United Nations Force in the Congo was considerably facilitated by the fact that it was possible for the Secretary-General to draw on the experience of the United Nations Emergency Force in Gaza and on the conclusions regarding various questions of principle and law which had been reached on the basis of that experience. The Congo operation being far more complicated and far bigger than the Gaza operation, it is likely that it will lead to a new series of valuable experiences which should be fully utilized by the United Nations, by appropriate informal planning within the administration.

III. THE UNITED NATIONS AND THE COLD WAR

On various points the preceding observations have touched upon the ideological conflicts and the conflicts of power which divide our world of today.

There is no reason to elaborate here the way in which these major conflicts have influenced proceedings within the United Nations and even the constitutional pattern which has developed in practice. One word may, however, be said about the possibilities of substantive action by the United Nations in a split world.

Fundamental though the differences splitting our world are, the areas which are not committed in the major conflicts are still considerable. Whether the countries concerned call themselves non-committed, neutral, neutralist or something else, they have all found it not to be in harmony with their role and interests in world politics to tie their policies, in a general sense, to any one of the blocs or to any specific line of action supported by one of the sides in the major conflict. The reasons for such attitudes vary. That, however, is less important in this special context than the fact that conflicts arising within the non-committed areas offer opportunities for solutions which avoid an aggravation of big Power differences and can remain uninfluenced by them. There is thus a field within which international conflicts may be faced and solved with such harmony between the power blocs as was anticipated as a condition for Security Council action in San Francisco. Agreement may be achieved because of a mutual interest among the big Powers to avoid having a regional or local conflict drawn into the sphere of bloc politics.

With its constitution and structure, it is extremely difficult for the United Nations to exercise an influence on problems which are clearly and definitely within the orbit of present day conflicts between power blocs. If a specific conflict is within that orbit, it can be assumed that the Security Council is rendered inactive, and it may be feared that even positions taken by the General Assembly would follow lines strongly influenced by considerations only indirectly related to the concrete difficulty under consideration. Whatever the attitude of the General Assembly and the Security Council, it is in such cases also practically impossible for the Secretary-General to operate effectively with the means put at his disposal, short of risking seriously to impair the usefulness of his office for the Organization in all the other cases for which the services of the United Nations Secretariat are needed.

This clearly defines the main field of useful activity of the United Nations in its efforts to prevent conflicts or to solve conflicts. Those efforts must aim at keeping newly arising conflicts outside the

sphere of bloc differences. Further, in the case of conflicts on the
margin of, or inside, the sphere of bloc differences, the United
Nations should seek to bring such conflicts out of this sphere
through solutions aiming, in the first instance, at their strict localization. In doing so, the Organization and its agents have to lay
down a policy line, but this will then not be for one party against
another, but for the general purpose of avoiding an extension or
achieving a reduction of the area into which the bloc conflicts
penetrate.

Experience indicates that the preventive diplomacy, to which the
efforts of the United Nations must thus to a large extent be directed,
is of special significance in cases where the original conflict may be
said either to be the result of, or to imply risks for, the creation of
a power vacuum between the main blocs. Preventive action in such
cases must in the first place aim at filling the vacuum so that it will
not provoke action from any of the major parties, the initiative for
which might be taken for preventive purposes but might in turn
lead to counter-action from the other side. The ways in which a
vacuum can be filled by the United Nations so as to forestall such
initiatives differ from case to case, but they have this in common:
temporarily, and pending the filling of a vacuum by normal means,
the United Nations enters the picture on the basis of its non-
commitment to any power bloc, so as to provide to the extent
possible a guarantee in relation to all parties against initiatives
from others.

The special need and the special possibilities for what I here
call preventive United Nations diplomacy have been demonstrated
in several recent cases, such as Suez and Gaza, Lebanon and
Jordan, Laos and the Congo.

A study of the records of the conflicts to which I have just
referred shows how it has been possible to use the means and
methods of the United Nations for the purposes I have indicated.
In all cases, whatever the immediate reason for the United Nations
initiative, the Organization has moved so as to forestall developments which might draw the specific conflict, openly or actively,
into the sphere of power bloc differences. It has done so by introducing itself into the picture, sometimes with very modest means,
sometimes in strength, so as to eliminate a political, economic and
social, or military vacuum.

The view expressed here as to the special possibilities and

responsibilities of the Organization in situations of a vacuum has reached an unusually clear expression in the case of the Congo. There, the main argument presented for United Nations intervention was the breakdown of law and order, the rejection of the attempt to maintain order by foreign troops, and the introduction of the United Nations Force so as to create the basis for the withdrawal of the foreign troops and for the forestalling of initiatives to introduce any other foreign troops into the territory with the obvious risks for widening international conflict which would ensue.

Whether the Congo operation is characterized as a case of preventive diplomacy, or as a move in order to fill a vacuum and to forestall the international risks created by the development of such a vacuum, or as a policy aimed at the localization of a conflict with potentially wide international repercussions, is not essential. Whatever the description, the political reality remains. It is a policy which is justified by the wish of the international community to avoid this important area being split by bloc conflicts. It is a policy rendered possible by the fact that both blocs have an interest in avoiding such an extension of the area of conflict because of the threatening consequences, were the localization of the conflict to fail.

Those who look with impatience at present-day efforts by the United Nations to resolve major international problems are inclined to neglect, or to misread, the significance of the efforts which can be made by the United Nations in the field of practical politics in order to guide the international community in a direction of growing stability. They see the incapacity of the United Nations to resolve the major bloc conflicts as an argument against the very form of international cooperation which the Organization represents. In doing so, they forget what the Organization has achieved and can achieve, through its activities regarding conflicts which are initially only on the margin of, or outside, the bloc conflicts, but which, unless solved or localized, might widen the bloc conflicts and seriously aggravate them. Thus the Organization in fact also exercises a most important, though indirect, influence on the conflicts between the power blocs by preventing the widening of the geographical and political area covered by these conflicts and by providing for solutions whenever the interests of all parties in a localization of conflict can be mobilized in favor of its efforts.

The Organization in this way also makes a significant contribution in the direction of an ultimate solution of the differences between the power blocs, as it is obvious that it is a condition for an improvement in the situation that the area to which those differences apply, as a minimum requirement, is not permitted to expand and, so far as possible, is reduced.

It is with this background that the initiative for United Nations intervention in the Congo conflict was taken under Article 99 of the Charter, for the first time applied fully, according to its letter and in the spirit in which it must have been drafted. It is also in this light that one has to view the fact that not only the first but also the subsequent decisions in the Security Council regarding the Congo have been taken by votes in which the power bloc conflicts have not been reflected.

These observations are of special interest when we turn to the consideration of questions regarding which the power bloc interests openly clash. I have in mind especially disarmament. In general terms, it is not surprising that, in the case of problems so deeply related to the security of many nations and to the predominant Powers within the different blocs, negotiations have presented extraordinary difficulties. On the other hand, it is also evident that there is a latitude within which a shared interest in avoiding an aggravation of the situation overrides the specific security interests of any one party and within which, for that reason, agreement may be possible.

De facto, we have seen such an agreement developing in the field of nuclear tests. I believe that there are also other questions within the field of disarmament regarding which success is possible for new efforts to reach agreement, on at least so much of a common *de facto* policy as is indicated by the mutual interest to avoid a widening of the substantive basis for the present day race towards a world crisis. Approached in this way, disarmament seems to offer important possibilities, still incompletely explored, of a gradual reduction of the area in which clashing security interests so far have rendered formal agreement impossible.

There is no contradiction between this application to the disarmament problem of the philosophy and practices successfully tried by the United Nations in specific conflicts and the view that there can be no solution to the disarmament problem short of the acceptance of total disarmament under satisfactory control by both sides. The pragmatic approach and the, so to say, global one are

20

not at variance, for it is obvious that efforts to avoid a widening of the field of conflict and to reduce the area in which concrete agreement for the moment is impossible should at all events be integrated into a wider, more far-reaching plan under which the security interests of the parties can be balanced out against each other in ways that will make it possible for the parties to reach the ideal target of total disarmament.

It is certainly not productive to approach the disarmament problem solely on a pragmatic basis, without integration of the steps taken into a plan ultimately aiming at full disarmament. Likewise, however, it seems unrealistic to approach the total problem oblivious of the fact that all political experience and all previous negotiation show that the road to progress lies in the direction of efforts to contain and reduce the area of disagreement by mobilizing such common interests as may exist and as may override other and special interests tending in the opposite direction.

The Members of the General Assembly will excuse me for presenting these general observations on a problem to which the Assembly has devoted so much attention. I have done so only because it seems to me that the experiences from other political fields in which the United Nations has acted with success have a bearing also on a field like this one where, so far, the Organization has failed to achieve results.

IV. ROLE IN ECONOMIC DEVELOPMENT

The responsibilities and possibilities of the Organization in the exercise of preventive diplomacy apply also to the economic sphere. Far less dramatic in their impact as the economic activities must be, they are of decisive long-term significance for the welfare of the international community. In the end, the United Nations is likely to be judged not so much by the criterion of how successfully it has overcome this or that crisis as by the significance of its total contribution towards building the kind of world community in which such crises will no longer be inevitable.

This aim, naturally, cannot be reached overnight, nor can it be considerably furthered by any institutional or constitutional reforms of the United Nations. It cannot even be achieved by the political resolution of the conflicts which today divide the major Powers. Essential though such a political resolution would be, it would not by itself ensure stability and peace in the face of the dangerous economic and social vacuum created and maintained by the enormous gap which separates countries at different stages of development.

In the enduring task of bridging the gulf between countries, all Member nations, whether developed or under-developed, whether in the East or the West, have a common interest. This common interest is recognized by everyone. It is clearly stated in the Charter of the United Nations, in which countries pledge themselves to take joint and separate action in cooperation with the Organization to promote 'higher standards of living, full employment and conditions of economic and social progress and development'. It is reflected in all of the debates of the Economic and Social Council as well as of the General Assembly on the relevant items. It has borne fruit in a host of activities within the United Nations and its sister institutions. And yet, in considering the rate of progress that has been made in relation to the task that remains to be achieved, it is difficult to escape a feeling of disappointment.

It is true that the mere recognition of the community of interest in the economic development of under-developed countries itself represents a major step forward. And the expressions of common interest in economic development are no lip service. The achievements of the United Nations family in the economic and social field, as generously supported by Member governments, demonstrates their seriousness. However, it must, in the context of a newly emerging Africa, be registered, in a spirit of candid realism, that the rate of achievement is not at all commensurate with the needs.

The coincidence of interest in the economic field stems from the economic interdependence of the world community. The degree of interdependence has been increasing rapidly, partly as the inevitable outcome of an accelerating rate of advance in science and technology, partly owing to the emergence of the countries of the continents of Asia and of Africa to independence and full participation in the affairs of the world at large, but, to a significant degree, also as a result of economic forces making for a growing integration of the world community.

For the first time in history, the concept of a world economy has come to take on a significant meaning not only for the student of economics but also for the statesman and the layman.

Unfortunately, this growing interdependence has recently been reflected much less in efforts and activities within the United Nations than outside it. The United Nations can welcome regional arrangements among neighbouring or like-minded countries. As long as such arrangements are so designed as to reinforce rather than to supplant the common effort towards establishing conditions of economic and social progress, they have an important role to play. A real danger arises, however, when such regional arrangements are so envisaged as to make them fall within the sphere of bloc conflict. In that case, efforts which properly should embody and be supported by a common interest may instead lead to a weakening of the uniting force of that interest and aggravate the split. This, obviously, is the reverse of the major purpose and function of the United Nations in its efforts to provide for a growing measure of political stability.

Just as it is clearly within the interests of the entire world community to prevent the widening of the area of conflict in cases of political crises, so it must be in the interests of all constantly to seek to widen rather than to restrict the area of coincidence of economic interest within the United Nations. Unless this is done, the entire world, and not just one or the other side, is bound to lose. As I noted in my statement to the Economic and Social Council at its thirtieth session, 'the United Nations Organization remains the only universal agency in which countries with widely differing political institutions and at different stages of economic development may exchange views, share their problems and experiences, probe each other's reactions to policies of mutual interest, and initiate collective action'.

It was this recognition of the growing area of coincidence of economic interest which was at the basis of my proposal and of the Council's decision that it hold its thirtieth session at the Ministerial level in order to undertake, at the beginning of a new decade, a broad examination of the direction to be taken by the United Nations to meet the challenge of both national and collective responsibility for economic growth and development.

At its thirteenth session,* the General Assembly adopted resolution 1316 (XIII) calling upon Member States to undertake a review of accomplishments to date and to chart their future courses of cooperative action for the purpose of giving further impetus to the economic development of the less developed countries. At the

* 1958.

national level also, many countries, both developed and under-developed, have found it useful to establish long-term plans for economic growth as guide-lines for economic policy, and others have established national commissions on economic and social goals and policies.

In the light of these events, and in the light of the changes that have taken place in the national economic and political landscape since the Charter was first signed, it was my belief that the Economic and Social Council might usefully explore the question of the desirability and feasibility of some United Nations undertaking to chart the future course of cooperative action to implement the economic and social objectives of the Charter.

A common stand has not yet been reached on the possibility or advisability of harmonizing and coordinating national economic policies. Even the idea of regular and systematic consultation with a view to achieving fuller knowledge of the facts and the issues is new. In view of the very modest and very recent progress in harmonization of national economic policies, even within regional groupings of like-minded countries, it is not surprising that no consensus on the possibility or desirability of harmonizing or coordinating national economic policies within the framework of the United Nations should as yet exist.

And yet, though the objective is not within immediate reach, and though I do not wish to underestimate the obstacles, the importance of a harmonization of national economic development policies within the United Nations must be stressed. Even though the session at the Ministerial level did not produce the results that some may have hoped, it did represent a beginning. It did lead to a useful exchange of views. It did provide an opportunity for contacts between Ministers in charge of economic questions, some of whom have only limited alternative possibilities of making such direct contacts. It did lead to at least one important step looking towards better coordination in the future of policies of economic projections. Thus, this meeting, with its achievements—and its shortcomings— may be regarded as opening the door to new efforts to explore and utilize for common ends the wide area of common economic interests, at the same time as it demonstrates the difficulties we encounter and the early stage of evolution at which we still find ourselves.

Until now, the economic analyses undertaken by the Secretariat and consequently the debates within the Economic and Social Council and the General Assembly have been concerned essentially with past and present trends. Now, with the program of work in economic projections initiated by the Council, we may hope that, as we succeed in ascertaining the constituent elements of policies of economic growth, the Organization will be able to make an important contribution towards widening the bounds of the area of co-incidence of interest within the United Nations, thus helping to harmonize decisions of governments in the field of national policy and in the promotion of rapid and stable development for all.

V. INSTRUMENT FOR THE OVERRIDING COMMON INTEREST

In the Introduction to my Report to the General Assembly at its fourteenth session* I discussed the role of the United Nations. In that context I said:

> 'The work of today within and for the United Nations is a work through which the basis may be laid for increasingly satisfactory forms of international cooperation and for a future international system of law and order, for which the world is not yet ripe.'

I continued:

> 'It has so often been said that the world of today is one which requires organized international cooperation on a basis of universality that one repeats it with hesitation. However, there are reasons to do so. It still seems sometimes to be forgotten that—whatever views may be held about the United Nations as an institution—the principle of organized international cooperation on a basis of universality which is at present reflected in this Organization is one which has emerged from bitter experiences and should now be considered as firmly established.'

In the previous parts of this Introduction I have tried to outline my views on some specific problems arising for the Organization at the present juncture, which may well, in the perspective of history,

* See Introduction to the Annual Report 1958-1959, pages 220 et seq.

come to be regarded as a turning point. Especially, I have wished to draw the attention of the Members to the scope for possible diplomatic and political action by the Organization in a split world and to the desirability of the widening of that scope by patient and persistent action, using as the lever the community of interests which is created by the desire of everybody to limit the area of conflict, to reduce the risk of conflicts and to create a basis for joint action for solution, or at least localization, of conflicts.

Recent developments—reflected in a revolutionary technical evolution of arms for destruction, in the entry of new major regions of the world in full strength into international politics and in new and world-wide economic interdependence—have given to the Organization, and what it represents as an instrument in the hands of Member governments, greatly increased responsibilities, but also increased usefulness.

The Organization and its activities can be viewed on different levels. It provides Member governments with a highly developed, continuously operating conference and negotiation machinery. However, to a growing extent it has provided them also with an effective executive organ for joint action. In this latter respect, the evolution has taken a course somewhat different from the one envisaged in San Francisco, but, as recent developments have shown, the departure as to methods is not considerable and the conformity as to aims is complete. Finally, the Organization is also the embodiment of an ideal and the symbol of an approach to international life which recognizes the common interest of all in the rejection of the use of force, in any form, as a means for settling disputes and in adherence to the principles of law, justice, and human rights.

The Organization has often in the past been faced, and is likely in its continued work again and again to be faced, with situations in which a compromise with these last-mentioned principles might seem to facilitate the achievement of results in negotiations or to promise an easier success for the Organization in its executive efforts to resolve a problem. It is for the Members themselves to judge to what extent the Organization, in particular cases, has accepted such compromises and to what extent it has remained faithful to the principles and ideals which it embodies.

It is my firm conviction that any result bought at the price of a compromise with the principles and ideals of the Organization, either by yielding to force, by disregard of justice, by neglect of common interests or by contempt for human rights, is bought at too high a price. That is so because a compromise with its principles and purposes weakens the Organization in a way representing a definite loss for the future that cannot be balanced by any immediate advantage achieved.

The United Nations has increasingly become the main platform—and the main protector of the interests—of those many nations who feel themselves strong as members of the international family but who are weak in isolation. Thus, an increasing number of nations have come to look to the United Nations for leadership and support in ways somewhat different from those natural in the light of traditional international diplomacy. They look to the Organization as a spokesman and as an agent for principles which give them strength in an international concert in which other voices can mobilize all the weight of armed force, wealth, an historical role and that influence which is the other side of a special responsibility for peace and security. Therefore, a weakening of the Organization, resulting from an attempt to achieve results at the cost of principles, is a loss not only for the future but also immediately in respect of the significance of the Organization for the vast majority of nations and in respect of their confidence in the Organization on which its strength in our present-day world ultimately depends.

There are in the Charter elements of a thinking which, I believe, belongs to an earlier period in the development of the world community. I have in mind especially the concept that the permanent members of the Security Council should not only, as is natural, be recognized as carrying special responsibility for peace and security, but that, further, these permanent members, working together, should represent a kind of 'built-in' directing group for the world community as organized in the United Nations.

The fifteen years which have passed since the founding of the United Nations have witnessed a different development. In the first place, we have seen a split among the permanent members which, in fact, has created the major war risk of today and considerably hampered the development of the Organization. But, further, we have experienced a growth into independence of a majority of States of two great continents, with other interests, other traditions and other concepts of international politics than those of the countries of Europe and the Americas. Who can deny that today the countries of Asia or the countries of Africa, acting in a common spirit, represent powerful elements in the international community, in their ways as important as any of the big Powers, although lacking in their military and economic potential?

The United Nations is an organic creation of the political situation facing our generation. At the same time, however, the international community has, so to say, come to political self-consciousness in the Organization and, therefore, can use it in a meaningful way in order to influence those very circumstances of which the Organization is a creation.

It is impossible for anyone to say where the international community is heading and how the United Nations will change in the further course of evolution of international politics. But it can safely be said that international cooperation will become increasingly essential for the maintenance of peace, progress and international justice. It can also safely be said that if the United Nations firmly adheres to its principles and purposes, with flexibility and intelligent adjustment to needs as regards procedure, Members engaged in this cooperation will increasingly turn to the Organization for assistance. Therefore, they will find it increasingly necessary to maintain its strength as an instrument for the world community in their efforts to reduce those areas of major conflict where the Organization so far has been powerless, as well as in efforts to resolve problems, arising outside or on the margin of these areas, in a spirit reflecting the overriding common interest.

This concept of the role and of the future of the United Nations may go beyond the conventional thinking which sees in the Organization only, or mainly, a machinery for negotiation, but I am convinced of its realism and I am convinced also that the Organization and its Member nations would act rightly and wisely if they acted consistently with this concept in mind, even if temporarily it may seem to point out a road full of risks and of difficulties which they may doubt that the Organization is yet strong enough to overcome.

STATEMENTS OF REPLY TO
ATTACKS UPON HIS OFFICE AND CONDUCT OF OPERATIONS IN THE CONGO

September 1960–February 1961

*The following selections have been made as represen-
tative of the many statements of reply to which the
Secretary-General was forced after he and the Secretariat came under constantly repeated Soviet fire in
the fall of 1960. The first two statements are concerned
primarily with the responsibilities of his own Office
in relation to the USSR demand that he resign and be
replaced by a three-man directorate or troika. The
statement of 17 October cuts through the turbulent
surface manifestations of anarchy and competing
political ambitions with which all the Congo debate
had been occupied to the heart of the United Nations
program in the Congo and to its spirit. The two
Security Council statements are reaffirmations of the
Charter purposes and principles governing the conduct
of the operation. These were made not only in answer
to Soviet attacks, but also in the face of criticisms
from the Western side for opposite reasons and of
moves by a few African and Asian states to use the
Organization for political ends in ways that would
have violated the Charter.*

'. . . A QUESTION NOT OF A MAN BUT OF AN INSTITUTION'

*Statement before the General Assembly in reply to
Chairman Krushchev and others, 26 September 1960.*

When I asked for the privilege of exercising my right of reply at
this stage of the general debate, it was not because I wanted to use

this opportunity to correct any factual mistakes or misrepresentations. That should be unnecessary in the light of the very full debates in the Security Council and at the very recent emergency special session. . . .

My reason for taking the floor now is another one. I felt that, before the debate goes any further, it would be appropriate for me to make clear to the Assembly what, in my view, is and is not the problem before the Assembly in certain respects on which the Secretary-General has been addressed by some speakers.

In those respects the General Assembly is facing a question not of any specific actions but of the principles guiding United Nations activities. In those respects it is a question not of a man but of an institution.

Just one week ago the General Assembly adopted a resolution regarding the Congo operation. It did so after a thorough debate and a full presentation of facts. As that is the situation it may well be asked why those same facts should now be brought out again in the Assembly as a basis for new and far-reaching conclusions, perhaps involving even a question of confidence.

The question before the General Assembly is no longer one of certain actions but one of the principles guiding them. Time and again the United Nations has had to face situations in which a wrong move might have tended to throw the weight of the Organization over in favor of this or that specific party in a conflict of a primarily domestic character. To permit that to happen is indeed to intervene in domestic affairs contrary to the letter and the spirit of the Charter.

To avoid doing so is to be true to the letter and spirit of the Charter, whatever disappointment it might cause those who might have thought that they could add to their political weight by drawing the United Nations over to their side.

This is, of course, the basic reason for the principle spelled out at the very first stage of the Congo operation, and approved by the Security Council, to the effect that the United Nations Force is not under the orders of a government requesting its assistance and cannot be permitted to become a party to any internal conflict, be it one in which the government is engaged or not. It is common experience that nothing, in the heat of emotion, is regarded as more partial by one who takes himself the position of a party than strict impartiality.

Further, as I have said, this is a question not of a man but of an institution. Use whatever words you like, independence, impartiality, objectivity—they all describe essential aspects of what, without exception, must be the attitude of the Secretary-General. Such an attitude, which has found its clear and decisive expression in Article 100 of the Charter,* may at any stage become an obstacle for those who work for certain political aims which would be better served or more easily achieved if the Secretary-General compromised with this attitude. But if he did how gravely he would then betray the trust of all those for whom the strict maintenance of such an attitude is their best protection in the world-wide fight for power and influence. Thus, if the office of the Secretary-General becomes a stumbling block for anyone, be it an individual, a group or a government, because the incumbent stands by the basic principle which must guide his whole activity, and if, for that reason, he comes under criticism, such criticism strikes at the very office and the concepts on which it is based. I would rather see that office break on strict adherence to the principle of independence, impartiality and objectivity than drift on the basis of compromise. That is the choice daily facing the Secretary-General. It is also the choice now openly facing the General Assembly, both in substance and in form. I believe that all those whose interests are safeguarded by the United Nations will realize that the choice is not one of the convenience of the moment but one which is decisive for the future, their future.

One last word. Sometimes one gets the impression that the Congo operation is looked at as being in the hands of the Secretary-General, as somehow distinct from the United Nations. No: this is your operation, gentlemen. And this is true whether you represent the African and Asian member countries, which carry the main burden for the Force and for its Command, or speak and act for other parts of the world. There is nothing in the Charter which puts responsibility of this kind on the shoulders of the Secretary-General or makes him the independent master of such an operation. It was the Security Council which, without any dissenting vote, gave this mandate to the Secretary-General on 14 July. It was the Security Council which, on 22 July, commended his report on the principles that should be applied. It was the Security Council, on 9 August, which, again without any dissenting vote, confirmed the authority

* See 'The International Civil Servant', pages 329 et seq. and 'Executive Action and an International Secretariat', pages 365 et seq.

given to the Secretary-General. Again, just a week ago, the General Assembly, without any dissenting vote, requested the Secretary-General to continue to take vigorous action. Indeed, as I said, this is your operation, gentlemen. It is for you to indicate what you want to have done. As the agent of the Organization I am grateful for any positive advice, but if no such positive advice is forthcoming— as happened in the Security Council on 21 August, when my line of implementation had been challenged from outside—then I have no choice but to follow my own conviction, guided by the principles to which I have just referred.

'I SHALL REMAIN IN MY POST . . .'

Statement to the General Assembly, 3 October 1960

The Head of the Soviet Delegation to the General Assembly, this morning, in exercising his right of reply, said, among many other things, that the present Secretary-General has always been biased against the socialist countries, that he has used the United Nations in support of the colonial Powers fighting the Congolese Government and Parliament in order to impose 'a new yoke on the Congo,' and finally, that if I, myself, and I quote, 'do not muster up enough courage to resign, so to say in a chivalrous manner, then the Soviet Union will draw the necessary conclusions from the obtained situation.' In support of this challenge the representative of the Soviet Union said that it is not proper for a man who has 'flouted elementary justice to hold such an important post as that of the Secretary-General'. And later on he found reason to say to the delegates of this session that they should not 'submit to the clamorous phrases pronounced here' by me 'in attempts to justify the bloody crimes perpetrated against the Congolese people'.

The General Assembly can rightly expect an immediate reply from my side to a statement so directly addressed to me and regarding a matter of such potential significance.

The Assembly has witnessed over the last weeks how historical truth is established; once an allegation has been repeated a few times, it is no longer an allegation, it is an established fact, even if no evidence has been brought out in order to support it. However, facts are facts, and the true facts are there for whosoever cares for truth. Those who invoke history will certainly be heard by history. And they will have to accept its verdict as it will be pronounced on the basis of the facts by men free of mind and firm in their conviction that only on a scrutiny of truth can a future of peace be built.

I have no reason to defend myself or my colleagues against the accusations and judgments to which you have listened. Let me say only this, that *you*, all of you, are the judges. No single party can claim that authority. I am sure you will be guided by truth and justice. In particular, let those who know what the United Nations has done and is doing in the Congo, and those who are not pursuing aims proper only to themselves, pass judgment on our actions there. Let the countries who have liberated themselves in the last fifteen years speak for themselves.

I regret that the intervention to which I have found it necessary to reply has again tended to personalize an issue which, as I have said, in my view is not a question of a man but of an institution. The man does not count, the institution does. A weak or non-existent executive would mean that the United Nations would no longer be able to serve as an effective instrument for active protection of the interests of those many Members who need such protection. The man holding the responsibility as chief executive should leave if he weakens the executive; he should stay if this is necessary for its maintenance. This, and only this, seems to me to be the substantive criterion that has to be applied.

I said the other day that I would not wish to continue to serve as Secretary-General one day longer than such continued service was, and was considered to be, in the best interest of the Organization.* The statement this morning seems to indicate that the Soviet Union finds it impossible to work with the present Secretary-General. This may seem to provide a strong reason why I should resign. However, the Soviet Union has also made it clear that, if the present Secretary-General were to resign now, they would not wish to elect a new incumbent but insist on an arrangement which—and this is my firm conviction based on broad experience—would make it impossible to maintain an effective executive. By resigning, I would, therefore, at the present difficult and dangerous juncture throw the Organization to the winds. I have no right to do so because I have a responsibility to all those States Members for which the Organization is of decisive importance, a responsibility which overrides all other considerations.

* Refers to a brief statement 18 September, 1960, reserving his right to return to the matter later in the debate.

It is not the Soviet Union or, indeed, any other big Powers who need the United Nations for their protection; it is all the others. In this sense the Organization is first of all *their* Organization, and I deeply believe in the wisdom with which they will be able to use it and guide it. I shall remain in my post during the term of my office as a servant of the Organization in the interests of all those other nations, as long as *they* wish me to do so.

In this context the representative of the Soviet Union spoke of courage. It is very easy to resign; it is not so easy to stay on. It is very easy to bow to the wish of a big Power. It is another matter to resist. As is well known to all members of this Assembly, I have done so before on many occasions and in many directions. If it is the wish of those nations who see in the Organization their best protection in the present world, I shall now do so again.

STATEMENT ON UN OPERATIONS IN THE CONGO BEFORE THE GENERAL ASSEMBLY

17 October 1960

In my first intervention during the general debate I reserved my right to ask for the floor at a later stage for such clarifications and comments as might seem indicated. I thank you, Mr. President, for giving me this opportunity of saying a few words at this final stage of the debate.

The distinguished President of the Republic of Guinea said in his speech last Monday: 'The Congo is part of the life of humanity; the fate reserved for millions of men, women and children should be looked at more closely. Let less be said of Messrs. Lumumba, Kasavubu, Mobutu, Ileo and the others, but let more be pondered seriously to find a true and just solution for the problems of the people which only yearns for well-being, peace and progress, as do all people all over.'

Much has been said in this debate regarding the Congo, its problems and the United Nations effort in support of the independence, integrity, peace and progress of the Congo. Much has been

said which has been ill-founded. Whether this has been the result
of misinformation, of an emotional engagement or of tactical considerations but flimsily related to the interests of the Congo, I leave
to others to consider. Following the statement of President Sekou
Touré which I just quoted, I would, instead of taking up your time
with setting straight a record mainly concerned with basically
superficial and temporary problems, wish to fill out the picture of
the General Assembly by talking about what has not been mentioned: the needs of the people of the Congo and the work of the
United Nations in assistance of the authorities whose responsibility
it is to meet those needs.

In the confusing fights and conflicts which have now been going
on for more than three months in the Congo among political
dignitaries of that country, an impression has grown that few have
realized that to lead and govern is not a privilege to be sought for
but a burden of responsibility to be assumed.

It is not those names which we read about in the papers which
are tied to the painstaking daily efforts to maintain a minimum of
order, to keep an administration—on a minimum level—running,
to forestall epidemics and cure disease, to keep the transport system
working, to feed the hungriest, to see to it that the many workers
for the state are in a position to pay for the necessities of their
families. No, that work has been undertaken by many who are
nameless, by Congolese officials who are never mentioned and
whose names will probably never be known to the world. They have
chosen to serve instead of to rule, they have chosen to subordinate
themselves instead of searching for power. May I pay tribute to
these men and to what they have done to give life and sense to the
independence of the Congo. It is those with whom the United
Nations has had to work, it is those we have been able to consult,
and those we have tried to assist.

In doing so, we have been accused of serving the interest of
foreign elements, of working hand-in-hand with imperialists, and
of impeding the legitimate authorities. We have been accused of
substituting ourselves for those authorities, of seeking power for
the United Nations in the Congo and of reinstituting some kind of
colonialism. Let nobody be misled. Those many men, from many
nations in Africa, Asia, Europe and the transatlantic countries, who
are serving the United Nations in the Congo, why are they there?
They have left their families. They do not solicit merits for future

advancement in the home countries to which they want to return. They work against the heaviest odds under a continuous nerve strain, they have endless working days, they do not know whether all that they do will not be swept aside one of these days by new waves of political unrest. And yet, they give the best they can. May I pay them a tribute as pioneers for that growing group of men all over the world who regard service to the fellow members of the community of mankind to be a reward in itself, giving sense to their efforts and to their life—guided by faith in a better future and maintaining the strict norms of behavior which the Charter requests of an international civil servant. Blame them for their shortcomings, if you will; say that they should do more, if you believe that you are entitled to say so; criticize this or that decision they have taken, because in your perspective another decision might have been better, but do not throw doubt on their honesty and seriousness, do not impugn their motives and, especially, do not try to depict them as enemies of the very cause—the well-being of the Congolese people in a life of peace and true independence—for which they are giving so much and, in worldly terms, as individuals, receiving little or nothing.

I wish to say this as an act of justice, necessary if this Organization is to live up to the moral standards it professes and if it is to be able to count in the future on the services of those for whom those standards are a creed which it is their duty to uphold in practical action.

Much of the debate has had as its obvious background this or that specific United Nations emergency step with supposed political implications—or even motives. The listener may have got the impression that what the United Nations is doing in the Congo is really crystallized and summed up in those few actions. In my perspective they are details in a vast pattern of activity; important though they may be in themselves, they are only highly publicized events which have occurred when, in the course of the political complications of the situation, the activities of the Organization, because of the principles which it must maintain, momentarily may seem to have collided with some specific party interest.

With the collapse and disintegration of the *Armée Nationale Congolaise* as a stabilizing factor, there are now instead on an emergency basis close to 20,000 men of the United Nations Force in the Congo, found necessary to maintain a minimum assurance for the life of the people and, thus, carrying a burden normally assumed by the national security forces. This complicated operation, rendered possible very largely through the generosity and sacrifices of other African States is also heavily dependent on a highly qualified cadre of officers of very many nations and on highly developed and costly technical advice. The Force could not be there without one of the biggest airlifts in history which we could arrange only by drawing on the resources of the most powerful countries of the world. The Force is serviced by technicians with the most qualified technical schooling and machinery available. And yet it is feeble in relation to its own tasks. Indeed, this is a strange background for statements to the effect that the Force should and could be withdrawn or that its tasks could be taken over by the national security forces or by a few of the units now making up part of it.

But, the activities of the Force are, I hope, a quickly passing phase in the United Nations effort to give to the Congo its full and real independence and to re-establish its integrity. Already now, and increasingly so, the civilian operation is of decisive importance. And in that civilian operation what has been achieved has required the service of all the agencies in the United Nations, to their full capacity.

In the vastness of the Congo where so much movement depends on air services, everything would have been grounded in the last three months but for the air traffic control, the radio and navigation aids, the weather forecasting and telecommunications provided by the International Civil Aviation Organization, the International Telecommunication Union and the World Meteorological Organization. Even the food and milk so generously provided by Member States for supply to children and refugees—when supplies were not interrupted by political disturbances—have been largely carried in United Nations planes to country-wide distribution points where local authorities and Red Cross took over. The early breakdown of surface transport which caused local shortages of food, has been overcome by United Nations personnel, who saw to the dredging of the river and re-opening of the ocean port, who moved pilots by helicopter to increase their effective working hours, who reactivated the oil pipe-lines between port and capital, and who are supervising workshops and maintenance of harbors and railways. Some of these engineers have been diverted to the preparation of a program of public works for the relief of unemployment. International Labor

Office programs are dealing with a number of crucial labor and social security fields. Hospitals, abandoned by their medical staff, have been quickly restored to use by medical units provided by Red Cross societies of many countries, and the elementary health services have been maintained by the World Health Organization. Plans and actions for the reopening of schools and the organization of secondary and technical education have largely depended on the activities of the United Nations Educational, Scientific and Cultural Organization. Plans for maintaining agricultural services are being developed through the Food and Agriculture Organization. Research institutions of continental value, whose prestige is world-wide, are being protected and maintained through the United Nations. Plans are being drawn for the training of tomorrow's doctors, teachers and civil servants so that the Congo may make the maximum use of its reservoir of youth, its greatest and most durable asset. All these vitally essential services are rendered under the United Nations flag, thus eliminating any risks that they create a dependence of the Congo on any specific foreign Powers or that outside elements be permitted to establish what might develop into vested interests in the country. They, thereby, effectively help in establishing and strengthening its true independence.

You may ask, where then the Government and the administration are to be found in this picture. I think I have already given the reply. We have tried to consult to all the extent there was anybody who could be consulted—and who paid any attention to the needs. We have cooperated on a continuous basis of great intimacy with a number of Central Government officials. We have avoided taking decisions for which we could not get authoritative approval, but when a specific situation reached the stage of acute crisis, requiring immediate counter-action, and when we could not find those whose support we wished to have, we have had to act as responsible human beings facing a desperate emergency. You try to save a drowning man without prior authorization and even if he resists you; you do not let him go even when he tries to strangle you. I do not believe that anyone would wish the Organization to follow other rules than those you apply to yourself when faced with such a situation.

I said in the Congo, some time ago, that the birth of an independent Congo had come to coincide with the birth of true cooperation of the United Nations family of agencies in the service of a Member nation. As a spokesman for all these administrations I can say that we are proud that we have been permitted to serve in this way, but I should add that we will be even prouder when, through all the joint efforts, the stage has been reached when our services are no longer necessary in the Congo and we can leave the country solely and fully in the good hands of its own people, with its independence, peace and prosperity safeguarded by its own means.

The end of all political effort must be the well-being of the individual in a life of safety and freedom. In the case of the Congo, as elsewhere, the means to this end are in the first place the independence, peace, integrity and prosperity of the country. In turn, this goal requires the maintenance and progress of economic life, the functioning of a good judiciary system, a soundly working administration, all under the responsibility of a government, stable thanks to its firm roots in the free will of the people, expressed and developed in democratic forms. This is the perspective in which the effort of the United Nations must be seen. This perspective should determine our judgment and give us the sense of proportion necessary if we are to avoid substituting the means for the ends and the interests of the man or the group for those of the people.

EXTRACT FROM STATEMENT ON UN OPERATIONS IN THE CONGO BEFORE THE SECURITY COUNCIL

7 December 1960

The UN sent troops and civilian technicians to the Congo for clearly defined Charter aims and under clearly defined Charter principles.

The aim was to protect life and property within the Congo, in danger after the breakdown of the national security system, so as to eliminate the reasons given for the Belgian military intervention and thereby to reduce what internationally had to be regarded as a serious threat to peace and security.

The principles were that the Organization in the pursuit of this aim should maintain a position of strict neutrality in relation to all domestic problems of a political nature in which the Organization under the Charter had no right to interfere. This meant that neither the UN Force, nor the civilian operation, could be used by any person or faction in pursuit of his or their political aims; thus, the UN Force was not to be an instrument for anybody in order to exert his political authority. This further meant that the UN and its representatives had no right to further any specific political solutions of domestic problems of the Congo, such problems having to be resolved solely by the Congolese themselves in accordance with their own free will and in democratic forms.

The aims and the principles thus defined have been strictly maintained by me and my collaborators all through the operation. There have been no shifts in policy or changes of approach. Nor have we been 'lackeys' of anybody or shown 'servility' to any interest.

Of course, we have been accused of all this, and from all sides, although the terminology may have varied. What is more natural; by maintaining our aim, and by being faithful to the principles of the UN, we were bound to cause disappointment to those who have wished to abuse the Organization and we were bound to be regarded also as enemies or obstacles by those who found that the very neutrality of the UN represented an obstacle to their aims. It is common experience to everyone who has tried to pursue a line of independence and objectivity in human affairs that he comes under criticism from those who believe that they would have had a greater chance of success for their own special aims, if it had not been for this attitude.

Thus nobody should be surprised by the attacks which in rich measure have been directed against the UN operation in succession by leading personalities in the Congo of various factions, and by public opinion or governments from the East to the West. And nobody should from that criticism, or from the way its center has shifted from one point to the other, permit himself to draw the conclusion that the UN policy has shifted. Nor should anybody permit himself to look at any one criticism, thus voiced, as objective in the sense that it is detached from political aims or pressures. That does not mean that I claim any infallibility for what the UN has done in the Congo—of course mistakes have been made—but what I do claim is that such possible mistakes have not reflected any change of policy implying a departure from the aims and principles proper to the Organization. It should be a reason for reflection that the very day the Soviet Union repeats its well-known criticism against the Secretary-General and his representatives we are under equally heavy criticism from people whom the Soviet Union in the same document characterizes as those to whom we show servile subservience.

All the misunderstandings, all the wilful misrepresentations, all the efforts to make what is done now suspected could be treated lightly as a part of a political game in which, I believe, the players themselves must regard all these various statements only as moves and not as statements of fact, if it were not for their effect on this Organization and its authority. I believe, and many believe with me, that this Organization in all its frailty represents the sole approach which may give us a chance to reduce the risk that the constant frictions—large and small—which characterize the life of our present-day world, build up to a tension easily triggered into a clash in which we would all be engulfed. I also believe that it is essential for the growth of a human society in which the dignity of the human being will be respected that every effort is made to make this step in the direction of an organized world community a success. In these circumstances I may be excused if I express the deepest worry at seeing the way in which this Organization is abused in words, and abused as an instrument for purposes contrary to the Charter.

We have been accused of servility in relation to the West, of softness in relation to the East, of supporting this or that man in the Congo whom one group or another on the world scene has chosen to make its symbol, or for assisting another man to whom another group has chosen to tie their hopes for the success of interests they wish to safeguard. However, this is no excessive price to be paid for avoiding the thing for which no one in my position should be forgiven: to compromise, in any political interest, with the aims and principles of this Organization. It has not been done and it will not be done with my knowledge or acquiescence. I can only repeat what I said in the General Assembly that I would rather see the office of the Secretary-General break on this principle than drift on compromise. May these observations be accepted as a reply to the criticism of the Secretariat which we find repeated in the Soviet statement, and also as a reply to all those who now criticize us so freely for the very opposite reasons. . . .

EXTRACT FROM STATEMENT ON UN
OPERATIONS IN THE CONGO BEFORE
THE SECURITY COUNCIL

15 February 1961

... For seven or eight months, through efforts far beyond the imagination of those who founded this Organization, it has tried to counter tendencies to introduce the big Power conflict into Africa and put the young African countries under the shadow of the Cold War. It has done so with great risks and against heavy odds. It has done so at the cost of very great personal sacrifices for a great number of people. In the beginning the effort was successful, and I do not now hesitate to say that on more than one occasion the drift into a war with foreign power intervention of the Korean or Spanish type was avoided only thanks to the work done by the Organization, basing itself on African solidarity. We countered effectively efforts from all sides to make the Congo a happy hunting ground for national interests. To be a road-block to such efforts is to make yourself the target of attacks from all those who find their plans thwarted. In the case of some the opposition against the United Nations line was for a while under the surface, but it was not long before it broke out in the open. In other cases the disappointment in meeting this unexpected obstacle broke out at once in violent and vocal attacks on the Organization. From both sides the main accusation was a lack of objectivity. The historian will undoubtedly find in this balance of accusations the very evidence of that objectivity we were accused of lacking, but also of the fact that very many Member nations have not yet accepted the limits put on their national ambitions by the very existence of the United Nations and by the membership of that Organization.

Now, under basically identical although superficially more dramatic circumstances, we have again reached the point where a local armed conflict is threatening in forms which are only too likely to lead to a widening of the conflict into the international arena. I have no new solutions to offer to you. Still, I firmly believe that, as in July and August last year, the only way in which the continent of Africa and its countries can counter a tragic development into an international conflict, perhaps on a world-wide scale, is by rallying around common aims within the framework of the United Nations.

African solidarity within the United Nations was the reply to the threats last year; I am firmly convinced that it still is the only reply.

THE INTERNATIONAL CIVIL
SERVANT IN LAW AND IN FACT

Lecture delivered to Congregation at Oxford University,
*30 May 1961.**

I

In a recent article Mr. Walter Lippmann tells about an interview in Moscow with Mr. Krushchev. According to the article, Chairman Krushchev stated that 'while there are neutral countries, there are no neutral men,' and the author draws the conclusion that it is now the view of the Soviet Government 'that there can be no such thing as an impartial civil servant in this deeply divided world, and that the kind of political celibacy which the British theory of the civil servant calls for, is in international affairs a fiction.'

Whether this accurately sums up the views held by the Soviet Government, as reflected in the interview, or not, one thing is certain: The attitude which the article reflects is one which we find nowadays in many political quarters, communist and non-communist alike, and it raises a problem which cannot be treated lightly. In fact, it challenges basic tenets in the philosophy of both the League of Nations and the United Nations, as one of the essential points on which these experiments in international cooperation represent an advance beyond traditional 'conference diplomacy' is the introduction on the international arena of joint permanent organs, employing a neutral civil service, and the use of such organs for executive purposes on behalf of all the members of the organizations. Were it to be considered that the experience shows that this radical innovation in international life rests on a false assumption, because 'no man can be neutral,' then we would be thrown back to 1919, and a searching re-appraisal would become necessary.

II

The international civil service had its genesis in the League of Nations but it did not spring full-blown in the Treaty of Versailles and the Covenant. The Covenant was in fact silent on the

* Reprinted by permission of the Clarendon Press, Oxford.

international character of the Secretariat. It contained no provisions comparable to those of Article 100 of the Charter and simply stated:

> 'The permanent Secretariat shall be established at the Seat of the League. The Secretariat shall comprise a Secretary-General and such secretaries and staff as may be required.'

In the earliest proposals for the Secretariat of the League, it was apparently taken for granted that there could not be a truly international secretariat but that there would have to be nine national secretaries, each assisted by a national staff and performing, in turn, the duties of Secretary to the Council, under the supervision of the Secretary-General. This plan, which had been drawn up by Sir Maurice Hankey, who had been offered the post of Secretary-General of the League by the Allied Powers, was in keeping with the precedents set by the various international bureaux established before the war which were staffed by officials seconded by Member countries on a temporary basis.

It was Sir Eric Drummond, first Secretary-General of the League, who is generally regarded as mainly responsible for building upon the vague language of the Covenant a truly international secretariat. The classic statement of the principles he first espoused is found in the report submitted to the Council of the League by its British member, Arthur Balfour:

> 'By the terms of the Treaty, the duty of selecting the staff falls upon the Secretary-General, just as the duty of approving it falls upon the Council. In making his appointments, he had primarily to secure the best available men and women for the particular duties which had to be performed; but in doing so, it was necessary to have regard to the great importance of selecting the officials from various nations. Evidently, no one nation or group of nations ought to have a monopoly in providing the material for this international institution. I emphasize the word "international," because the members of the Secretariat once appointed are no longer the servants of the country of which they are citizens, but become for the time being the servants only of the League of Nations. Their duties are not national but international.'

Thus, in this statement, we have two of the essential principles of an international civil service: (1) its international composition and (2) its international responsibilities. The latter principle found its legal expression in the Regulations subsequently adopted which enjoined all officials 'to discharge their functions and to regulate their conduct with the interests of the League alone in view' and prohibited them from seeking or receiving 'instructions from any Government or other authority external to the Secretariat of the League of Nations.'

Along with the conception of an independent, internationally responsible staff, another major idea was to be found: the international Secretariat was to be solely an administrative organ, eschewing political judgments and actions. It is not at all surprising that this third principle should have originated with a British Secretary-General. In the United Kingdom, as in certain other European countries, a system of patronage, political or personal, had been gradually replaced in the course of the nineteenth century by the principle of a permanent civil service based on efficiency and competence and owing allegiance only to the State which it served. It followed that a civil service so organized and dedicated would be non-political. The civil servant could not be expected to serve two masters and consequently he could not, in his official duties, display any political allegiance to a political party or ideology. Those decisions which involved a political choice were left to the Government and to Parliament; the civil servant was the non-partisan administrator of those decisions. His discretion was a limited one, bound by the framework of national law and authority and by rules and instructions issued by his political superiors. True, there were choices for him, since neither legal rules nor policy decisions can wholly eliminate the discretion of the administrative official, but the choices to be made were confined to relatively narrow limits by legislative enactment, Government decision and the great body of precedent and tradition. The necessary condition was that there should exist at all times a higher political authority with the capacity to take the political decisions. With that condition it seemed almost axiomatic that the civil service had to be 'politically celibate' (though not perhaps politically virgin). It could not take sides in any political controversy and, accordingly, it could not be given tasks which required it to do so. This was reflected in the basic statements laying down the policy to govern the international Secretariat. I may quote two of them:

'We recommend with special urgency that, in the interests of the League, as well as in its own interests, the Secretariat should not extend the sphere of its activities, that in the preparation of the work and the decisions of the various organizations of the League, it should regard it as its first duty to collate the relevant documents, and to prepare the ground for these decisions without suggesting what these decisions should be; finally, that once these decisions have been taken by the bodies solely responsible for them, it should confine itself to executing them in the letter and in the spirit.'[*]

'Une fois les décisions prises, le rôle du Secrétariat est de les appliquer. Ici encore, il y a lieu de faire une distinction entre application et interprétation, non pas, à coup sûr, que je demande au Secrétariat de ne jamais interpréter; c'est son métier! Mais je lui demande, et vous lui demanderez certainement tous, d'interpréter le moins loin possible, le plus fidèlement possible, et surtout de ne jamais substituer son interprétation à la vôtre.'[†]

Historians of the League have noted the self-restraining role played by the Secretary-General. He never addressed the Assembly of the League and in the Council 'he tended to speak . . . as a Secretary of a committee and not more than that.'[‡] For him to have entered into political tasks which involved in any substantial degree the taking of a position was regarded as compromising the very basis of the impartiality essential for the Secretariat.

True, this does not mean that political matters as such were entirely excluded from the area of the Secretariat's interests. It has been reported by Sir Eric Drummond and others that he played a role behind the scenes, acting as a confidential channel of communication to Governments engaged in controversy or dispute, but this behind-the-scenes role was never extended to taking action in a politically controversial case that was deemed objectionable by one of the sides concerned.

III

The legacy of the international Secretariat of the League is marked in the Charter of the United Nations. Article 100 follows

[*] Report of Committee Four, records of the Second Assembly.
[†] Statement by M. Noblemaire, Second Assembly, 1 October 1921.
[‡] Proceedings of Conference on Experience in International Administration, Washington, D.C., Carnegie Endowment, 1943.

almost verbatim the League regulations on independence and international responsibility—barring the seeking or receiving of instructions from States or other external authority. This was originally proposed at San Francisco by the four sponsoring powers—China, the USSR, the United Kingdom and the United States—and unanimously accepted. The League experience had shown that an international civil service, responsible only to the Organization, was workable and efficient. It had also revealed as manifested in the behaviour of German and Italian Fascists, that there was a danger of national pressures corroding the concept of international loyalty. That experience underlined the desirability of including in the Charter itself an explicit obligation on officials and governments alike to respect fully the independence and the exclusively international character of the responsibilities of the Secretariat.

It was also recognized that an international civil service of this kind could not be made up of persons indirectly responsible to their national governments. The weight attached to this by the majority of Members was demonstrated in the Preparatory Commission, London, when it was proposed that appointments of officials should be subject to the consent of the government of the Member State of which the candidate was a national. Even in making this proposal, its sponsor explained that it was only intended to build up a staff adequately representative of the governments and acceptable to them. He maintained that prior approval of officials was necessary, in order to obtain the confidence of their governments which was essential to the Secretariat, but once the officials were appointed, the exclusively international character of their responsibilities would be respected. However, the great majority of Member States rejected this proposal, for they believed that it would be extremely undesirable to write into the regulations anything that would give national governments particular rights in respect of appointments and thus indirectly permit political pressures on the Secretary-General.

Similarly in line with Article 100, the Preparatory Commission laid emphasis on the fact that the Secretary-General 'alone is responsible to the other principal organs for the Secretariat's work,' and that all officials in the Organization must recognize the exclusive authority of the Secretary-General and submit themselves to rules of discipline laid down by him.

The principle of the independence of the Secretariat from national pressures was also reinforced in the Charter by Article 105, which provides for granting officials of the Organization 'such privileges and immunities as are necessary for the independent exercise of their functions in connection with the Organization'. It was in fact foreseen at San Francisco that in exceptional circumstances there might be a clash between the independent position of a member of the Secretariat and the position of his country, and consequently that an immunity in respect of official acts would be necessary for the protection of the officials from pressure by individual governments and to permit them to carry out their international responsibilities without interference.

In all of these legal provisions, the Charter built essentially on the experience of the League and affirmed the principles already accepted there. However, when it came to the functions and authority of the Secretary-General, the Charter broke new ground.

In Article 97 the Secretary-General is described as the 'chief administrative officer of the Organization', a phrase not found in the Covenant, though probably implicit in the position of the Secretary-General of the League. Its explicit inclusion in the Charter made it a constitutional requirement—not simply a matter left to the discretion of the organs—that the administration of the Organization shall be left to the Secretary-General. The Preparatory Commission observed that the administrative responsibility under Article 97 involves the essential tasks of preparing the ground for the decisions of the organs and of 'executing' them in cooperation with the Members.

Article 97 is of fundamental importance for the status of the international Secretariat of the United Nations, and thus for the international civil servant employed by the Organization, as together with Articles 100 and 101 it creates for the Secretariat a position, administratively, of full political independence. However, it does not, or at least it need not represent an element in the picture which raises the question of the 'neutrality' of the international civil servant. This is so because the decisions and actions of the Secretary-General as chief administrative officer naturally can be envisaged as limited to administrative problems outside the sphere of political conflicts of interest or ideology, and thus as maintaining the concept of the international civil servant as first developed in the League of Nations.

However, Article 97 is followed by Article 98, and Article 98 is followed by Article 99. And these two Articles together open the door to the problem of neutrality in a sense unknown in the history of the League of Nations.

In Article 98 it is, thus, provided not only that the Secretary-General 'shall act in that capacity' in meetings of the organs, but that he 'shall perform such other functions as are entrusted to him by these organs'. This latter provision was not in the Covenant of the League. It has substantial significance in the Charter, for it entitles the General Assembly and the Security Council to entrust the Secretary-General with tasks involving the execution of political decisions, even when this would bring him—and with him the Secretariat and its members—into the arena of possible political conflict. The organs are, of course, not required to delegate such tasks to the Secretary-General but it is clear that they *may* do so. Moreover, it may be said that in doing so the General Assembly and the Security Council are in no way in conflict with the spirit of the Charter—even if some might like to give the word 'chief administrative officer' in Article 97 a normative and limitative significance—since the Charter itself gives to the Secretary-General an explicit political role.

It is Article 99 more than any other which was considered by the drafters of the Charter to have transformed the Secretary-General of the United Nations from a purely administrative official to one with an explicit political responsibility. Considering its importance, it is perhaps surprising that Article 99 was hardly debated: most delegates appeared to share Smuts' opinion that the position of the Secretary-General 'should be of the highest importance and for this reason a large measure of initiative was expressly conferred.' Legal scholars have observed that Article 99 not only confers upon the Secretary-General a right to bring matters to the attention of the Security Council but that this right carries with it, by necessary implication, a broad discretion to conduct inquiries and to engage in informal diplomatic activity in regard to matters which 'may threaten the maintenance of international peace and security.'

It is not without some significance that this new conception of a Secretary-General originated principally with the United States rather than the United Kingdom. It has been reported that at an early stage in the preparation of the papers that later became the Dumbarton Oaks proposals, the United States gave serious consideration to the idea that the Organization should have a President as well as a Secretary-General. Subsequently, it was decided to propose only a single officer, but one in whom there would be combined both the political and executive functions of a President with the internal administrative functions that were previously accorded to a Secretary-General. Obviously, this is a reflection, in some measure, of the American political system, which places authority in a chief executive officer who is not simply subordinated to the legislative organs but who is constitutionally responsible alone for the execution of legislation and in some respects for carrying out the authority derived from the constitutional instrument directly.

The fact that the Secretary-General is an official with political power as well as administrative functions had direct implications for the method of his selection. Proposals at San Francisco to eliminate the participation of the Security Council in the election process were rejected precisely because it was recognized that the role of the Secretary-General in the field of political and security matters properly involved the Security Council and made it logical that the unanimity rule of the permanent Members should apply. At the same time, it was recognized that the necessity of such unanimous agreement would have to be limited only to the selection of the Secretary-General and that it was equally essential that he be protected against the pressure of a Member during his term in office. Thus a proposal for a three-year term was rejected on the ground that so short a term might impair his independent role.

The concern with the independence of the Secretary-General from national pressures was also reflected at San Francisco in the decision of the Conference to reject proposals for Deputies Secretary-General appointed in the same manner as the Secretary-General. The opponents of this provision maintained that a proposal of this kind would result in a group of high officials who would not be responsible to the Secretary-General but to the bodies which elected them. This would inevitably mean a dilution of the responsibility of the Secretary-General for the conduct of the Organization and would be conducive neither to the efficient functioning of the Secretariat nor to its independent position. In this action and other related decisions, the drafters of the Charter laid emphasis on the personal responsibility of the Secretary-General; it is he who is solely responsible for performing the functions entrusted to him for the appointment of all members of the Secretariat and for assuring the organ that the Secretariat will carry out their tasks under his exclusive authority. The idea of a 'Cabinet system' in which responsibility for administration and political functions would be distributed among several individuals was squarely rejected.

It is also relevant in this connection that the provision for 'due regard to geographical representation' in the recruitment of the Secretariat was never treated as calling for political or ideological representation. It was rather an affirmation of the idea accepted since the beginning of the League Secretariat that the staff of the Organization was to have an international composition and that its basis would be as 'geographically' broad as possible. Moreover, as clearly indicated in the language of Article 101, the 'paramount consideration in the employment of the staff' should be the necessity of securing the highest standards of efficiency, competence and integrity. This terminology is evidence of the intention of the drafters to accord priority to considerations of efficiency and competence over those of geographical representation, important though the latter be.

To sum up, the Charter laid down these essential legal principles for an international civil service:

It was to be an international body, recruited primarily for efficiency, competence and integrity, but on as wide a geographical basis as possible;

It was to be headed by a Secretary-General who carried constitutionally the responsibility to the other principal organs for the Secretariat's work;

And finally, Article 98 entitled the General Assembly and the Security Council to entrust the Secretary-General with tasks going beyond the *verba formalia* of Article 97—with its emphasis on the administrative function—thus opening the door to a measure of political responsibility which is distinct from the authority explicitly accorded to the Secretary-General under Article 99 but in keeping with the spirit of that article.

This last-mentioned development concerning the Secretary-General, with its obvious consequences for the Secretariat as such, takes us beyond the concept of a non-political civil service into an area where the official, in the exercise of his functions, may be forced to take stands of a politically controversial nature. It does this, however, on an international basis and, thus, without departing from the basic concept of 'neutrality'; in fact, Article 98, as well

22

as Article 99, would be unthinkable without the complement of
Article 100 strictly observed both in letter and spirit.

Reverting for a moment to our initial question, I have tried to
emphasize the distinction just made. If a demand for neutrality is
made, by present critics of the international civil service, with the
intent that the international civil servant should not be permitted
to take a stand on political issues, in response to requests of the
General Assembly or the Security Council, then the demand is in
conflict with the Charter itself. If, however, 'neutrality' means that
the international civil servant, also in executive tasks with political
implications, must remain wholly uninfluenced by national or group
interests or ideologies, then the obligation to observe such neutrality
is just as basic to the Charter concept of the international civil
service as it was to the concept once found in the Covenant of the
League. Due to the circumstances then prevailing the distinction to
which I have just drawn attention probably never was clearly made
in the League, but it has become fundamental for the interpretation
of the actions of the Secretariat as established by the Charter.

The criticism to which I referred at the beginning of this lecture
can be directed against the very Charter concept of the Secretariat
and imply a demand for a reduction of the functions of the Secretariat to the role assigned to it in the League and explicitly mentioned
in Article 97 of the Charter; this would be a retrograde development
in sharp conflict with the way in which the functions of the international Secretariat over the years have been extended by the main
organs of the United Nations, in response to arising needs. Another
possibility would be that the actual developments under Articles 98
and 99 are accepted but that a lack of confidence in the possibility
of personal 'neutrality' is considered to render necessary administrative arrangements putting the persons in question under special
constitutional controls, either built into the structure of the Secretariat or established through organs outside the Secretariat.

IV

The conception of an independent international civil service,
although reasonably clear in the Charter provisions, was almost
continuously subjected to stress in the history of the Organization.
International tensions, changes in governments, concern with
national security, all had their inevitable repercussions on the still

fragile institution dedicated to the international community. Governments not only strove for the acceptance of their views in the organs of the Organization, but they concerned themselves in varying degrees with the attitude of their nationals in the Secretariat. Some governments sought in one way or another to revive the substance of the proposal defeated at London for the clearance of their nationals prior to employment in the Secretariat; other governments on occasion demanded the dismissal of staff members who were said to be inappropriately representative of the country of their nationality for political, racial or even cultural reasons.

In consequence, the Charter Articles underwent a continual process of interpretation and clarification in the face of pressures brought to bear on the Secretary-General. On the whole the results tended to affirm and strengthen the independence of the international civil service. These developments involved two complementary aspects: first, the relation between the Organization and the Member States in regard to the selection and employment of nationals of those States; and second, the relation between the international official, his own State and the international responsibilities of the Organization. It is apparent that these relationships involved a complex set of obligations and rights applying to the several interested parties.

One of the most difficult of the problems was presented as a result of the interest of several national governments in passing upon the recruitment of their nationals by the Secretariat. It was of course a matter of fundamental principle that the selection of the staff should be made by the Secretary-General on his own responsibility and not on the responsibility of the national governments. The interest of the governments in placing certain nationals and in barring the employment of others had to be subordinated, as a matter of principle and law, to the independent determination of the Organization. Otherwise there would have been an abandonment of the position adopted at San Francisco and affirmed by the Preparatory Commission in London.

On the other hand, there were practical considerations which required the Organization to utilize the services of governments for the purpose of obtaining applicants for positions and, as a corollary of this, for information as to the competence, integrity and general suitability of such nationals for employment. The United Nations could not have an investigating agency comparable to those available to national governments, and the Organization had therefore to accept assistance from governments in obtaining information and records concerning possible applicants. However, the Secretary-General consistently reserved the right to make the final determination on the basis of all the facts and his own independent appreciation of these facts.

It may be recalled that this problem assumed critical proportions in 1952 and 1953 when various authorities of the United States Government, host to the United Nations Headquarters, conducted a series of highly publicized investigations of the loyalty of its nationals in the Secretariat. Charges were made which, although relating to a small number of individuals and largely founded upon inference rather than on direct evidence or admissions, led to proposals which implicitly challenged the international character of the responsibilities of the Secretary-General and his staff. In certain other countries similar proposals were made and in some cases adopted in legislation or by administrative action.

In response, the Secretary-General and the Organization as a whole affirmed the necessity of independent action by the United Nations in regard to selection and recruitment of staff. The Organization was only prepared to accept information from governments concerning suitability for employment, including information that might be relevant to political considerations such as activity which would be regarded as inconsistent with the obligation of international civil servants. It was recognized that there should be a relationship of mutual confidence and trust between international officials and the governments of Member States. At the same time, the Secretary-General took a strong position that the dismissal of a staff member on the basis of the mere suspicion of a government of a Member State or a bare conclusion arrived at by that government on evidence which is denied the Secretary-General would amount to receiving instructions in violation of his obligation under Article 100, paragraph 1, of the Charter 'not to receive in the performance of his duties instructions from any government'. It should be said that, as a result of the stand taken by the Organization, this principle was recognized by the United States Government in the procedures it established for hearings and submission of information to the Secretary-General regarding U.S. citizens.

A risk of national pressure on the international official may also be introduced, in a somewhat more subtle way, by the terms and duration of his appointment. A national official, seconded by his government for a year or two with an international organization, is evidently in a different position psychologically—and one might say, politically—from the permanent international civil servant who does not contemplate a subsequent career with his national government. This was recognized by the Preparatory Commission in London in 1945 when it concluded that members of the Secretariat staff could not be expected 'fully to subordinate the special interests of their countries to the international interest if they are merely detached temporarily from national administrations and dependent upon them for their future'. Recently, however, assertions have been made that it is necessary to switch from the present system, which makes permanent appointments and career service the rule, to a predominant system of fixed-term appointments to be granted mainly to officials seconded by their governments. This line is prompted by governments which show little enthusiasm for making officials available on a long-term basis, and, moreover, seem to regard—as a matter of principle or, at least, of 'realistic' psychology —the international civil servant primarily as a national official representing his country and its ideology. On this view, the international civil service should be recognized and developed as being an 'intergovernmental' secretariat composed principally of national officials assigned by their governments, rather than as an 'international' secretariat as conceived from the days of the League of Nations and until now. In the light of what I have already said regarding the provisions of the Charter, I need not demonstrate that this conception runs squarely against the principles of Articles 100 and 101.

This is not to say that there is not room for a reasonable number of 'seconded' officials in the Secretariat. It has in fact been accepted that it is highly desirable to have a number of officials available from governments for short periods, especially to perform particular tasks calling for diplomatic or technical backgrounds. Experience has shown that such seconded officials, true to their obligations under the Charter, perform valuable service but as a matter of good policy it should, of course, be avoided as much as possible to put them on assignments in which their status and nationality might be embarrassing to themselves or the parties concerned. However, this is quite different from having a large portion of the Secretariat— say, in excess of one-third—composed of short-term officials. To have so large a proportion of the Secretariat staff in the seconded category would be likely to impose serious strains on its ability to function as a body dedicated exclusively to international responsibilities. Especially if there were any doubts as to the principles ruling their work in the minds of the governments on which their future might depend, this might result in a radical departure from the basic concepts of the Charter and the destruction of the international civil service as it has been developed in the League and up to now in the United Nations.

It can fairly be said that the United Nations has increasingly succeeded in affirming the original idea of a dedicated professional service responsible only to the Organization in the performance of its duties and protected insofar as possible from the inevitable pressures of national governments. And this has been done in spite of strong pressures which are easily explained in terms of historic tradition and national interests. Obviously, however, the problem is ultimately one of the spirit of service shown by the international civil servant and respected by Member governments. The International Secretariat is not what it is meant to be until the day when it can be recruited on a wide geographical basis without the risk that then some will be under—or consider themselves to be under—two masters in respect of their official functions.

V

The independence and international character of the Secretariat required not only resistance to national pressures in matters of personnel, but also—and this was more complex—the independent implementation of controversial political decisions in a manner fully consistent with the exclusively international responsibility of the Secretary-General. True, in some cases implementation was largely administrative; the political organs stated their objectives and the measures to be taken in reasonably specific terms, leaving only a narrow area for executive discretion. But in other cases—and these generally involved the most controversial situations—the Secretary-General was confronted with mandates of a highly general character, expressing the bare minimum of agreement attainable in the organs. That the execution of these tasks involved the exercise of political judgment by the Secretary-General was, of course, evident to the Member States themselves.

It could perhaps be surmised that virtually no one at San Francisco envisaged the extent to which the Members of the Organization would assign to the Secretary-General functions which necessarily required him to take positions in highly controversial political matters. A few examples of these mandates in recent years will demonstrate how wide has been the scope of authority delegated to the Secretary-General by the Security Council and the General Assembly in matters of peace and security.

One might begin in 1956 with the Palestine armistice problem when the Security Council instructed the Secretary-General 'to arrange with the parties for adoption of any measures' which he would consider 'would reduce existing tensions along the armistice demarcation lines.' A few months later, after the outbreak of hostilities in Egypt, the General Assembly authorized the Secretary-General immediately to 'obtain compliance of the withdrawal of foreign forces.' At the same session he was requested to submit a plan for a United Nations Force to 'secure and supervise the cessation of hostilities,' and subsequently he was instructed 'to take all ... necessary administrative and executive action to organize this Force and dispatch it to Egypt.'

In 1958 the Secretary-General was requested 'to dispatch urgently an Observation Group . . . to Lebanon so as to insure that there is no illegal infiltration of personnel or supply of arms or other matériel across the Lebanese borders.' Two months later he was asked to make forthwith 'such practical arrangements as would adequately help in upholding the purposes and principles of the Charter in relation to Lebanon and Jordan.'

Most recently, in July 1960, the Secretary-General was requested to provide military assistance to the Central Government of the Republic of the Congo. The basic mandate is contained in a single paragraph of a resolution adopted by the Security Council on 13 July 1960, which reads as follows:

'*The Security Council*

. . . .

'2. *Decides* to authorize the Secretary-General to take the necessary steps, in consultation with the Government of the Republic of the Congo, to provide the Government with such military assistance, as may be necessary, until, through the efforts of the Congolese Government with the technical assistance of the United Nations, the national security forces may be able, in the opinion of the Government, to meet fully their tasks.'

The only additional guidance was provided by a set of principles concerning the use of United Nations Forces which had been evolved during the experience of the United Nations Emergency Force. I had informed the Security Council before the adoption of the resolution that I would base any action that I might be required to take on these principles, drawing attention specifically to some of the most significant of the rules applied in the UNEF operation. At the request of the Security Council I later submitted an elaboration of the same principles to the extent they appeared to me to be applicable to the Congo operation. A report on the matter was explicitly approved by the Council, but naturally it proved to leave wide gaps; unforeseen and unforeseeable problems, which we quickly came to face, made it necessary for me repeatedly to invite the Council to express themselves on the interpretation given by the Secretary-General to the mandate. The needs for added interpretation referred especially to the politically extremely charged situation which arose because of the secession of Katanga and because of the disintegration of the Central Government, which, according to the basic resolution of the Security Council, was to be the party in consultation with which the United Nations activities had to be developed.

These recent examples demonstrate the extent to which the Member States have entrusted the Secretary-General with tasks that have required him to take action which unavoidably may have to run counter to the views of at least some of these Member States. The agreement reached in the general terms of a resolution, as we have seen, no longer need obtain when more specific issues are presented. Even when the original resolution is fairly precise, subsequent developments, previously unforeseen, may render highly controversial the action called for under the resolution. Thus, for example, the unanimous resolution authorizing assistance to the Central Government of the Congo offered little guidance to the Secretary-General when that Government split into competing centers of authority, each claiming to be the Central Government and each supported by different groups of Member States within and outside the Security Council.

A simple solution for the dilemmas thus posed for the Secretary-General might seem to be for him to refer the problem to the political organ for it to resolve the question. Under a national parliamentary regime, this would often be the obvious course of action for the executive to take. Indeed, this is what the Secretary-General must also do whenever it is feasible. But the serious problems arise precisely because it is so often not possible for the organs themselves to resolve the controversial issue faced by the Secretary-General. When brought down to specific cases involving a clash of interests and positions, the required majority in the Security Council or General Assembly may not be available for any particular solution. This will frequently be evident in advance of a meeting and the Member States will conclude that it would be futile for the organs to attempt to reach a decision and consequently that the problem has to be left to the Secretary-General to solve on one basis or another, on his own risk but with as faithful an interpretation of the instructions, rights and obligations of the Organization as possible in view of international law and the decisions already taken.

It might be said that in this situation the Secretary-General should refuse to implement the resolution, since implementation would offend one or another group of Member States and open him to the charge that he has abandoned the political neutrality and impartiality essential to his office. The only way to avoid such criticism, it is said, is for the Secretary-General to refrain from execution of the original resolution until the organs have decided the issue by the required majority (and, in the case of the Security Council, with the unanimous concurrence of the permanent members) or he, maybe, has found another way to pass responsibility over on to governments.

For the Secretary-General this course of action—or more precisely, non-action—may be tempting; it enables him to avoid criticism by refusing to act until other political organs resolve the dilemma. An easy refuge may thus appear to be available. But would such refuge be compatible with the responsibility placed upon the Secretary-General by the Charter? Is he entitled to refuse to carry out the decision properly reached by the organs, on the ground that the specific implementation would be opposed to positions some Member States might wish to take, as indicated, perhaps, by an earlier minority vote? Of course the political organs may always instruct him to discontinue the implementation of a resolution, but when they do not so instruct him and the resolution remains in effect, is the Secretary-General legally and morally free to take no action, particularly in a matter considered to affect international peace and security? Should he, for example, have abandoned the operation in the Congo because almost any decision he made as to the composition of the Force or its role would have been contrary to the attitudes of some Members as reflected in debates, and maybe even in votes, although not in decisions?

The answers seem clear enough in law; the responsibilities of the Secretary-General under the Charter cannot be laid aside merely because the execution of decisions by him is likely to be politically controversial. The Secretary-General remains under the obligation to carry out the policies as adopted by the organs; the essential requirement is that he does this on the basis of his exclusively international responsibility and not in the interest of any particular State or groups of States.

This presents us with the crucial issue; is it possible for the Secretary-General to resolve controversial questions on a truly international basis without obtaining the formal decision of the organs? In my opinion and on the basis of my experience, the answer is in the affirmative; it is possible for the Secretary-General to carry out his tasks in controversial political situations with full regard to his exclusively international obligation under the Charter and without subservience to a particular national or ideological attitude. This is not to say that the Secretary-General is a kind of delphic oracle who alone speaks for the international community. He has available for his task varied means and resources.

Of primary importance in this respect are the principles and purposes of the Charter which are the fundamental law accepted by and binding on all States. Necessarily general and comprehensive, these principles and purposes still are specific enough to have practical significance in concrete cases.

The principles of the Charter are, moreover, supplemented by the body of legal doctrine and precepts that have been accepted by States generally, and particularly as manifested in the resolutions of United Nations organs. In this body of law there are rules and precedents that appropriately furnish guidance to the Secretary-General when he is faced with the duty of applying a general mandate in circumstances that had not been envisaged by the resolution.

Considerations of principle and law, important as they are, do not of course suffice to settle all the questions posed by the political tasks entrusted to the Secretary-General. Problems of political judgment still remain. In regard to these problems, the Secretary-General must find constitutional means and techniques to assist him, insofar as possible, in reducing the element of purely personal judgment. In my experience I have found several arrangements of value to enable the Secretary-General to obtain what might be regarded as the representative opinion of the Organization in respect of the political issues faced by him.

One such arrangement might be described as the institution of the permanent missions to the United Nations, through which the Member States have enabled the Secretary-General to carry on frequent consultations safeguarded by diplomatic privacy.

Another arrangement, which represents a further development of the first, has been the advisory committees of the Secretary-General, such as those on UNEF and the Congo, composed of representatives of governments most directly concerned with the activity involved, and also representing diverse political positions and interests. These advisory committees have furnished a large measure of the guidance required by the Secretary-General in carrying out his mandates relating to UNEF and the Congo operations. They have provided an essential link between the judgment of the executive and the consensus of the political bodies.

VI

Experience has thus indicated that the international civil servant may take steps to reduce the sphere within which he has to take stands on politically controversial issues. In summary, it may be said that he will carefully seek guidance in the decisions of the main organs, in statements relevant for the interpretation of those decisions, in the Charter and in generally recognized principles of law, remembering that by his actions he may set important precedents. Further, he will submit as complete reporting to the main organs as circumstances permit, seeking their guidance whenever such guidance seems to be possible to obtain. Even if all of these steps are taken, it will still remain, as has been amply demonstrated in practice, that the reduced area of discretion will be large enough to expose the international Secretariat to heated political controversy and to accusations of a lack of neutrality.

I have already drawn attention to the ambiguity of the word 'neutrality' in such a context. It is obvious from what I have said that the international civil servant cannot be accused of lack of neutrality simply for taking a stand on a controversial issue when this is his duty and cannot be avoided. But there remains a serious intellectual and moral problem as we move within an area inside which personal judgment must come into play. Finally, we have to deal here with a question of integrity or with, if you please, a question of conscience.

The international civil servant must keep himself under the strictest observation. He is not requested to be a neuter in the sense that he has to have no sympathies or antipathies, that there are to be no interests which are close to him in his personal capacity or that he is to have no ideas or ideals that matter for him. However, he is requested to be fully aware of those human reactions and meticulously check himself so that they are not permitted to influence his actions. This is nothing unique. Is not every judge professionally under the same obligation?

If the international civil servant knows himself to be free from such personal influences in his actions and guided solely by the common aims and rules laid down for, and by the Organization he serves and by recognized legal principles, then he has done his duty, and then he can face the criticism which, even so, will be unavoidable. As I said, at the final last, this is a question of integrity, and if integrity in the sense of respect for law and respect for truth were to drive him into positions of conflict with this or that interest, then that conflict is a sign of his neutrality and not of his failure to observe neutrality—then it is in line, not in conflict, with his duties as an international civil servant.

Recently, it has been said, this time in Western circles, that as the international Secretariat is going forward on the road of international thought and action, while Member States depart from it, a gap develops between them and they are growing into being mutually hostile elements; and this is said to increase the tension in the world which it was the purpose of the United Nations to diminish. From this view the conclusion has been drawn that we may have to switch from an international Secretariat, ruled by the principles described in this lecture, to an intergovernmental Secretariat, the members of which obviously would not be supposed to work in the direction of an internationalism considered unpalatable to their governments. Such a passive acceptance of a nationalism rendering it necessary to abandon present efforts in the direction of internationalism symbolized by the international civil service— somewhat surprisingly regarded as a cause of tension—might, if accepted by the Member nations, well prove to be the Munich of international cooperation as conceived after the first World War and further developed under the impression of the tragedy of the second World War. To abandon or to compromise with principles on which such cooperation is built may be no less dangerous than to compromise with principles regarding the rights of a nation. In both cases the price to be paid may be peace.

PRESS CONFERENCE COMMENTS
ARISING FROM LECTURE AT OXFORD

From transcript, 12 June 1961

QUESTION: In your widely commented-upon Oxford University speech about two weeks ago you warned that to abandon or compromise with the principles on which international cooperation is based, as symbolized in an independent international civil service, might well prove to be the Munich of international cooperation. You also pointed out two basic principles in the Charter: that decisions were to be political and that the administration and implementation were to be lifted out of the realm of the political. I want to ask you whether you consider these principles applicable to any political decisions taken on nuclear tests, on disarmament, or on any possible arrangement for the United Nations in Berlin.

THE SECRETARY-GENERAL: I believe that the principles do apply whenever you want an impartial implementation or execution of a decision which has been reached or an agreement which has been established. You may remember that at the last press conference I made a distinction between what I called a natural veto, which is based on substance, and an artificial and imposed veto.

(He had said: 'There is a real veto problem and there is an artificial one. The real veto problem, for which in fact the word "veto" is a misnomer is based on the fact that there are questions which cannot be solved without agreement between the big

Powers, especially, in this case, between the predominant
military Powers.

There is the artificial veto problem, that is to say, the attempt
by this or that Power to make its consent essential for questions
which naturally should be solved, let us say, on a majority
basis.

On the first point neither you nor I can change anything
because there we are up against a hard fact. It is a real problem
and it can be solved only by agreement and by the will to agree
among the big Powers.

As regards the other question, what I call the artificial veto
problem, it is my firm and strong feeling that the introduction
and development of such a problem is harmful to international
cooperation because it stymies a development which could take
place on majority decisions here in this Organization or on
some other kind of objective basis.')

I believe one could develop the theme further in the light of
your question and say that, as regards agreements, or basic decisions,
of course the cooperation of all parties concerned is necessary, and,
for that reason, to a greater or lesser extent, a political element
enters basically into the operation. On the other hand, once an
agreement is reached or a decision taken with the necessary support
—that is to say, when you reach the stage of execution—it is just
as essential that all parties should be able to feel that the execution
will not give rise to new negotiations or, so to speak, tear up the
agreement or decision.

Therefore my conclusion is that the principles I tried to develop,
especially the principle of the international character of an executive,
do apply to all operations in which parties to an agreement or
decision should feel assured that the decision will be carried out in
a way which is not partisan.

I believe very strongly that the basic principle of internationalism,
as established especially in Article 100, is decisive, because if it were
not applied, if it were not respected, what would we have? We
would have executives or Secretariats which in fact were a lower-
level government and party representation. That being so, of course,
you would have not an impartial execution of a decision or an agreement, but you would have, in a sense, a continued negotiation or a
continued effort to reach decisions. And there you can see how the

very logic of the situation indicates the need of the international character which I mentioned. If we were to lose the international character of the executive part of the operation, of the Secretariats, I think that it would mean a very serious slowing-down of the execution of agreements and the carrying through of decisions. And, when I talked about those principles in somewhat dramatic terms, it was because of the fear which I feel for what we may risk if in this way the whole process of international cooperation were to be slowed down.

*   *   *

.... QUESTION: Mr. Secretary-General, in connection with what you have just said, I would like to ask you a question on a sort of broader aspect. We have seen during the past few months the emergence of a theory of international relations which actually goes back behind the theory of Thomas Hobbes, namely, that objectivity or neutrality is irreconcilable with the working of the human mind and that there is not a single neutral person on this globe. Now, in connection with this new theory, I would like to ask you two questions. First, as a man who was a neutral even in a neutral country, what do you think about the possibility of the freedom of the individual from dependence on ideologies or loyalties to one particular country? And second, what do you think can be done to counter this new theory in order to make possible the theoretical and practical working of international organizations?

THE SECRETARY-GENERAL: In a sense, I have said what I feel can be said about the neutrality of an executive and the neutrality of an international civil servant in the speech at Oxford to which reference has been made. But you put the question in more personal terms, and I may try to explain myself in personal terms.

It may be true that in a very deep, human sense there is no neutral individual, because, as I said at Oxford, everyone, if he is worth anything, has to have his ideas and ideals—things which are dear to him, and so on. But what I do claim is that even a man who is in that sense not neutral can very well undertake and carry through neutral actions, because that is an act of integrity. That is to say, I would say there is no neutral man, but there is, if you have integrity, neutral action by the right kind of man. And 'neutrality' may develop, after all, into a kind of *jeu de mots*. I am not a neutral as regards the Charter; I am not neutral as regards facts. But that is not what we mean. What is meant by 'neutrality' in this kind of debate, is of course, neutrality in relation to interests; and there I do claim that there is no insurmountable difficulty for anybody with the proper kind of guiding principles in carrying through such neutrality one hundred per cent.

*   *   *

. . . . QUESTION: A part of the discussion this morning seems to have centered on an interpretation I was looking for of a statement made [in] your Oxford speech. There you raised the question that once the possibility of the impartiality of an international civil servant is questioned there may be—and you go into a sentence which implies a need for changes, constitutional or otherwise, to meet the possibility . . . I wondered—whereas you have previously indicated that a resignation would be forthcoming if the majority of the Assembly should vote against you on a crucial issue—does this represent a sort of *de facto* evolution of the Charter as a constitution or would such an interpretation be beyond what you were saying in the Oxford speech?

THE SECRETARY-GENERAL: I think that in fact you mix two problems here. What I meant . . . is covered by the trite expression, 'Caesar's wife must not even be suspected.' Under such circumstances any international service should be willing to submit itself to all checks and controls which are found constitutionally advisable. That is one thing and I would be quite happy to have it. You may remember that I have at various stages during the Congo operation, for example, invited decisions to the effect that there would be what I called a sharing of responsibilities. You can also say that such a sharing of responsibilities means that the people will have the chance to look at the spirit, the way in which decisions are carried out so as to ascertain that there is this neutrality of action to which I referred. That is really what I had in mind here.

You bring up the other question, the question, of, so to say, the standing offer of resignation. That represents a *de facto* development. It does not have any precedent. There is nothing in the Charter indicating that form. You may perhaps say that it is built on a kind of parliamentary theory in the interpretation of the Charter, a parliamentary theory which, however, I have never, so to say, spelled out. We have a situation where one of the permanent members has ceased cooperation. What should the consequences be? Obviously the General Assembly comes into the picture, too. The Security Council is not the only one to decide in such matters. I am not in the position to extend Article 97* to cover the whole period of the service of the Secretary-General. That certainly would be absolutely preposterous for the Secretary-General to do. But he must, on the other hand, take into account the hard facts of the situation. Bringing the General Assembly into the question the way I did, I think that, if you want to translate it into constitutional terms—I should not like to formalize it myself but you may want to do so—it is reasonable to say that if the Secretary-General has lost the support of one of the permanent members of the Security Council, which presumably is one of the conditions for his functioning, and if, moreover, he does not have the support of at least two-thirds of the General Assembly, he is no longer in a position to function.

* Art. 97 says, 'The Secretary-General shall be appointed by the General Assembly upon the recommendation of the Security Council.' The vote in the Security Council is subject to the veto rule.

INTRODUCTION TO THE
ANNUAL REPORT 1960-1961

17 August 1961

I. THE CHOICE

Debates and events during the year since the publication of the last report to the General Assembly have brought to the fore different concepts of the United Nations, the character of the Organization, its authority and its structure.

On the one side, it has in various ways become clear that certain Members conceive of the Organization as a static conference machinery for resolving conflicts of interests and ideologies with a view to peaceful coexistence, within the Charter, to be served by a Secretariat which is to be regarded not as fully internationalized but as representing within its ranks those very interests and ideologies.

Other Members have made it clear that they conceive of the Organization primarily as a dynamic instrument of governments through which they, jointly and for the same purpose, should seek such reconciliation but through which they should also try to develop forms of executive action, undertaken on behalf of all Members, and aiming at forestalling conflicts and resolving them, once they have arisen, by appropriate diplomatic or political means, in a spirit of objectivity and in implementation of the principles and purposes of the Charter.

Naturally, the latter concept takes as its starting point the conference concept, but it regards it only as a starting point, envisaging the possibility of continued growth to increasingly effective forms of active international cooperation, adapted to experience, and served by a Secretariat of which it is required that, whatever the background and the views of its individual members, their actions be guided solely by the principles of the Charter, the decisions of the main organs, and the interests of the Organization itself.

The first concept can refer to history and to the traditions of national policies of the past. The second can point to the needs of the present and of the future in a world of ever-closer international interdependence where nations have at their disposal armaments of hitherto unknown destructive strength. The first one is firmly anchored in the time-honoured philosophy of sovereign national States in armed competition of which the most that may be expected in the international field is that they achieve a peaceful coexistence. The second one envisages possibilities of inter-governmental action overriding such a philosophy, and opens the road towards more developed and increasingly effective forms of constructive international cooperation.

It is clearly for the governments, Members of the Organization, and for these governments only, to make their choice and decide on the direction in which they wish the Organization to develop. However, it may be appropriate to study these two concepts in terms of the purposes of the Organization as laid down in the Charter, and, in this context, also to consider the character and significance of the decisions of the Organization as well as its structure.

II. CHARTER PURPOSES AND PRINCIPLES

The purposes and principles of the Charter are set out in its Preamble and further developed in a series of articles, including some which may seem to be primarily of a procedural or administrative nature. Together, these parts of the Charter lay down some basic rules of international ethics by which all Member States have committed themselves to be guided. To a large extent, the rules reflect standards accepted as binding for life within States. Thus, they appear, in the main, as a projection into the international arena and the international community of purposes and principles already accepted as being of national validity. In this sense, the Charter takes a first step in the direction of an organized international community, and this independently of the organs set up for international cooperation. Due to different traditions, the state of social development and the character of national institutions, wide variations naturally exist as to the application in national life of the principles reflected in the Charter, but it is not too difficult to recognize the common elements behind those differences. It is therefore not surprising that such principles of national application could be transposed into an agreed basis also for international behaviour and cooperation.

In the Preamble to the Charter, Member nations have reaffirmed their faith 'in the equal rights of men and women and of nations large and small', a principle which also has found many other expressions in the Charter.

Thus, it re-states the basic democratic principle of equal political rights, independently of the position of the individual or of the Member country in respect of its strength, as determined by territory, population or wealth. The words just quoted must, however, be considered as going further and imply an endorsement as well of a right to equal economic opportunities.

It is in the light of the first principle that the Charter has established a system of equal votes, expressing 'the sovereign equality of all its Members', and has committed the Organization to the furtherance of self-determination, self-government and independence. On the same basis, the Charter requires universal respect for and observance of human rights and fundamental freedoms for all 'without distinction as to race, sex, language or religion'.

It is in the light of the latter principle—or, perhaps, the latter aspect of the same basic principle—that the Charter, in Article 55, has committed the Members to the promotion of higher standards of living, full employment and conditions of economic and social progress and development as well as to solutions of international economic and related problems. The pledge of all Members to take joint and separate action, in cooperation with the Organization, for the achievement of these purposes has been the basis for the far-reaching economic and technical assistance channelled through or administered by the Organization, and may rightly be considered as the basic obligation reflected also in such economic and technical assistance as Member governments have been giving, on a bilateral basis, outside the framework of the Organization.

It would seem that those who regard the Organization as a conference machinery, 'neutral' in relation to the direction of policies on a national or international basis and serving solely as an instrument for the solution of conflicts by reconciliation, do not pay adequate attention to those essential principles of the Charter to which reference has just been made. The terms of the Charter are explicit as regards the equal political rights of nations as well as of individuals and, although this second principle may be considered only as implicit in the terms of the Charter, they are clear also as regards the demand for equal economic opportunities for all individuals and nations. So as to avoid any misunderstanding, the Charter directly states that the basic democratic principles are applicable to nations 'large and small' and to individuals without distinction 'as to race, sex, language and religion', qualifications that obviously could be extended to cover also other criteria such as, for example, those of an ideological character which have been used or may be used as a basis for political or economic discrimination.

In the practical work of the Organization these basic principles have been of special significance in relation to countries under colonial rule or in other ways under foreign domination. The General Assembly has translated the principles into action intended to establish through self-determination a free and independent life as sovereign States for peoples who have expressed in democratic forms their wish for such a status. Decisive action has in many cases been taken by Member governments, and then the United Nations has had only to lend its support to their efforts. In other cases, the main responsibility has fallen on the Organization itself. The resolution on colonialism, adopted by the General Assembly at its fifteenth session, may be regarded as a comprehensive re-statement in elaborated form of the principle laid down in the Charter. Results of developments so far have been reflected in the birth of a great number of new national States and a revolutionary widening of the membership of the Organization.

The demand for equal economic opportunities has, likewise, been—and remains—of special significance in relation to those very countries which have more recently entered the international arena as new States. This is natural in view of the fact that, mostly, they have been in an unfavourable economic position, which is reflected in a much lower *per capita* income, rate of capital supply and degree of technical development, while their political independence and sovereignty require a fair measure of economic stability and economic possibilities in order to gain substance and full viability.

In working for the translation into practical realities in international life of the democratic principles which are basic to the Charter, the Organization has thus assumed a most active role and it has done so with success, demonstrating both the need and the possibilities for such action.

Further, in the Preamble to the Charter it is stated to be a principle and purpose of the Organization 'to establish conditions under which justice and respect for the obligations arising from treaties and other sources of international law can be maintained'. In these words—to which, naturally, counterparts may be found in other parts of the Charter—it gives expression to another basic democratic principle, that of the rule of law. In order to promote this principle, the Charter established the International Court of Justice, but the principle permeates the approach of the Charter to international problems far beyond the sphere of competence of the Court. As in national life, the principle of justice—which obviously implies also the principle of objectivity and equity in the consideration of all matters before the General Assembly or the Security Council—must be considered as applicable without distinction or discrimination, with one measure and one standard valid for the strong as well as for the weak. Thus, the demand of the Charter for a rule of law aims at the substitution of right for might and makes of the Organization the natural protector of rights which countries without it might find it more difficult to assert and to get respected.

The principle of justice can be regarded as flowing naturally from the principles of equal political rights and equal economic opportunities, but it has an independent life and carries, of itself, the world community as far in the direction of an organized international system as the two first-mentioned principles. It has deep roots in the history of the efforts of man to eliminate from international life the anarchy which he had already much earlier overcome on the national level, deeper indeed than the political and economic principles which, as is well known, were much later to get full acceptance also in national life. Long before the United Nations and long before even the League of Nations, governments were working towards a rule of justice in international life through which they hoped to establish an international community based on law, without parliamentary or executive organs, but with a judicial procedure through which law and justice could be made to apply.

The Charter states and develops the three principles mentioned here as a means to an end: 'to save succeeding generations from the scourge of war'. This adds emphasis to the concept, clearly implied in the Charter, of an international community for which the Organization is an instrument and an expression and in which anarchic tendencies in international life are to be curbed by the introduction of a system of equal political rights, equal economic opportunities and the rule of law. However, the Charter goes one step further, drawing a logical conclusion both from the ultimate aim of the Organization and from the three principles. Thus, it outlaws the use of armed force 'save in the common interest'. Obviously, the Charter cannot, on the one side, establish a rule of law and the principle of equal rights for 'nations large and small', and, on the other hand, permit the use of armed force for national ends, contrary to those principles and, therefore, not 'in the common interest'. Were nations, under the Charter, to be allowed, by the use of their military strength, to achieve ends contrary to the principle of the equality of Members and the principle of justice, it would obviously deprive those very principles of all substance and significance. One practical expression of this approach, which may be mentioned here, is that the organs of the United Nations have consistently maintained that the use of force, contrary to the Charter as interpreted by those organs, cannot be permitted to yield results which can be accepted as valid by the Organization and as establishing new rights.

In the Charter, the right to the use of force is somewhat more extensive than may seem to be the case from a superficial reading of the phrase 'save in the common interest'. Thus, apart from military action undertaken pursuant to a decision of the Security Council for repression of aggression—that is, for upholding the basic Charter principles—the Charter opens the door to the use of armed force by a nation in exercise of its inherent right to resist armed attack. This is a point on which, both in theory and in practice, the development of international law is still at a very early stage. As is well known, no agreement has been reached on a definition of aggression, beyond that found in Article 2, paragraph 4, of the Charter,* and the Organization has several times had to face situations in which, therefore, the rights and wrongs in a specific case of conflict have not been clarified. It would be a vitally important step forward if wider agreement could be reached regarding the criteria to be applied in order to distinguish between legitimate and illegitimate use of force. History is only too rich in examples of armed aggression claimed as action in self-defence. How could it be otherwise, when most cases of armed conflict are so deeply rooted

---

* 'All members shall refrain in their international relations from the threat or use of force against the territorial integrity or political independence of any state, or in any other manner inconsistent with the Purposes of the United Nations.'

in a history of clashes of interests and rights, even if, up to the fatal moment of the first shot, those clashes have not involved recourse to the use of armed force?

In recognition of this situation and in the light of historical experience, the Charter makes yet another projection into international life of solutions to conflicts tested in national life, and establishes the final principle that the Organization shall 'bring about by peaceful means and in conformity with the principles of justice and international law, adjustment or settlement of international disputes or situations which might lead to a breach of the peace'. This principle, as quoted here from Article 1 of the Charter, is further developed specifically in Article 33, which requires parties to any dispute, the consequence of which is likely to endanger the maintenance of international peace and security, to 'seek a solution by negotiation, enquiry, mediation, conciliation, arbitration, judicial settlement, resort to regional agencies or arrangements, or other peaceful means of their own choice'. It is in this sphere that the Security Council has had, and is likely to continue to have, its main significance, both directly as a forum before which any dispute threatening peace and security can be brought up for debate and as an organ which directly, or through appropriate agents, may assist the parties in finding a way out and, by preventive diplomacy, may forestall the outbreak of an armed conflict. It seems appropriate here to draw attention especially to the right of the Security Council under Article 40 to 'call upon the parties concerned to comply with such provisional measures as it deems necessary or desirable' for the prevention of any aggravation of a situation threatening peace and security, and to the obligation of Members to comply with a decision on such measures.

It is in the light of the approach to international coexistence in our world today, which is thus to be found in the Charter, that judgment has to be passed on the validity of the different conceptions of the Organization which in recent times have become increasingly apparent. As already pointed out, the basic principles regarding the political equality of nations and their right to equal economic opportunities are difficult to reconcile with the view that the Organization is to be regarded only as a conference machinery for the solution, by debate and joint decisions, of conflicts of interest or ideology. It seems even more difficult to reconcile these principles with a view according to which equality among Members should be reflected in the establishment of a balance between power blocs or other groupings of nations. The same difficulty is apparent as regards the principle of justice and the principle prohibiting the use of armed force. It is easier to apply the conference concept to the principle of prevention of conflict through negotiation, but also on this point the difficulties become considerable if it is recognized that such solutions as may be sought by the Organization should be solutions based on the rules of equality and justice.

III. RESPECT FOR AUTHORITY OF THE ORGANIZATION

The General Assembly, the Security Council and other collective organs of the United Nations have features in common with a standing international diplomatic conference, but their procedures go beyond the forms of such a conference and show aspects of a parliamentary or quasi-parliamentary character.

While decisions of a conference, in order to commit its participants, must be based on their subsequent acceptance of the decisions, the organs of the United Nations act on the basis of voting, with the decisions being adopted if supported by a majority. However, the decisions of the Assembly have, as regards Member States, only the character of recommendation (except for financial assessments and certain other types of organizational action) so that obligations like those arising out of an agreement, coming into force after a conference, do not normally flow from them. But although the decisions, legally, are only recommendations, they introduce an important element by expressing a majority consensus on the issue under consideration.

Naturally, such a formula leaves scope for a gradual development in practice of the weight of the decisions. To the extent that more respect, in fact, is shown to General Assembly recommendations by the Member States, they may come more and more close to being recognized as decisions having a binding effect on those concerned, particularly when they involve the application of the binding principles of the Charter and of international law.

Both those who regard a gradual increase in the weight of decisions of the General Assembly as necessary, if progress is to be registered in the direction of organized peaceful coexistence within the

Charter, and those who oppose such a development, have to recognize that, with certain variations in individual cases, the practice still is very close to the restrictive Charter formula. Experience shows that even countries which have voted for a certain decision may, later on, basing themselves on its character of merely being a recommendation, refuse to follow it or fail to support its implementation, financially or in other respects.

What has been said applies generally to the collective organs of the Organization, but, as is well known, the Charter has gone one step further beyond the conference concept, in the direction of the parliamentary concept, in the case of the Security Council. In Article 25, Member States of the United Nations have agreed to 'accept and carry out the decisions of the Security Council in accordance with the present Charter,' thus by agreement, making the decisions of the Council mandatory, except, of course, when such decisions take the form of 'recommendations' within the terms of Chapter VI or certain other articles of the Charter. They have further, in Article 49, undertaken to 'join in affording mutual assistance in carrying out the measures decided upon by the Security Council.'

This agreed mandatory nature of certain Security Council decisions might have led to a demand for unanimity in the Council, a unanimity which was the rule for the Council of the League of Nations. Even so, however, the arrangement would have gone beyond the conference principle with its requirement that no decision reached in an international organ should be binding on an individual Member short of his agreement. With the present arrangements, requiring a majority of seven and the concurring votes of the permanent members, a bridge between the traditional conference approach and a parliamentary approach is provided by the commitment in Article 25 to agree to the carrying out of the decisions in the Council which should be considered as giving the Council its authority by general delegation as indeed stated in Article 24, paragraph 1.*

What clearly remains within the Council of the traditional conference and agreement pattern is the condition that its decisions of

---

* 'In order to ensure prompt and effective action by the United Nations, its Members confer on the Security Council primary responsibility for the maintenance of international peace and security, and agree that in carrying out its duties under this responsibility the Security Council acts on their behalf.'

a non-procedural character must be supported by the unanimous vote of the five permanent members, thus avoiding for those members the risk of being bound by a decision of the Council which has not met with their agreement. It may be observed that this special position for the permanent members, apart from other reasons, has the justification that, without such a rule, the other Members of the Organization, in complying with a Security Council decision, might find themselves unwillingly drawn into a big Power conflict.

In spite of the delegated authority which the Council may be considered as exercising, and the condition that decisions must be agreed to by the permanent members, the experience of the Organization, as regards the implementation of Council decisions, is uneven and does not indicate full acceptance in practice of Article 25. In this case also, examples can be given of a tendency to regard decisions, even when taken under Chapter VII, as recommendations binding only to the extent that the party concerned has freely committed itself to carry them out; there is here a clear dichotomy between the aims of the Charter and the general political practice at its present stage of development. Such cases refer not only to Members outside the Council, or, perhaps, Members inside the Council, who have not supported a specific decision, but also to Members within the Council who have cast their votes in favour of a decision but who later on are found to reserve for themselves at least a right to interpret the decision in ways which seem to be at variance with the intentions of the Council. The ambiguity of this situation emerges with special force in cases where such attitudes have been taken by permanent members of the Council, who are considered to shoulder the responsibility for the maintenance of peace and security which is reflected in the special position they hold within the Council. Obviously, the problem whether the intended legal weight is given to decisions of the Security Council arises in practice not only in cases of non-compliance but also in cases of a refusal to shoulder the financial consequences of a decision of the Council.

These observations—which have been limited to a reminder of the Charter rules and a factual reminder also of the experiences in practice—point to a situation which in any evaluation of the United Nations must be given the most serious consideration by Members. For the judgment on the various concepts of the United Nations which are put forward, it is one thing to note what the Charter stipulates; it is an entirely different but ultimately more important question as to what the situation is in practice and what, in fact, is the weight given to decisions of the Organization when they go beyond the conference pattern of agreement.

For those who maintain the conference concept of the Organization, it is natural to side-step the mandatory nature of decisions by the Security Council. For those who take a different view, it is equally natural and essential to work for a full and general acceptance of the Charter rules. Were those to be right who hold that the Charter on the points discussed here, and, maybe, also as regards the five basic principles discussed in the first part of this Introduction, is ahead of our time and the political possibilities which it offers, such a view still would not seem to justify the conclusion that the clear approach of the Charter should be abandoned. Rather, it would indicate that Member nations jointly should increase their efforts to make political realities gradually come closer to the pattern established by the Charter.

In the light of such considerations, the significance of the outcome of every single conflict on which the Organization has to take a stand, and the weight given to its decisions in such a conflict stand out very clearly. A failure to gain respect for decisions or actions of the Organization within the terms of the Charter is often called a failure for the Organization. It would seem more correct to regard it as a failure of the world community, through its Member nations and in particular those most directly concerned, to cooperate in order, step by step, to make the Charter a living reality in practical action as it is already in law.

Were such cooperation, for which the responsibility naturally rests with each single Member as well as with all Members collectively, not to come about, and were the respect for the obligations flowing from Article 25 of the Charter, to be allowed to diminish, this would spell the end of the possibilities of the Organization to grow into what the Charter indicates as the clear intention of the founders, as also of all hopes to see the Organization grow into an increasingly effective instrument, with increasing respect for recommendations of the General Assembly as well.

What this would mean for the value of the Organization as protector of the aims, principles and rights it was set up to further and safeguard, is obvious. The effort through the Organization to find a way by which the world community might, step by step, grow into organized international cooperation within the Charter, must either progress or recede. Those whose reactions to the work of the Organization hamper its development or reduce its possibilities of effective action, may have to shoulder the responsibility for a return to a state of affairs which governments had already found too dangerous after the first World War.

IV. EXECUTIVE ACTION AND AN INTERNATIONAL SECRETARIAT

The growth of the United Nations out of the historic conference pattern—which, as observed earlier in this Introduction, at all events naturally remains the starting point in all efforts of the Organization —is clearly reflected in what, in the light of experience, may seem to be a lack of balance in the Charter. While great attention is given to the principles and purposes, and considerable space is devoted to an elaboration of what may be called the parliamentary aspects of the Organization, little is said about executive arrangements. This does not mean that the Charter in any way closes the door to such arrangements or to executive action, but only that, at the stage of international thinking crystallized in the Charter, the conference approach still was predominant, and that the needs for executive action, if the new Organization was to live up to expectations and to its obligations under the Charter, had not yet attracted the attention they were to receive in response to later developments.

The key clause on the executive side may be considered to be Article 24, in which it is said that 'in order to assure prompt and effective action by the United Nations, its Members confer on the Security Council primary responsibility for the maintenance of international peace and security.' On that basis the Security Council is given the right, under Article 29, to establish such subsidiary organs as it deems necessary for the performance of its functions, the right under Article 40 to decide on so-called provisional measures, the right to use, for the purposes of the Charter, under certain conditions, armed forces made available to the Council, the right under Article 48 to request from governments action on the Council's behalf, as well as the right to request of the Secretary-General to 'perform such . . . functions as are entrusted to him' by the Council.*

Quoted from Article 98.

The various clauses here briefly enumerated open a wide range of possibilities for executive action undertaken by, and under the aegis of, the Security Council. However, no specific machinery is set up for such action by the Council, apart from the Military Staff Committee, with planning responsibilities in the field of the possible use of armed force by the Security Council under Chapter VII of the Charter. In fact, therefore, the executive functions and their form have been left largely to practice, and it is in the field of the practices of the Organization that cases may be found in the light of which it is now possible to evaluate the ways in which the Organization may develop its possibilities for diplomatic, political or military intervention of an executive nature in the field.

The forms used for executive action by the Security Council— or when the Council has not been able to reach decisions, in some cases, by the General Assembly—are varied and are to be explained by an effort to adjust the measures to the needs of each single situation. However, some main types are recurrent. Sub-committees have been set up for fact-finding or negotiation on the spot. Missions have been placed in areas of conflict for the purpose of observation and local negotiation. Observer groups of a temporary nature have been sent out. And, finally, police forces under the aegis of the United Nations have been organized for the assistance of the governments concerned with a view to upholding the principles of the Charter. As these, or many of these, arrangements require centralized administrative measures, which cannot be performed by the Council or the General Assembly, Members have to a large extent used the possibility to request the Secretary-General to perform special functions by instructing him to take the necessary executive steps for implementation of the action decided upon. This has been done under Article 98, as quoted above, and has represented a development in practice of the duties of the Secretary-General under Article 97. The character of the mandates has, in many cases, been such that in carrying out his functions the Secretary-General has found himself forced also to interpret the decisions in the light of the Charter, United Nations precedents and the aims and intentions expressed by the Members. When that has been the case, the Secretary-General has been under the obligation to seek guidance, to all possible extent, from the main organs; but when such guidance has not been forthcoming, developments have sometimes led to situations in which he has had to shoulder responsibility for certain limited political functions, which may be considered to be in line with the spirit of Article 99 but which legally have been based on decisions of the main organs themselves, under Article 98, and thus the exclusive responsibility of Member States acting through these organs. Naturally, in carrying out such functions the Secretariat has remained fully subject to the decisions of the political bodies.

This whole development has lately become a matter of controversy, natural and, indeed, unavoidable in the light of differences of approach to the role of the Organization to which attention has been drawn earlier in this Introduction. While the development is welcomed by Member nations which feel a need of growth as regards the possibilities of the Organization to engage in executive action in protection of the Charter principles, it is rejected by those who maintain the conference concept of the Organization. The different opinions expressed on the development are only superficially related to this or that specific action and the way in which it is considered to have been carried through. They are also only superficially related to the choice of means used for translating decisions into action. The discussion regarding the development of executive functions is basically one confronting the same fundamentally different concepts of the Organization and its place in international politics, which could be seen also in the different attitudes towards the legal weight of decisions of the Organization.

It is in this context that the principle embodied in Article 100 of the Charter is of decisive significance. This principle, which has a long history, establishes the international and independent character of the Secretariat. Thus, it is said that the Secretary-General and the staff of the Secretariat 'shall not seek or receive instructions from any government or from any other authority external to the Organization,' and that they 'shall refrain from any action which might reflect on their position as international officials responsible only to the Organization.' In the same Article, the Members of the United Nations undertake to respect 'the exclusively international character of the responsibilities of the Secretary-General and the staff and not to seek to influence them in the discharge of their responsibilities.'

The significance of the principle stated in Article 100 is a dual one. It envisages a Secretariat so organized and developed as to be able to serve as a neutral instrument for the Organization, were its main organs to wish to use the Secretariat in the way which has been mentioned above and for which Article 98 has opened possibilities. But in doing so, the principle also indicates an intention to use the Secretariat for such functions as would require that it have an exclusively international character.

In the traditional conference pattern, participants in a meeting are mostly serviced by a Secretariat drawn from the same countries as the participants themselves, and constituting a mixed group regarding which there is no need to demand or maintain an exclusively international character. It is therefore natural that those who favour the conference approach to the United Nations tend to give to Article 100 another interpretation than the one which the text calls for, especially in the light of its historical background and its background also in other clauses of the Charter.

There is no reason to go more deeply into this special problem here. Suffice it to say that, while the Organization, if regarded as a standing diplomatic conference, might well be serviced by a fully international Secretariat but does not need it, the other approach to the Organization and its role cannot be satisfied with anything less than a Secretariat of an exclusively international character, and thus cannot be reconciled with a Secretariat composed on party lines and on the assumption that the interests represented in the main organs in this manner should be represented and advocated also within the Secretariat. Thus, again, the choice between conflicting views on the United Nations Secretariat is basically a choice between conflicting views on the Organization, its functions and its future.

In order to avoid possible misunderstandings, it should be pointed out here that there is no contradiction at all between a demand for a truly international Secretariat and a demand, found in the Charter itself, for as wide a 'geographical' distribution of posts within the Secretariat as possible. It is, indeed, necessary precisely in order to maintain the exclusively international character of the Secretariat, that it be so composed as to achieve a balanced distribution of posts on all levels among all regions. This, however, is clearly something entirely different from a balanced representation of trends or ideologies. In fact if a realistic representation of such trends is considered desirable, it can and should be achieved without any assumption of political representation within the ranks of the Secretariat, by a satisfactory distribution of posts based on geographical criteria.

The exclusively international character of the Secretariat is not tied to its composition, but to the spirit in which it works and to its insulation from outside influences as stated in Article 100. While it may be said that no man is neutral in the sense that he is without opinions or ideals, it is just as true that, in spite of this, a neutral Secretariat is possible. Anyone of integrity, not subjected to undue pressures, can, regardless of his own views, readily act in an 'exclusively international' spirit and can be guided in his actions on behalf of the Organization solely by its interests and principles, and by the instructions of its organs.

V. SCOPE OF THE ORGANIZATION'S ACTIVITIES

After this brief review of the principles of the Organization, of the character of its decisions and of its structure, especially as regards arrangements for executive action, presented only as a background for the consideration of what basic concepts and approaches should guide the development of the Organization, it may be appropriate, in conclusion, to give attention to the activities of the Organization and their relevance to the current international situation.

For years the Organization has been a focal point for efforts to achieve disarmament. This may still be considered as the main standing item on the agenda of the General Assembly. However, in recent years these efforts of the Organization have been running parallel to other efforts which are either outside of it or only loosely tied to the work of the United Nations. This may be justified on the basis that a very limited number of countries hold key positions in the field of armaments, so that any effort on a universal basis and by voting, to reach a decision having practical force, would be ineffective, unless founded on a basic agreement between those few parties mostly concerned. Therefore, direct negotiations between those countries are an essential first step to the solution, through the United Nations, of the disarmament problem, and do not in any way derogate from the responsibilities or rights of the Organization.

The situation may serve as an example of a problem which has become increasingly important in the life of the Organization: the right way in which to balance the weight of the big Powers and

24+

their security interests against the rights of the majority of Member nations. Such a majority naturally cannot expect the big Powers, in questions of vital concern to them, with their superior military and economic strength, automatically to accept a majority verdict. On the other hand, the big Powers cannot, as members of the world community, and with their dependence on all other nations, set themselves above, or disregard the views of, the majority of nations. An effort to balance the big Power element and the majority element is found in the Charter rules regarding the respective competence of the General Assembly and the Security Council and regarding the special position of the big Powers within the Council. Other efforts to solve the same problem are reflected in the way in which the disarmament problem has been attacked in recent years. No fully satisfactory or definitive formula has been found, but it must be sought, and it is to be hoped that when the time comes for a Charter revision, agreement may be reached on a satisfactory solution.

What is true of the disarmament problem is, of course, true also of those more specific questions in which security interests of big Powers are or may be directly involved, as for example the Berlin problem. The community of nations, represented in the United Nations, has a vital interest in a peaceful solution, based on justice, of any question which—like this one—unless brought to a satisfactory solution, might come to represent a threat to peace and security. However, the problem of the balance to be struck between the rights and obligations of the big Powers and the rights and obligations of all other nations applies, in a very direct way, also to this problem which is now so seriously preoccupying the minds of all peoples and their leaders. The United Nations, with its wide membership, is not, and can, perhaps, not aspire to be a focal point in the debate on an issue such as the Berlin question, or in the efforts to solve it, but the Organization cannot, for that reason, be considered as an outside party which has no right to make its voice heard should a situation develop which would threaten those very interests which the United Nations is to safeguard and for the defense of which it was intended to provide all Member nations with an instrument and a forum.

Reference has already been made in this Introduction to the work of the Organization devoted to furthering self-determination, self-government and independence for all peoples. In that context it was recalled that the General Assembly, at its last session, adopted a resolution regarding the colonial problem which elaborates the basic principles of the Charter in their application to this problem.

This is, likewise, a question which for years has been before the General Assembly and it is likely to remain a major item until a final result is achieved which reflects full implementation of the basic principles in the direction indicated by last year's resolution. Experience has shown that peaceful progress in that direction cannot be guaranteed solely by decisions of the General Assembly or the Security Council, within the framework of a conference pattern. Executive action is necessary, and neither the General Assembly nor the Security Council—which has had to deal with situations in which the liquidation of the colonial system has led to acute conflict—has abstained from such action in support of the lines upheld. As in the past, executive action by the Organization in the future will undoubtedly also be found necessary if it is to render the service expected from it under the terms of the Charter.

It is in conflicts relating to the development towards full self-government and independence that the Organization has faced its most complicated tasks in the executive field. It is also in the case of executive action in this context that different concepts of the Organization and of its decisions and structure have their most pointed expressions. As regards this specific aspect of the work of the United Nations, the front line has not been the usual one between different bloc interests, but more one between a great number of nations with aims natural especially for those which recently have been under colonial rule or under other forms of foreign domination, and a limited number of powers with other aims and predominant interests. This seems understandable if one takes into account that a majority of nations wishes to stand aside from the big Power conflicts, while power blocs or big Powers tend to safeguard their positions and security by efforts to maintain or extend an influence over newly emerging areas. The United Nations easily becomes a focal point for such conflicting interests, as the majority looks to the Organization for support in their policy of independence also in relation to such efforts, while power blocs or countries with other aims may see in the United Nations an obstacle in the way of their policies to the extent that the Organization provides the desired support. How this is reflected in the attitude towards the development of the executive functions of the United Nations can be illustrated by numerous examples. It may be appropriate in this context to say in passing a word about the problem of the Congo and the activities of the United Nations in that country.

Different interests and Powers outside Africa have seen in the Congo situation a possibility of developments with strong impact on their international position. They have, therefore, naturally, held strong views on the direction in which they would like to see developments in the Congo turn and—with the lack of political traditions in the country and without the stability which political institutions can get only by being tested through experience—the doors have been opened for efforts to influence developments by supporting this or that faction or this or that personality. True to its principles, the United Nations has had to be guided in its operations solely by the interest of the Congolese people and by their right to decide freely for themselves, without any outside influences and with full knowledge of facts. Therefore, the Organization, throughout the first year of its work in the Congo, up to the point when Parliament reassembled and invested a new national Government, has refused —what many may have wished—to permit the weight of its resources to be used in support of any faction so as thereby to prejudge in any way the outcome of a choice which belonged solely to the Congolese people. It has also had to pursue a line which, by safe-guarding the free choice of the people, implied resistance against all efforts from outside to influence the outcome. In doing so, the Organization has been put in a position in which those within the country who felt disappointed in not getting the support of the Organization were led to suspect that others were in a more favoured position and, therefore, accused the Organization of partiality, and in which, further, such outside elements as tried to get or protect a foothold within the country, when meeting an obstacle in the United Nations, made similar accusations. If, as it is sincerely to be hoped, the recent national reconciliation, achieved by Parliament and its elected representatives of the people, provides a stable basis for a peaceful future in a fully independent and unified Congo, this would definitely confirm the correctness of the line pursued by the United Nations in the Congo. In fact, what was achieved by Parliament early in August may be said to have done so with sufficient clarity. It is a thankless and easily misunderstood role for the Organization to remain neutral in relation to a situation of domestic conflict and to provide active assistance only by protecting the rights and possibilities of the people to find their own way, but it remains the only manner in which the Organization can serve its proclaimed purpose of furthering the full independence of the people in the true and unqualified sense of the word.

The United Nations may be called upon again to assist in similar ways. Whatever mistakes in detail and on specific points critics may ascribe to the Organization in the highly complicated situation in the Congo, it is to be hoped that they do not lead Members to revise the basic rules which guide the United Nations' activities in such situations, as laid down in the first report of the Secretary-General to the Security Council on the Congo question, which the Council, a year ago, found reason, unanimously, to commend.

Closely related to a policy aiming at self-government and independence for all is the question of economic and technical assistance, especially during the first years of independence of a new Member State. The United Nations and its agencies and affiliated organs have at their disposal only very modest means for the purpose, but a rich experience has been gathered and the personnel resources are not inconsiderable.

Last year the Economic and Social Council and the General Assembly had to consider proposals designed to open up new possibilities for the Organization to respond to the demands of Member governments facing all the problems of newly achieved independence. Naturally, the problems which are of special importance for such countries are basically the same as those which face all countries which have been left behind in economic development. Therefore, the urgent attention required by newly independent countries in this respect can in no way justify a discrimination in their favour against other countries with similar difficulties.

This year the General Assembly will have before it proposals initiated by the Scientific Advisory Committee and endorsed by the Economic and Social Council, for a conference under United Nations aegis, intended to provide possibilities for a break-through in the application of the technical achievements of present times to the problems of the economically less developed countries. It is sincerely to be hoped that, in the interest of international cooperation and the acceleration of the economic progress of those countries, this proposal will meet with the approval of the General Assembly.

So far, the economic and technical activities of the United Nations have been less influenced by the conflict between different concepts of the role of the Organization than its activities in other fields. However, it is impossible to isolate the economic and technical problems from the general question discussed in this Introduction. While receiving countries should have full freedom to take assistance from whatever source they find appropriate, they should not be barred, if they so wish, from getting all the assistance they need through United Nations channels or under United Nations aegis. The Organization is far from being able to meet all such demands, as donor nations continue to show a strong preference for bilateral approaches on a national or a group basis. Again, the problem arises of the basic concept of the United Nations. With the conference approach to the work of the Organization a choice is made also in favor of bilateral assistance, while the alternative approach opens the door to a development under which international assistance, in implementation of the principle of equal economic opportunities for all, would be channelled through the Organization or its related agencies to all the extent that this is desired by the recipient countries and is within the capacity of the Organization.

Basic to the United Nations approach to economic and technical assistance is the principle, under all circumstances, that, although the Organization has to follow its own rules and maintain its own independence, its services are exclusively designed to meet the wishes of the recipient government, without the possibility of any ulterior motives and free from the risk of any possible influence on the national or international policies of that government. Whatever development the executive activities of the Organization may show in the field, there should never be any suspicion that the world community would wish or, indeed, could ever wish to maintain for itself, through the United Nations, a position of power or control in a Member country. Were political groups in a country really to believe in such a risk, the explanation would seem to be that, as has indeed happened in the case of governments of Member countries with long established independence, they may find it difficult to accept the judgment of the majority of the nations of the world as to what in a specific situation is necessary in order to safeguard international peace and security, when such a judgment appears to be in conflict with the immediate aims of the group. With growing respect for the decisions of the Organization and growing understanding of its principles, the risks for such misinterpretations should be eliminated.

This Introduction has limited itself to general observations on questions of principle, leaving all problems of detail to the report itself. This has seemed appropriate in view of the fact that the Organization has now reached a stage in its development where Member nations may find it timely to clarify their views on the direction in which they would like to see the future work of the Organization develop.

LAST WORDS TO THE STAFF

From Dag Hammarskjöld's last speech, which
was made to the Secretariat staff on the occasion of
Staff Day in the General Assembly Hall,
8 September 1961.

... The general world situation and its repercussions on the Organization have unavoidably left their mark on the Secretariat. In particular the discussions in the last session of the General Assembly have raised far-reaching questions on the nature of the Secretariat. What is at stake is a basic question of principle: Is the Secretariat to develop as an international secretariat, with the full independence contemplated in Article 100 of the Charter, or is it to be looked upon as an inter-governmental—not international—secretariat, providing merely the necessary administrative services for a conference machinery? This is a basic question and the answer to it affects not only the working of the Secretariat but the whole of the future of international relations.

If the Secretariat is regarded as truly international, and its individual members as owing no allegiance to any national government, then the Secretariat may develop as an instrument for the preservation of peace and security of increasing significance and responsibilities. If a contrary view were to be taken, the Secretariat itself would not be available to Member governments as an instrument, additional to the normal diplomatic methods, for active and growing service in the common interest.

I have dealt with this question at some length in various statements, most recently and fully in the Introduction to the Annual Report. It is a question which the Secretariat itself cannot answer as it is up to the Member governments to decide what kind of Secretariat they want. But the quality and spirit of our work will necessarily greatly influence the reply.

In a situation like the one now facing all peoples of the world, as represented in this Organization, it is understandable that staff members should sometimes feel frustrated and even depressed. In that they are not different from their fellow beings in other positions influenced by the trend of world events. There is only one answer to the human problem involved, and that is for all to maintain their professional pride, their sense of purpose, and their confidence in the higher destiny of the Organization itself, by keeping to the highest standards of personal integrity in their conduct as international civil servants and in the quality of the work that they turn out on behalf of the Organization. This is the way to defend what they believe in and to strengthen this Organization as an instrument of peace for which they wish to work. Dejection and despair lead to defeatism—and defeat.

. . . . It is true that we are passing through a period of unusual threats to human society and to peace. The dangers are too well known for me to add any comments here. If anything, you hear and see too much about them in the headlines of every paper. It is also true that the role of the Organization is necessarily a modest one, subordinated as it must be to governments, and through governments to the will of the peoples.

But, although the dangers may be great and although our role may be modest, we can feel that the work of the Organization is *the* means through which we all, jointly, can work so as to reduce the dangers. It would be too dramatic to talk about our task as one of waging a war for peace, but it is quite realistic to look at it as an essential and—within its limits—effective work for building dams against the floods of disintegration and violence.

Those who serve the Organization can take pride in what it has done already in many, many cases. I know what I am talking about if I say, for example, that short of the heavy work in which each of you has had his or her part, the Congo would by now have been torn to pieces in a fight which in all likelihood would not have been limited to that territory, but spread far around, involving directly or indirectly many or all of the countries from which you come. I also know what the activities of the Organization in the economic and social fields have meant for the betterment of life of millions, and for the creation of a basis for a happier future.

This is not said in a spirit of boastful satisfaction with what this Organization has been able to do—which, alas, falls far short of the needs—but as a realistic evaluation of the contribution we all of us, individually, have been permitted to make through our work for this Organization. It is false pride to register and to boast to the world about the importance of one's work, but it is false humility,

24*

and finally just as destructive, not to recognize—and recognize with gratitude—that one's work has a sense. Let us avoid the second fallacy as carefully as the first, and let us work in the conviction that our work *has* a meaning beyond the narrow individual one and *has* meant something for man. . . .

STATEMENT AT UNITED NATIONS DAY CONCERT, 24 OCTOBER 1960

This was the last of the statements made by Dag Hammarskjöld at the annual observances of United Nations Day. It was recorded at the time and repeated eleven months later during the memorial ceremony in the General Assembly Hall for him and those who had died with him on 18 September 1961. The Philadelphia Orchestra returned to play again on this occasion Beethoven's Ninth Symphony.

It is the tradition that the Organization marks United Nations Day with a concert including the final movement of Beethoven's Ninth Symphony. Today we shall, for the first time in this hall, listen to the symphony in its entirety.

It is difficult to say anything, knowing that the words spoken will be followed by this enormous confession of faith in the victorious human spirit and in human brotherhood, a confession valid for all times and with a depth and wealth of expression never surpassed. However, this concert is in celebration of United Nations Day and it has been felt that a few words may remind us of the purpose for which we have assembled.

When the Ninth Symphony opens we enter a drama full of harsh conflict and dark threats. But the composer leads us on, and in the beginning of the last movement we hear again the various themes repeated, now as a bridge towards a final synthesis. A moment of silence and a new theme is introduced, the theme of reconciliation and joy in reconciliation. A human voice is raised in rejection of all that has preceded and we enter the dreamt kingdom of peace. New voices join the first and mix in a jubilant assertion of life and all that it gives us when we meet it, joined in faith and human solidarity.

On his road from conflict and emotion to reconciliation in this final hymn of praise, Beethoven has given us a confession and a credo which we, who work within and for this Organization, may well make our own. We take part in the continuous fight between conflicting interests and ideologies which so far has marked the history of mankind, but we may never lose our faith that the first movements one day will be followed by the fourth movement. In that faith we strive to bring order and purity into chaos and anarchy. Inspired by that faith we try to impose the laws of the human mind and of the integrity of the human will on the dramatic evolution in which we are all engaged and in which we all carry our responsibility.

The road of Beethoven in his Ninth Symphony is also the road followed by the authors of the Preamble of the Charter. It begins with the recognition of the threat under which we all live, speaking as it does of the need to save succeeding generations from the scourge of war which has brought untold sorrow to mankind. It moves on to a reaffirmation of faith in the dignity and worth of the human person. And it ends with the promise to practice tolerance and live together in peace with one another as good neighbors and to unite our strength to maintain peace.

This year, the fifteenth in the life of the Organization, is putting it to new tests. Experience has shown how far we are from the end which inspired the Charter. We are indeed still in the first movements. But no matter how deep the shadows may be, how sharp the conflicts, how tense the mistrust reflected in what is said and done in our world of today as reflected in this hall and in this house, we are not permitted to forget that we have too much in common, too great a sharing of interests and too much that we might lose together, for ourselves and for succeeding generations, ever to weaken in our efforts to surmount the difficulties and not to turn the simple human values, which are our common heritage, into the firm foundation on which we may unite our strength and live together in peace.

May this be enough as a reminder of the significance of this day. And may now the symphony develop its themes, uniting us in its recognition of fear and its confession of faith.

INDEX

Acheson, Dean, 143
Advisory Committees to Secretary-General, see under Scientific, Congo, UNEF
Africa, attitudes, problems and relationships of, 16, 17, 18, 19, 115–116, 120, 146, 196, 212–219, 231–241, 245, 275, 277, 289, 293–297, 307, 312–313, 322, 327, 328, 372
Age of Enlightenment, 50, 131
Alliances and the UN, 15, 144, 204, 205
Almqvist, Agnes, see under Hammarskjöld
Almqvist, Carl Jonas Love, 70, 152
American Association for the United Nations, 40
American Jewish Committee, 126
American Revolution, 48, 194
Arab League, 191, 220
Arab Refugees, see Palestine Question
Arab States, 173, 189–193, 269–270; see also Middle East and Palestine Question
Arbitral Awards, Convention for, 291
Arctic, military flights over and inspection zone proposal, 177–181
Armistice Agreements, see Palestine Question
Arms Race, see Disarmament
Aronson, Stina, 247
Asia, attitudes, problems and relationships of, 16, 19, 115–116, 120–122, 134, 135, 146, 196, 212–219, 266, 275, 277, 289, 307, 312–313
Assembly, UN, see General Assembly
Atomic Bombs, see Nuclear Tests
Atomic Energy, advisory committee, see Scientific; UN conferences on peaceful uses of, 11, 101, 102, 112, 170–171
Atoms for Peace Award, 194
Atoms for Peace Plan, 170
Auden, W. H., quotation from, 91
Austria, 58

Baghavad-Gita, quotation from, 40
Balfour, Arthur, quotation from, 330
Beethoven's Ninth Symphony, 379–380
Bergman, Bo, 247
Berlin, question of, 17, 200, 201, 206, 220, 262, 267–268, 349–350, 370
Bernadotte, Count Folke, 31, 32
Beskow, Bo, 160
Big Powers and UN, 16, 20, 145, 178–181, 271, 274, 312, 319, 363, 369–371; see also Cold War, Veto power
Bilateral Aid, see Economic and Social Development

Bilateral Diplomacy, 49; changed requirements of, 50–51; war as ultimate resource of, 50; see also Multilateral Diplomacy
Bohr, Niels, 197, 198
Bolivia, UN technical assistance report on, 116
Buber, Martin, quotation from, 186
Buddhism, 212, 215, 218

Cambodia, 12, 264, 289
Cambridge University, 184, 185, 187
Cameroons, Republic of the, 231, 293
Canadian Broadcasting Corp. (CBC), 134, 135
Carlyle, Thomas, citation from, 86; 87, 90
Carnegie Endowment, citation from proceedings, 332
Charles IX of Sweden, 65; Charles XII, 65, 151
Charter, amendment of, 144, 147, 298, 370; collective self-defense, 143, 203, see also Art. 51 below; disarmament, 257, 258, 369; domestic jurisdiction clause, 43, 315; economic and social progress, 276, 279, 282, 307, 309, 356; enforcement powers, 204, 256–257; equality of rights and votes, 297, 356–357; flexibility of, 95–96, 210–211, 223–224, 256; human rights provisions, 105, 356; independence of Secretariat, 316, 321, 333–334, 338–342, 367–368; peaceful settlement with justice, 122, 203, 358–360; political responsibilities of Secretary-General and Secretariat, 335–338, 345–346, 367–368; powers of principal organs, 93–94, 96–97, 204–205, 255–257, 268, 370; respect for authority of Organization, 361–365; respect for national independence and integrity, 203, 296; self-determination, 120–121, 370–371; tolerance, 130; Articles 1 and 2, see Purposes and Principles below; Article 10, 145; Article 11, 145; Article 12, 145; Article 24, 362, 365; Article 25, 362, 363, 364; Article 28, 173; Article 29, 365; Article 33, 16, 221, 360; Article 36, 221; Article 40, 360, 365; Article 48, 365; Article 49, 362; Article 51, 143, 145; Article 55, 292, 356; Article 76, 293; Article 97, 334, 335, 337, 353, 366; Article 98, 334, 335, 337, 338, 365, 366, 367, 368; Article 99, 226, 305, 335, 337, 338, 367; Article 100,